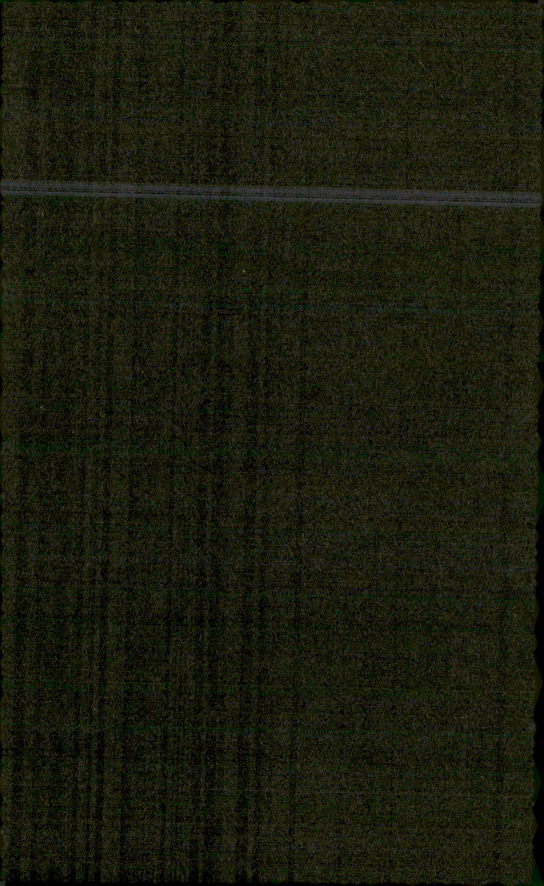

Brutal
Choreographies

J. Brooks Bouson

BRUTAL CHOREOGRAPHIES

Oppositional
Strategies and
Narrative Design
in the
Novels of
Margaret
Atwood

The
University of
Massachusetts
Press
Amherst

Copyright © 1993 by
The University of Massachusetts Press
All rights reserved
Printed in the United States of America
LC 93–2964
ISBN 0–87023–845–0
Designed by Mary Mendell
Set in Galliard by Keystone Typesetting, Inc.
Printed and bound by Thomson-Shore, Inc.
Library of Congress Cataloging-in-Publication Data
Bouson, J. Brooks.
Brutal choreographies : oppositional strategies and narrative
design in the novels of Margaret Atwood / J. Brooks Bouson.
p.   cm.
Includes bibliographical references and index.
ISBN 0–87023–845–0 (alk. paper)
1. Atwood, Margaret Eleanor, 1939– —Political and social views.
2. Feminism and literature—Canada—History—20th century.   3. Women
and literature—Canada—History—20th century.   4. Psychoanalysis
and literature.   5. Narration (Rhetoric)   I. Title.
PR9199.3.A8Z56   1993
813'.54—dc20   93–2964
                    CIP

British Library Cataloguing in Publication data are available.

For my mother

Contents

anadian author Margaret Atwood (b. 1939) has written best sellers—*The Handmaid's Tale* and *Cat's Eye*—and her novels and poetry have given rise to a regular Atwood industry among academic literary critics. A novelist with both popular and literary appeal, Atwood provokes her readers to confront issues that are of special importance to women, such as domestic and sexual violence, pornography, eating disorders, mastectomy, and problems with body-self image. And in all of her fiction, Atwood—who is deeply concerned about the uneven and potentially damaging power relations that occur in the parent-child situation, heterosexual romance, and female friendship— relentlessly focuses attention on the gender and power politics that govern women's lives.

My aim in *Brutal Choreographies* is to offer a chronological reading of Atwood's novels, clarifying the relationships among the novels and providing a close analysis of their psychological and political concerns and preoccupations. I place emphasis on Atwood's family and romance dramas, her evolving story of the female self-in-crisis, her novelistic subversion of romantic love ideology, and her ongoing critique of gender and power politics. I also consider the oppositional strategies used in Atwood's novels: their punitive plotting and their enactments of female revenge fantasies; their dialogic resistance to romantic discourse; and their self-conscious manipulation and sabotage of the romance plot and other traditional narrative forms and formulas. Because Atwood does not shun what she calls the "story of the disaster which is the world" ("End to Audience" 350), the stories she tells are often brutal, portraying female victimization at the hands of the male lover or husband, the mother, or the best girlfriend. But if her novels have the power to disturb, compel, and at times even brutalize her readers, they are also carefully choreographed, and, indeed, call attention to their preoccupation with form and design.

The fact that Atwood, in characters like Fish and Professor Pieixoto, openly parodies academic discourse can be a bit unnerving to the academic commentator on Atwood. Although she has described the academic critic as "a kind of reader made visible" (Jean Ross 24), Atwood also has said, with considerable exasperation, "You can read any text any way. You can read it standing on your head. You can use it for toilet paper. It's not a statement about the text. It's a statement about the user" (Hancock 276). My intention in *Brutal Choreographies* is to provide a critical reading of Atwood's novels and to read her work with my feet planted firmly on the ground. Because Atwood is a novelist whose career spans the emergence and evolution of the second wave of feminism and the conservative backlash against it, and because her novels engage in interesting ways with the oppositional culture of the women's movement, I find feminist theory—in particular Anglo-American theory—helpful in situating and elucidating Atwood's fiction. I also draw on psychoanalysis in my discussion of the recurring self, romance, and family dramas in Atwood's novels. And I am indebted to the rich and immensely varied scholarly conversation surrounding Atwood's novels, not only for the valuable insights American and Canadian scholars have provided about the themes, patterns, and subversive strategies of Atwood's fiction, but also for the important clues they provide about the emotional and interpretive demands of her art.

I have other debts to acknowledge as well. I owe much to the many women students at Mundelein College (which is now part of Loyola University) who reacted with such energy and enthusiasm when I taught courses on Atwood and who helped me clarify my own emotional and interpretive responses to Atwood's fiction. And I would like to thank the Margaret Atwood Society, an organization that provided me with a sustaining sense of community while I worked on this project. Thanks are also due to Loyola University, both for granting me a summer stipend so I could complete this book and for aiding in its publication. Parts of the chapter on *Lady Oracle* appeared in my book, *The Empathic Reader* (University of Massachusetts Press, 1989), and parts of the chapter on *The Edible Woman* in *Style* (Summer 1990). I am grateful for permission to reuse this material, which I have significantly revised for this study.

Brutal
Choreographies

T hat Margaret Atwood is an irrepressible storyteller and literary code breaker is evident in her comic description of her development as a writer in the essay, "Great Unexpectations." When in 1960 at the age of nineteen she "wanted to be— no, worse—was determined to be" a writer, she was "scared to death" not only because the prospects for being both a Canadian and a writer were "dim," but also because she was a woman (xiii–xiv). It is true that in some ways her sex was an advantage. For although the male writer in Canada was branded "a sissy," writing was "not quite so unthinkable for a woman, ranking as it did with flower painting and making roses out of wool." Moreover, because Canada was a "cultural backwater," it had been spared the "wave of Freudianism that had washed over the United States" in the 1950s; thus, "Canadian women were not yet expected to be fecund and passive in order to fulfill themselves" (xiv).

And yet, despite these cultural advantages, the story of the woman writer recorded in literary history pointed to the remarkable disadvantages of her chosen lifestyle. "I'd read the biographies, which were not encouraging. Jane Austen never married Mr. Darcy. Emily Brontë died young, Charlotte in childbirth. George Eliot never had children and was ostracized for living with a married man. Emily Dickinson flitted; Christina Rossetti looked at life through the wormholes in a shroud." And given the fact that women writers—like Mrs. Gaskell and Harriet Beecher Stowe—who managed to combine writing with "a normal life" were considered "second rate," the choices offered an aspiring writer like Atwood "were between excellence and doom on the one hand, and mediocrity and cosiness on the other." Also daunting was Robert Graves's depiction of the creative woman. In Graves's scheme, the woman who wanted to have a "chance of becoming a decent poet" had to take on the "attributes of the White Goddess" and spend her time "seducing men and then doing them in," an activity that "sounded a little strenuous, and appeared to rule out domestic bliss" (xiv, xv). Similarly troubling were the "new, high standards in self-destructiveness" for women writers set by authors like Sylvia Plath and Anne Sexton, which prompted others to ask Atwood "not whether but when" she was going to commit suicide (xvi).

Despite her "unexpectations," Atwood's own story, unlike that found in many of her novels, does have a happy ending. And yet, although she has successfully resisted the "postromantic collective delusion" of the unhappy, suicidal female artist and has opted for the "leaves-in-the-backyard" lifestyle she once thought "out of bounds," she is still plagued by the White Goddess who makes appearances in her life, "mainly as a fantasy projection on the part of certain male book reviewers, who seem to like the idea of my teeth sinking into some cringing male neck. I think of this as fifties nostalgia," Atwood remarks, sounding a lot like one of her fictional characters (xvi).

"A hard-hitting piece of writing by a man is liable to be thought of as merely realistic; an equivalent piece by a woman is much more likely to be labelled 'cruel' or 'tough,'" Atwood observes. "[T]here is no critical vocabulary for expressing the concept 'good/female.' Work by a male writer is often spoken of by critics admiring it as having 'balls'; ever hear anyone speak admiringly of work by a woman as having 'tits'?" ("On Being a 'Woman Writer'" 197, 198). Because Atwood is a woman writer who does not "use words in a soft, compliant way," she has been the target of repeated sexist attacks over the years (Hammond, "Interview" 29). "It *is* more difficult for a woman writer in this society than for a male writer," Atwood insists. "But not because of any innate mysterious hormonal or spiritual differences: it is more difficult because it has been made more difficult, and the stereotypes still lurk in the wings, ready to spring fully formed from the heads of critics, both male and female, and attach themselves to any unwary character or author that wanders by." Because women are expected to be morally better than men, the woman who is "not an angel" or who displays "any kind of strength or power, creative or otherwise," is perceived as "a witch, a Medusa, a destructive, powerful, scary monster." And so Atwood has been variously depicted by the media as "Margaret the Magician, Margaret the Medusa, Margaret the Man-eater, clawing her way to success over the corpses of many hapless men. Margaret the powerhungry Hitler, with her megalomaniac plans to take over the entire field of Canadian Literature" ("The Curse of Eve" 226, 227).

If Atwood has become, in the hands of some of her interviewers and reviewers, a kind of fictional character, she also actively opposes this fictionalizing tendency among her commentators, this attempt by others to appropriate—and misappropriate—her identity as a writer. "We are great categorizers and pigeonholers in our society, and one reason is to put people safely into pigeonholes and then dismiss them, thinking we have thereby summed them up," Atwood remarks (Ingersoll, "Evading" 538). Resisting the repeated attempts of her interviewers to exercise hermeneutic control over her, Atwood refuses to be transformed into a role model, a media stereotype, or a representative feminist. In the words of Camille Peri, "Atwood is a contrary woman: a nationalist who rankles nationalists, a feminist who rankles feminists. She is a master at exposing hypocrisy among the powerful, but can be curiously evasive when the subject is herself" (30). "Through the writing on Atwood there runs a series of questions: Who is Atwood? What is she up to? What is she up to *now*?" remarks Robert Fulford, in his comments on the "elusiveness" of Atwood's public stance and public personality, her "half-shy and half-assertive public manner" ("Images of Atwood" 95, 97). "Margaret Atwood will make one hell of an old lady," writes Fulford in his fantasy of Atwood's eightieth-birthday interview. "I'd like to be one of the young journalists who gather at her place on November 18, 2019. . . . I can't imagine what such people will want to ask her, but I can pretty well describe her answers—they'll be tart, aphoristic, defiant, confident" (*Best Seat* 200).

Because Atwood's "defensiveness is legend" and because she is an "evasive subject" to interview (Valerie Miner 175), she, like her fictional characters, actively invites others to interpret her, even as she refuses to be a character in the varied dramas her commentators have created for and around her. And yet, although Atwood vigorously resists the efforts of the "categorizers and pigeonholers," she does not deny the label often attached to her: that she is a "feminist" writer. But she also insists that the description does not "enclose" her, that she does not "consider it inclusive" (Ingersoll, "Evading" 538). And she is unwilling to adhere to a party line. "Am I a propagandist? No! Am I an observer of society? Yes! And no one who observes society can fail to make observations which are feminist. That is just based on real-life commonsense" (Jamkhandi 5).

Linked to Atwood's distrust of party lines is her long-standing aversion to the development of feminist criticism which awards points to works produced by women based on their "conformity or non-conformity to an ideological position" ("On Being a 'Woman Writer'" 192). Atwood adamantly refuses to be bound by a particular literary code or belief system. "[O]nce they start saying: 'Thou shalt write about this,' and 'Thou shalt not write about that,' 'Thou shalt not say, "The Empress has no clothes,"' 'Thou shalt not say, "This was a stupid, pig-headed way to behave,"' then I say no" (Meese 98). Opposing what she calls "ideological hardlines," Atwood is leery of "people telling people what they have to write," and she feels that it would be a mistake to impose "biological strait jackets" on women writers by arguing that only those writers who have a style that is considered to be "feminine or female" are "real women writers" (Meese 95, 96; *Atlantis* interview 207). "I think I'm against water-tight compartments. I'm against ghet-toization of anybody . . . and I'm against that kind of determinism that says because you are *this,* thou shalt be *so*—you know, because you have a womb, your style has to have a hole in the middle of it" (Draine 373).

An author who describes her "foundation," her "grounding," to be "the history of the novel as it has been written since the 18th century" ("Conversation" 175), Atwood, like many other contemporary women novelists, writes in a realist mode and thus implicitly writes against a very powerful story currently being told by some academic critics: that post-modernist fiction, with its disruptive stylistic innovations and its upend-ing of realistic conventions, is "feminist" art. "Because feminism has a stake in the undoing of hierarchy and containment," remarks Molly Hite, "it appears that writing commonly described in terms of its subver-sive newness, as avant-garde or postmodern, can also be described in terms of its subversive political implications, as 'feminine' or feminist writing." But given the fact that most postmodernist works are male-authored, "it would seem that in the contemporary period, fictional experimentation has everything to do with feminism and nothing to do with women—and emphatically nothing to do with women as points of origin, as authors" (16–17, 17). According to Alice Jardine, who claims that "[i]t is not something called the self that speaks, but language, the unconscious, the textuality of the text," the "question of whether a 'man' or a 'woman' wrote a text . . . becomes nonsensical" (58). But if post-modernists want to "persuade us that we should be suspicious of any notion of self or subjectivity," Jane Flax finds herself "suspicious of the motives of those who would counsel such a position at the same time as women have just begun to re-member their selves and to claim an agentic subjectivity available always before only to a few privileged white men" (220).

For Rita Felski, "The attempt to argue a necessary connection between feminism and experimental form, when not grounded in a biologistic thinking which affirms a spontaneous link between a 'feminine' textuality and the female body, relies on a theoretical sleight-of-hand that associates or equates the avant-garde and the 'feminine' as forms of marginalized dissidence. . . ." When linguistic subversion is defined as "feminine," the term is rendered "so broad as to become meaningless—almost any example of experimental literature in the last hundred years can be seen as 'feminine'" (5). Mapping onto "gender what are in fact class questions," the equation of the "feminine" and experimental writing "tacitly if not explicitly limits an oppositional culture to the reading and writing practices of an intellectual elite" (7, 6). Moreover, "it is both elitist and reductive to suggest that only certain highly specialized intellectual reading and writing practices can pierce the veil of ideological mystification" (61). In Felski's view, "the question of the most appropriate strategy for a feminist writing practice cannot be determined a priori, in relation to a concept of the 'feminine' text . . . but instead requires a theoretical approach which can address the social meanings and functions of literature in relation to women writers and readers" (19).

Rejecting the notion of a feminine style, Atwood argues that style is determined by literary movements, not by gender (*Atlantis* interview 206). A novelist who, in her own words, writes from the "ground up" and not "from some theory down" (Tennant 9), Atwood also insists on the social meanings and functions of literary production. "Novels have people; people exist in a social milieu; all of the cultural milieu gets into the novel," she remarks (Ingersoll, "Evading" 535). Aptly described as a writer concerned with "'manners,' that is the fashions, cultural signs, and modes of behavior specific to a social time" (Banerjee, "Atwood's Time" 514), Atwood is an astute observer of the mass culture and cultural trends. And for Atwood, who feels that it is a "luxury" to place politics and poetics in "two watertight compartments" ("Amnesty International" 394), the novel is also a reflector of its political surround.

From the protofeminism of *The Edible Woman* (1969), the cultural feminism of *Surfacing* (1972), and the examination of the cultural stereotypes placed on the female artist in *Lady Oracle* (1976), to the domestic and sexual warfare of *Life Before Man* (1979), the postfeminist and antifeminist backlash terrors of *Bodily Harm* (1981) and *The Handmaid's Tale* (1985), and the analysis of the potential power politics of female relationships in *Cat's Eye* (1988), Atwood's novels both reflect and reflect on the oppositional culture of the feminist movement. Like other contemporary women novelists, Atwood uses novelistic narrative to openly challenge the status quo. In her words, "a lot of the energy in women's writing . . . has come from being able to say things that once you couldn't say" and thus from "being able to see things that once you couldn't see, or that you would have seen but repressed, or that you would have seen and put another interpretation on" (Castro 231). Writing during the emergence and evolution of the women's movement and the backlash against it, Atwood clearly has benefited from what Rita Felski describes as the "feminist public sphere." "The women's movement," explains Felski, "has offered one of the most dynamic examples of a counter-ideology in recent years to have generated an oppositional public arena for the articulation of women's needs in critical opposition to the values of a male-defined society." Constituting "a discursive space" that is defined in terms of "the shared experience of gender-based oppression," the feminist public sphere offers "a critique of cultural values from the standpoint of women as a marginalized group within society" (166, 167).

Because Atwood is an author who self-consciously challenges the ideology of romantic love—which views romantic affiliation and/or marriage as a woman's primary means to self-definition and self-fulfillment—her woman-centered fiction has a strong oppositional appeal. But Atwood is also acutely aware of what Nancy Miller has called "the difficulty of curing plot of life, and life of certain plots" (46). Remarking on the "sexual-marital economy underlying the novel's dominant tradition," Joseph Boone observes that "the history of the English-language novel cannot really be separated from the history of the romantic wedlock ideal" and indeed that the "novelistic tradition of love and marriage" became "axiomatic of the genre" and "romanticized marriage . . . *the* ultimate signifier of personal and social well-being" (137, 65, 66). Although romantic wedlock has lost its privileged position in the twentieth-century novel, love-plot formulas and formats persist in depictions of the heterosexual relationship (134–37). But there is also a long counter-tradition in the history of the novel involving the demystification and undoing of the romantic love code. If the novel can "encode and perpetuate" the dominant ideology and thus conserve the status quo, remarks Boone, it is also "a genre that is potentially noncanonical, inherently multivocal, and profoundly invested in the ideological dismantling of a unitary worldview" (2, 4).

Aware that art is a repository for both the culturally endorsed and repressed, Atwood also recognizes the subversive, oppositional potentials of novelistic narrative and its ability to flout established social and literary conventions. In her short fiction, "Women's Novels," we find a telling example of the deliberate ways in which Atwood subverts the romantic love code in her novels. "Sometimes men put women in men's novels but they leave out some of the parts: the heads, for instance, or the hands. Women's novels leave out parts of the men as well. Sometimes it's the stretch between the belly button and the knees, sometimes it's the sense of humour. It's hard to have a sense of humour in a cloak, in a high wind, on a moor." Mocking the absurdities of the popular romance genre, Atwood's narrator responds to the description, *She had the startled eyes of a wild bird,*" by asking what kind of bird. "A screech owl, perhaps, or a cuckoo? It does make a difference. We do not need more literalists of the imagination. They cannot read *a body like a gazelle's* without thinking of intestinal parasites, zoos, and smells" (*Murder in the Dark* 34, 35–36). Because the novel incorporates conflicting social voices in dialogic exchange, it "always includes in itself the activity of coming to know another's word," according to Mikhail Bakhtin (*Dialogic Imagination* 353). Indeed, the dialogical word "reacts intensely to the word of the other person, answering it and anticipating it" (Bakhtin, *Problems* 163). And thus, despite the novel's "reputation as a compromised form that gives in too easily to the marriage plot and to romance," the novel, as Patricia Yaeger remarks, is a "multivoiced" form that invites the novelist "to parody other discourses" and that gives women writers "an opportunity to interrupt the speech practices, the ordinary patriarchal assumptions of everyday life" (*Honey-Mad Women* 183, 31). Indeed, Yaeger observes that Bakhtin, who draws attention to "the contestatory violence of everyday speech," insists on "the literary word's dynamism—on language as struggle, and literature as the magnification of that struggle" ("Afterword" 241).

If Atwood uses feminist-dialogic speech to resist romantic discourse and the novelistic form to interrupt the marriage and love plots, she is also aware of the staying power of the popular romance formula. "There's usually an area of reality in popular literature that's hooking into the reality in the lives of the readers," she remarks. Whereas the Harlequin romance reflects the belief that "everything can work out" and that "there is a Mr. Wonderful who does exist," the Gothic novel centers on " 'My husband is trying to kill me.' " Observing that the *Jane Eyre* story is "really still with us," Atwood asks how long the orphan Jane Eyre has to be married to Rochester "before she turns into the mad wife" (Hammond, "Margaret Atwood" 81). Believing that "popular art is material for serious art in the way that dreams are," Atwood self-consciously plugs into "the popular sensibility" (Sandler 10, 11) in her relentless examination of the ideological assumptions and scripts contained in novelistic narrative. Given the "long-standing and dismissive association of the popular with the feminine, an association which has been in evidence since the original emergence of a female reading public in the eighteenth century" (Felski 174), it is telling that Atwood has been criticized for having popular audience appeal. "People sometimes assume that because I have a larger audience than is usual for a literary writer, I must be writing non-literary books. You do get that form of snobbery from this or that mannikin of letters," Atwood remarks (Hancock 286).

With oppositional intent, Atwood uses the novel to sabotage the Gothic and romantic fantasies perpetuated in the popular women's culture and literature. Deliberately mixing literary and popular art in her fiction, Atwood also openly contests the masculine codes inscribed in traditional and popular fictional formats: *The Edible Woman,* for example, is an anticomedy, *Lady Oracle,* an anti-Gothic, and *Bodily Harm,* an antithriller. And she makes oppositional use of other conventional formats in her novels, such as the quest story in *Surfacing* or detective fiction in *Bodily Harm.* Atwood, then, is determined to tell what Molly Hite calls the "other side of the story," those "alternate versions" of culturally sanctioned stories that provide "an entirely different set of emphases and values" (4). Consistently challenging traditional textual practices, Atwood's novels construct what Anne Cranny-Francis calls a feminist "reading position"—that is, "the position assumed by a reader from which the text seems to be coherent and intelligible"—by revealing "the contradictions and injustices within the dominant gender discourse" and making visible "the strategies by which that discourse is naturalized, including genre conventions and narrative" (25, 25–26). The construction of a feminist reading position "may involve changing to some extent the conventions of the genre, reworking them to express a changed socio-historical (discursive) formation; and it may involve voicing a patriarchal discourse which is then contextualized or placed in dialogue with other discourses" (205). Because the construction within the text of a feminist reading position allows readers to "experience a different, transgressive way of perceiving the society in which they live," the "political practice of the text is extended beyond the confines of the particular narrative" (73).

Positioning herself both inside and outside masculinist culture and assumptions, Atwood is deliberately confrontational as she interprets women's lives. An example of the punitive strategies and feminist-dialogic speech that occur in her fiction is found in "Writing the Male Character," in which Atwood is supposedly reporting on a conversation she had with a male friend about why men "feel threatened" by women. "'I mean,' I said, 'men are bigger, most of the time, they can run faster, strangle better, and they have on the average a lot more money and power.'" If, in her friend's explanation, men are afraid of women because they fear that "women will laugh at them," women report that they are afraid of men for a very different reason: they are "afraid of being killed" (413). Effectively gaining active mastery over women's collective passive suffering, Atwood threatens men by laughing at them and by doing to them what they have long done to women. Revealing her awareness of what Tania Modleski describes as "the subversive potential of women's laughter" (*Women* 19), Atwood comments that "[a] man is not just a woman in funny clothes and a jock strap" nor "an alien or inferior form of life." Moreover, unlike other people who generalize about men, she would never say, "'Put a paper bag over their bodies and they're all the same.'" Neutralizing the male threat to women, she insists that men are "fun to play Scrabble with and handy for eating up the leftovers. I have heard some rather tired women express the opinion that the only good man is a dead man, but this is far from correct" (414). In a deliberate parody of some of her male critics' fantasies about her lethal powers as a female artist, Atwood asks if perhaps "men still think something they need will fall off them if they look too hard at certain supposedly malevolent combinations of words put together by women" (424).

If Atwood hits a kind of collective male nerve through the confrontational strategies of her fiction, she also, through her depictions of her female characters as objects of male desire or sexual commodities or passive victims, lays bare the cultural and literary script that assigns women the passive, self-effacing roles and encourages them to collude in their own oppression as they consent to femininity. "[W]omen *must either* consent *or* be seduced into consenting to femininity," writes Teresa de Lauretis in her analysis of the male Oedipal logic which is said to undergird traditional narrative (134). "[T]o say that narrative is the production of Oedipus is to say that each reader—male or female—is constrained and defined within the two positions of a sexual difference thus conceived: male-hero-human, on the side of the subject; and female-obstacle-boundary-space, on the other" (121). Recasting Laura Mulvey's observation that "sadism demands a story," de Lauretis insists: "'Story demands sadism, depends on making something happen, forcing a change in another person, a battle of will and strength, victory/defeat, all occurring in a linear time with a beginning and an end.' All of which is, to some extent, independent of women's consent" (132–33; see Mulvey 438). Although "women's consent may not be gotten easily," it is "finally gotten, and has been for a long time, as much by rape and economic coercion as by the more subtle and lasting effects of ideology, representation, and identification" (134). Urging "an interruption of the triple track by which narrative, meaning, and pleasure" are constructed from the point of view of Oedipus, de Lauretis lauds the feminist response that is not "anti-narrative or anti-Oedipal" but is "narrative and Oedipal with a vengeance, for it seeks to stress the duplicity of that scenario and the specific contradiction of the female subject in it" (157).

Concerned with the uses and abuses of power, Atwood focuses attention on the power politics that govern women's lives: the patterns of domination and subordination that occur not only in heterosexual romance but also in mother-daughter relationships and in women's friendships. And in works like *Bodily Harm* and *The Handmaid's Tale,* she turns her attention to the misogynistic practices of masculinist culture that oppress women. Narrative with a vengeance, Atwood's novels emphasize women's consent to femininity, and they also, in their relentless focus on the female experience of self, dramatize the vulnerable selfhood of women.

Insight into the troubled selfhood of Atwood's characters is provided by American psychoanalyst Heinz Kohut, whose landmark investigations into the "narcissistic" or "self disorder" gave rise to what is called psychoanalytic "self psychology" (see Bouson 11–29). Arguing that the individual's "essence is defined when seen as a self" ("Introspection" 94), Kohut describes the self as an experiential construct: as the "basis for our sense of being an independent center of initiative and perception, integrated with our most central ambitions and ideals and with our experience that our body and mind form a unit in space and a continuum in time" (*Restoration* 177). What marks the narcissistic disorder is a "[s]ignificant failure to achieve cohesion, vigour, or harmony" in the self or a "significant loss of these qualities after they had been tentatively established" (Kohut and Wolf 414). Lacking a cohesive sense of self, those who suffer from the narcissistic disorder are pathetically vulnerable. Indeed, they are subject to the "unnamable dread" of what Kohut calls "disintegration anxiety," an awful fear of body-self fragmentation and the loss of the self (*Restoration* 105, 104). Despite recent declarations about the "Death of the Self" (Waugh 1) by postmodern theorists, "[t]hose who celebrate or call for a 'decentered' self," as Jane Flax points out, "seem self-deceptively naive and unaware of the basic cohesion within themselves that makes the fragmentation of experiences something other than a terrifying slide into psychosis." In Flax's view, such writers "seem to confirm the very claims of those they have contempt for, that a sense of continuity or 'going on being' is so much a part of the core self that it becomes a taken-for-granted background. Persons who have a core self find the experiences of those who lack or have lacked it almost unimaginable" (218–19).

That women have been traditionally conceived as defective or deficient from male norms points to the narcissistic injuries women have long sustained in our culture. Suffering from a deficient sense of self, Atwood's characters are subject to the terrors of disintegration anxiety: to the "fear of being nothing"; the discovery of the "blank lady" within; the anxiety that the "core" self has been "invaded." Her characters may fear the loss of the self through immersion in socially constructed female roles as they perform the male-scripted feminine masquerade or as they consent to femininity. Or they may imagine that they are damaged or defective in some essential way as they struggle against the cultural codes that define and confine them. Indeed, the drama of the female self-in-crisis emerges in all of Atwood's novels as a kind of recurring textual anxiety, a repetition compulsion that is enacted and reenacted in narrative after narrative. What recurs are not just the terrors of a childhood spent in fear of the bad mother or one's best girl friends but also the cultural terrors implicit in fulfilling the prescribed roles of the dutiful daughter or passive wife or those of the sexual object or female victim.

Persistently depicting women as narcissistically injured and vulnerable, Atwood's narratives set out both to expose and fictively redress the wrongs done to women. One of the targets for fictive punishment in Atwood's art is the bad mother, who acts as a guardian and enforcer of the patriarchal codes that confine and injure women. Another is the male who is perceived as a potential rescuer but also as a possible persecutor or murderer. Recurring in Atwood's fiction like the repetition of a trauma, the bad unempathic mother and split good/bad male act as dangerous forces in the life of the heroine. They also act as potentially disruptive forces in the text and thus are defended against through various narrative strategies. The bad mother, for example, may be backgrounded or she may be strategically foregrounded—her badness dwelt upon—and then defensively killed off in the text. The fact that the good mother is often dead or absent points to the potency of the bad mother in Atwood's fictional world. Similarly, despite the various textual strategies used to master the male threat to female identity—such as the empowerment of the victimized female or the backgrounding or textual/sexual putdown of the potentially dangerous male—the female anxieties surrounding the unassimilable male remain a driving force in Atwood's fiction. Because "there is no good ending for a narrative whose story is governed by repetition" (Rimmon-Kenan 185), it is telling that Atwood's fiction returns again and again to the family and romance dramas and to a familiar cast of characters: the bad mother, the split male, the passive female victim. Atwood's fiction is governed by the compulsion to repeat because it deals with the basic fears and persisting conflicts that plague women in a male-dominant culture. But her narratives also provide outlets for female anger and resentment in their repeated enactments of fantasies of power and revenge. Indeed, Atwood's novels provide a uniquely female pleasure of the text in their constant stagings of such fantasies.

"Touch the page at your peril: it is you who are blank and innocent, not the page. Nevertheless you want to know, nothing will stop you," Atwood warns in "The Page" (*Murder in the Dark* 45). Commenting that when she reads a woman writer she feels she is "reading something closer to home," Atwood admits that "things that are closer to home have the power to make you a lot more nervous and anxious than things that are more remote" (Lyons 72). But she also states that she feels "good" when she finishes reading a book or seeing a play or film that is "well done" even if it is "swimming in blood and totally pessimistic," explaining that it is "the *well-doneness* that has that affect" on her (Hancock 286). If the Atwood novel, similarly, has the power to make critic/ readers anxious as it invites them to identify with female characters who are subject to disintegration anxiety and persecutory fears, it also invites them to form an identificatory bond with the author-designer by encouraging them to interpret and thematize, to focus attention on the complexities of narrative structure and on the evolving patterns of signification within the text. Potentially anxiety-provoking but also carefully choreographed, the Atwood novel draws attention to its "well-doneness" as it uses form and design to control and contain the female fears, anxieties, and anger that drive the narrative.

"Come with me, the writer is saying to the reader," writes Atwood. *"There is a story I have to tell you, there is something you need to know"* ("An End to Audience?" 348). As Atwood reads and interprets women's lives, she compulsively tells a story that she wants her readers to hear and respond to. My aim in the chapters that follow is to emphasize the recurring and interrelated self, family, romance, and female revenge dramas staged in Atwood's novels; to investigate Atwood's subversion of romantic love ideology and her manipulation of romantic and other narrative formats and formulas; and to analyze both the emotional demands and interpretive challenges of her highly controlled and designed but also angry, oppositional novelistic narratives.

twood wrote her first novel in 1963 when she was twenty-three. The novel—which she handwrote at night in her room in a Toronto rooming house and typed during the day at her job with a market research company—was set near a swamp. "It was very existential," as she describes it. "There was a lot of marsh gas in it. People committed suicide and also drowned. It ended with the female protagonist wondering whether or not to push one of the male characters off a roof, which would be perfectly acceptable now but was, then, considerably in advance of its age." Although "downcast" when she was unable to find a publisher for her novel, before long she began writing another novel about a market-research employee living in a Toronto rooming house ("Where Is How" 9; see also McCombs, "Up in the Air").

"I wrote *The Edible Woman* in the spring and summer of 1965, on empty examination booklets filched from the University of British Columbia, where I had been teaching freshman English for the previous eight months," Atwood remarks in her "Introduction" to the novel. "The title scene dates from a year earlier; I'd thought it up while gazing, as I recall, at a confectioner's display window full of marzipan pigs. It may have been a Woolworth's window full of Mickey Mouse cakes, but in any case I'd been speculating for some time about symbolic cannibalism. Wedding cakes with sugar brides and grooms were at that time of particular interest to me" (369). Like the story Atwood tells about her first, unpublished novel, which ends with the female protagonist thinking about pushing a male character off a roof, the story she tells about her first published novel—with its focus on the "symbolic cannibalism" of marriage in patriarchal society—registers protest as it reveals the cultural and literary expectations she openly challenged at the outset of her novel-writing career.

"*Edible Woman* was written in 1965, before the Women's Liberation Movement had begun," Atwood recalls. At the time, it was "still very much the model pattern, in Canada anyway, to take a crummy job and then marry to get away from it" (Oates 7). When her manuscript, which had been misplaced by the publisher, was finally published in 1969, "just in time to coincide with the rise of feminism in North America," some commentators wrongly assumed that her novel was "a product of the movement." It was, in fact, "protofeminist rather than feminist" inasmuch as there was "no women's movement in sight" when she composed the book ("Introduction" 370). While some lauded Atwood's novel for its feminism, others, invoking traditional gender expectations, viewed *The Edible Woman*'s critique of marriage and motherhood "as essentially 'young' or 'neurotic.' I would mature, they felt, and things (i.e., marriage and kids) would fall into place" (Oates 7). Caught in an inadvert act of repetition, such commentators, in effect, reenacted the central drama—and trauma—of the text by pronouncing Atwood's oppositional art as a sign of her rejection of her own femininity. These conflicting early readings of Atwood's novel, reflective of the changing cultural climate of the late 1960s, reveal how different interpretative communities can produce different constructions of the text, each having its own political aim: the culturally conservative reading of *The Edible Woman* concerned with maintaining the status quo, and the feminist intent on challenging traditional cultural and literary practices.

If the woman writer chooses to write a female-centered story "based in specifically female experience," comments Joanne Frye, "she is choosing a story that requires passivity and self-denial, a story with a prewritten ending: self existing *only* in relationship, with marriage and/or motherhood as the appropriate denouement, or the demise of the self" (3). Described by Atwood as a novel that makes "a negative statement about society" (Sandler 13), *The Edible Woman* does have a definite political and literary agenda. Focusing her narrative on traditional female rites of passage—courtship and marriage—Atwood is aware of the limitations imposed on theme and novelistic format by the masculine plot of desire, and she self-consciously resists the romantic love-plot formula. Atwood's oppositional intent is apparent in her description of *The Edible Woman* as an "anti-comedy." If in the "standard 18th-century comedy" the young couple must "trick or overcome" the "difficulty" of an individual "who embodies the restrictive forces of society" so they can get married, in *The Edible Woman,* in contrast, Peter—Marian MacAlpin's fiancé—embodies society's repressive forces. Because Peter "and the restrictive society are blended into one," Atwood remarks, the marriage resolution of the standard comedy would be "a tragic solution" for Marian (Gibson 20–21).

Unlike the traditional courtship novel in which the couple must overcome a series of frustrating obstacles to achieve the endpoint of marriage, *The Edible Woman* is patterned around, not a frustrated progression toward, but a frustrated movement away from romantic affiliation. *The Edible Woman* contradicts the traditional story of female maturation in which the "growth" of the heroine is viewed "as synonymous with the action of courtship," and marriage is regarded as the "climactic event" that "confers on the heroine her entire personal identity" (Boone 74). Enforcing the reader's discomfort with the romance scenario, Atwood's narrative elaborates on Marian's persecutory fears and disintegration anxiety as Peter assumes dominance over her. The novel contests the traditional story of female experience with its prescribed ending that insists on marriage and/or motherhood as the expected outcome for the female heroine. Instead, *The Edible Woman* shows how female passivity and submersion in the traditional wife and mother roles can lead not to self-fulfillment but to an intensifying sense of self-diminishment. Narrative with a vengeance, *The Edible Woman* focuses attention on the sexual objectification and potential victimization of Marian MacAlpin as she consents to femininity. But although Atwood presents her character as a potential victim, she also expresses her oppositional intent by disrupting the romance plot line, by interrupting romantic discourse, and by staging female revenge fantasies in *The Edible Woman.*

"Because all language is 'inherited' and because it is all socially and ideologically charged, the conflict of voices in a novel can reveal power structures and potential resistances to those structures," remarks Dale Bauer in her study of feminist dialogics (6). Through the dialogized female voices in the novel, Atwood both presents and undercuts the conservative messages given to Marian by the mid-1960s culture. Unlike Clara whose attitude toward her husband is "sentimental, like the love stories in the back numbers of women's magazines," Ainsley asserts that the "thing that ruins families . . . is the husbands" (134, 39). "[I]f I were you I'd get married in the States, it'll be so much easier to get a divorce when you need one," Ainsley tells Marian (86). But although Ainsley shuns marriage, she insists that every woman ought to have "at least one baby," sounding, when she makes this pronouncement, "like a voice on the radio saying that every woman should have at least one electric hair-dryer" (40). Ironically, while Ainsley accepts the inherited cultural belief that motherhood "fulfills" a woman's "deepest femininity," Clara urges Marian not to "believe what they tell you about maternal instinct"; moreover, Clara de-idealizes the mother-infant bond by comparing her baby to a leech or an octopus covered with suckers (40, 32, 31).

Enacting a pregiven feminine script as she begins to acquiesce to Peter, Marian finds herself speaking in a "soft flannelly" feminine voice that she barely recognizes as her own. "I'd rather leave the big decisions up to you," she says to him (92). Although Marian also speaks in an oppositional voice—"I've chopped Peter up into little bits. I'm camouflaging him as laundry and taking him down to bury him in the ravine," she tells Ainsley (94)—she learns to silence this voice when she is with Peter and subject to his social control. "I was about to make a sharp comment, but repressed it," Marian remarks. "Well you needn't bite my head off," she says to Peter, thinking to herself that she would have to "watch how she spoke" to him (64, 116). "[L]ife isn't run by principles but by adjustments," Marian tells herself (104), as she becomes increasingly dominated by Peter and thus assumes the preestablished feminine role assigned to her by romantic ideology: that of the passive sexual object.

Insistently exposing the female fears encoded in the traditional romance plot, *The Edible Woman* depicts Marian's intensifying paranoia as she becomes romantically involved with Peter. Explaining that one of the functions of the popular romance novel is to "deal with women's fears of and confusion about masculine behavior," Tania Modleski observes how such literature reflects the need of women to "read" men, to "engage in a continual deciphering of the motives" for their often frightening behavior (*Loving* 60, 34). That Marian's "reading" of Peter's behavior becomes increasingly infected with Gothic fears as he assumes dominance over her is telling. When Marian first attempts to "read" Peter, he appears ordinary enough. Fulfilling the culture's prescribed—and commodified—image of masculinity, he is "nicely packaged" (150): he resembles the young, well-groomed men in the cigarette ads and the plaid-jacketed sportsman in the Moose beer ad. And she imagines that Peter's attempts to have spontaneous sex with her—on a blanket in a field and on the sheepskin rug on his bedroom floor—are enactments of mass-culture fantasies found in men's magazines. "The field was, I guessed, a hunting story from one of the outdoorsy male magazines; I remembered he had worn a plaid jacket. The sheepskin I placed in one of the men's glossies, the kind with lust in pent-houses." But when Marian tries to "read" Peter's motive for wanting to have sex in the bathtub, her hidden fears surface. She imagines that he may have borrowed the idea for bathtub sex from "one of the murder mysteries he read as what he called 'escape literature'; but wouldn't that rather be someone drowned in the bathtub? A woman" (61).

Although Marian initially takes Peter at face value, she soon becomes preoccupied with discovering "what lay hidden under the surface, under the other surfaces" of Peter, "that secret identity which in spite of her many guesses and attempts and half-successes she was aware she had still not uncovered" (62, 120). It is suggestive that Marian fantasizes that Peter might secretly be the Underwear Man, an obscene phone caller who poses as a representative of Seymour Surveys doing a study on underwear. An otherwise normal man, the Underwear Man is "crazed" by the girdle advertisements found on buses, Marian imagines. "Society flaunted these slender laughing rubberized women before his eyes, urging, practically forcing upon him their flexible blandishments, and then refused to supply him with any. He had found when he had tried to buy the garment in question . . . that it came empty of the promised contents" (120). Pointing to one of the central premises—and anxieties—of *The Edible Woman,* Marian's comic-paranoid fantasy of the Underwear Man focuses attention on the cultural commodification of women, showing how men treat women as packaged goods, as objects of exchange and consumption.

The fact that Peter's grisly hunting story about killing a rabbit prefaces his pursuit of and proposal to Marian underlines the narrative's view of the sexual hunt as a form of predation. Describing how he gutted the animal after killing it with one shot, Peter tells how he slit the rabbit's stomach, grabbed "her" by the hind legs and then "gave her one hell of a crack, like a whip you see, and the next thing you know there was blood and guts all over the place. All over me, what a mess, rabbit guts dangling from the trees, god the trees were red for yards . . ." (70). Adumbrating *Surfacing*'s description of the "Americans," the "happy killers" who slaughter the heron and string it up like a lynch victim to "prove they could do it, they had the power to kill" (151, 138), Marian envisions Peter and his hunting friends as callous killers, their "mouths wrenched with laughter" (71). Unconsciously identifying with the rabbit in his story—"surprised" to find her feet moving, "wondering how they had begun" (73)—Marian flees only to be pursued and caught by Peter. In her "game of tag" (74) Marian unwittingly enacts the courtship ritual in which female flight attracts male pursuit and capture.

A precursor of the split good/bad male who repeatedly appears in Atwood's fiction, Peter is "ordinariness raised to perfection" (62), but he also harbors a secret, dangerous identity. Adept at masculine role-playing, Peter, when he becomes engaged to Marian, readily exchanges his "free-bachelor image for the mature-fiancé one," and he adjusts "his responses and acquaintances accordingly" (123). But Marian also begins to perceive Peter as a menacing presence. When she becomes the object of his sexual conquest as he is about to propose, she sees him as a sinister Gothic figure: his face is "strangely shadowed, his eyes gleaming like an animal's," his stare "intent, faintly ominous" (84). And when Peter proposes to her, she sees herself as "small and oval, mirrored in his eyes" (84), for as the object of male desire, Marian is subjected to the male gaze which seeks to assimilate, and thus erase, the female self. Trying to "read" Peter's dehumanizing gaze—he concentrates on her face "as though if he looked hard enough he would be able to see through her flesh and her skull and into the workings of her brain"—Marian imagines that he is "sizing her up as he would a new camera, trying to find the central complex of wheels and tiny mechanisms, the possible weak points, the kind of future performance to be expected: the springs of the machine. He wanted to know what made her tick" (153, 154). If Peter sounds "as though he'd just bought a shiny new car" when he becomes engaged, Marian, treated like a female commodity, gives him a "chrome-plated smile," her mouth feeling "stiff and bright and somehow expensive" (90).

When Peter, just before he asks Marian to marry him, acts as if she were a "stage-prop; silent but solid, a two-dimensional outline," she feels that he is not "ignoring" but instead "depending on" her (72). As a "stage-prop" and later as a "silent and smiling" object that Peter takes "pride in displaying" to his friends (181, 180), Marian is caught up in a masculine script which will slowly lead her to a frightening sense of self-alienation. For as Rita Felski observes in her remarks on the feminist narrative of self-discovery, the "internalization" of the notion of "female identity as supplementary to and supportive of a male figure" is indicative of "the deep-seated influence of patriarchal ideology." Moreover, the "sense of female identity as a lack, a problematic absence, offers no basis from which to challenge existing ideologies of gender as they are manifested at the level of commonsense assumptions and everyday practices" (129). Providing a psychological assessment of the inherent pathology of the traditional male/female relationship, *The Edible Woman* actively undercuts the popular romance formula which, as Tania Modleski observes, "insists upon and rewards feminine selflessness" by showing that the heroine achieves happiness "only by undergoing a complex process of self-subversion" (*Loving* 36–37). In *The Edible Woman,* Atwood reveals the dangerous gender politics inherent in the traditional marriage economy and in romantic discourse, which encodes and naturalizes the essentialist constructions of feminine selflessness and masculine self-assertion and conquest. The fact that the narrative shifts from first-person to third-person narration serves not only to emphasize Marian's self-alienation and threatened loss of self as she is objectified by the culture, but also to indicate that Marian's "sense of herself as sexual object makes her the object of someone else's discourse" (Greene, "Margaret Atwood's *The Edible Woman*" 105).

In an essaylike passage that both describes women's entrapment in masculine expectations and points to the central narcissistic anxiety dramatized in the text, Joe Bates chronicles the sad fate of women like his wife, Clara. When such a woman gets married, her "core"—the "centre of her personality, the thing she's built up; her image of herself"—gets "invaded." "Her feminine role and her core," as he explains, "are really in opposition, her feminine role demands passivity from her. . . . So she allows her core to get taken over by the husband. And when the kids come, she wakes up one morning and discovers she doesn't have anything left inside, she's hollow, she doesn't know who she is any more; her core has been destroyed" (242). To be "invaded" is to be rendered void within as the self is "taken over" and assimilated. While this passage clearly contains a political message—through Joe Bates, Atwood is telling her women readers to avoid such a fate—it also gives voice to the key anxiety found in the text. And by informing readers of the thematic significance of the nightmarish experiences Marian is undergoing, this passage is further designed to assuage potential reader anxiety about being enmeshed in the increasingly pathological world of the text.

Speaking a kind of body language, *The Edible Woman* reflects both the cultural identification of women with body and the pervasive fear of the uncontained, uncontrollable female body as it puts the "mature" female body on display and scrutinizes its isolated parts. At the office Christmas party, Marian examines the bodies of older women "with interest, critically, as though she had never seen them before." To Marian, the "mature" figure is a grotesque spectacle. "[N]ow she could see the roll of fat pushed up across Mrs. Gundridge's back by the top of her corset, the ham-like bulge of thigh, the creases around the neck, the large porous cheeks; the blotch of varicose veins glimpsed at the back of one plump crossed leg, the way her jowls jellied when she chewed. . . ." Observing the other women as they eat and talk, Marian is struck by their "dune-like contours of breast and waist and hip; their fluidity sustained some-where within by bones," and she is both fascinated with and repulsed by "the continual flux between the outside and the inside, taking things in, giving them out, chewing, words . . . babies, milk, excrement" (171).

Insistently the narrative thematizes Marian's anxiety—her "bridal nerves" (212)—as symptomatic of her repudiation of her femininity. But what subtends her rejection of the female body and bodily functions is a much deeper fear: what Adrienne Rich calls "matrophobia"—the fear "of *becoming one's mother*" (235). When Marian's distanced observa-tion of women with "mature" figures gives way to transient identifica-tion, the "matrophobia" underlying her reaction becomes apparent. Fantasizing that she is "one of them, her body the same, identical, merged with that other flesh," Marian feels "suffocated by this thick sargasso-sea of femininity" and fears she will be "sucked down" into "that liquid amorphous other." Anxious to reestablish the fixed bound-aries of the self to avoid this dreaded merger with the archaic mother, Marian wants "something solid, clear: a man . . . a fixed barrier" (172). In Nancy Chodorow's view, women have more fluid self-other bound-aries because in girlhood they tend "to remain part of the dyadic primary mother-child relationship" (166). But as Jean Wyatt remarks, females can also undergo the process Chodorow defines as unique to the male developmental track: "the process of negative identity formation," the "definition of the self as 'not-mother.'" Indeed, as Wyatt comments, women's fiction "is full of daughters who, like Chodorow's male chil-dren, define themselves through denial of the mother in them" (112, 113).

Although *The Edible Woman* omits the story of Marian's relationship with her mother and indeed depicts Marian as free from family stric-tures—for her family "no longer" seems "to belong to her" (173)—it nevertheless dramatizes the dangers of an extended symbiotic mother-daughter bond. It does this in the displaced, peripheral drama of the tyrannical landlady and her "cretinous," infantalized daughter, a "hulk-ing creature of fifteen or so" who is called "the child" by her mother and who wears a hair-ribbon "perched up on top of her gigantic body" (11). Marianne Hirsch, in her analysis of nineteenth-century novels in which the mother is "silenced, denigrated, simply eliminated, or written out," remarks that such "[m]aternal absence and silence is too much the condition of the heroine's development, too much the basis of the fiction itself; the form it takes is too akin to repression" (47). If in *The Edible Woman* the mother's absence is the condition of the daughter's development, the narrative also expresses repressed fears of the overbearing mother through the character of the landlady, who fits the "malevolent yet inconsequential" brand of maternal representation described by Hirsch (44). For although the landlady is the precursor of the hostile mother figure that occurs repeatedly in Atwood's fiction, she is easily mastered in the text. Operating by the "law of nuance," the landlady speaks for the official culture, making Marian feel as if she is "forbidden to do everything" (14). But the landlady is ultimately silenced by Ainsley, who asserts her right to speak in dialogic opposition to the repressive maternal voice. When the pregnant Ainsley accuses the landlady of being a "hypocrite" and a "bourgeois fraud" and claims she does not want her "exerting any negative pre-natal influences," Marian is surprised at how "easily" the landlady is "deflated" and wonders why she has been "slightly afraid of her" (230).

It is ironic that Marian perceives Peter as a "fixed barrier" against the amorphous world of femininity which she dreads. Because romantic love assigns her the male-defined feminine roles she wishes to escape and insists that she consent to femininity, her romantic affiliation with Peter leads not to heightened self-definition but to a frightening sense of self-diminishment. Fearing assimilation by the archaic mother, she finds herself, instead, being slowly assimilated—taken over—by Peter. As Peter increasingly dominates her and invades her "core" self, Marian becomes plagued by narcissistic fears of body-self disintegration. In a dream that occurs early in the text, she imagines that her body is dissolving: "I had looked down and seen my feet beginning to dissolve, like melting jelly, and had put on a pair of rubber boots just in time only to find that the ends of my fingers were turning transparent" (43). When she wakes up the morning after she has accepted Peter's proposal of marriage, she feels that her "mind" is "as empty as though someone had scooped out the inside" of her skull (84). Later, when she has dinner with Peter and experiences her first significant loss of appetite, she looks at her distorted image reflected in the bowl of a spoon, observing how her "huge torso" narrows "to a pinhead" at the spoon's handle end (150). This, in turn, recalls Marian's fantasy of the pregnant Clara as body, not mind-identified: as "a swollen mass of flesh with a tiny pinhead" (117).

Disintegration fears also emerge in Marian's response to Clara's pregnancy: she imagines that Clara is being "dragged slowly down into the gigantic pumpkin-like growth" that envelops her body or that she is "being absorbed in, or absorbed by, her tuberous abdomen" (117, 133). Having babies is psychically equivalent to a threat to the self, in Marian's view. For the pregnant Clara's body seems "somehow beyond her, going its own way without reference to any directions of hers," and during the "later, more vegetable stage" of her pregnancy, Marian tends to forget that Clara has "a mind at all or any perceptive faculties above the merely sentient and sponge-like" (36, 133).

That Marian, after she becomes engaged to Peter, feels trapped in a temporal sequence reveals how difficult it is to escape the inexorable logic of the romance plot. Marian imagines "time eddying and curling almost visibly around her feet, rising around her, lifting her body . . . and bearing her, slowly and circuitously but with the inevitability of water moving downhill, towards the distant, not-too-distant-anymore day they had agreed on . . . that would end this phase and begin another" (118). Plotting to forestall this closural moment, Atwood ushers Duncan into the text. But while Duncan functions structurally in the novel as the rival lover, he is no victim of romantic illusion. Mocking the myth of romantic attraction, Duncan claims that Fish picked up his notion that he will experience an "electric shock" when he meets the "right person" from "Some Enchanted Evening or D. H. Lawrence or something" (191). And for Duncan, lovemaking is "too literary," the "scenes have been done already." When he is with a "limp and sinuous and passionate" woman, he thinks, "oh god it's yet another bad imitation of whoever it happens to be a bad imitation of" and he loses interest or starts to laugh (195). In *The Edible Woman* Atwood not only presents a rival lover whose dialogic speech disrupts romantic discourse, but she also deliberately subverts the "double suitor convention" in which the heroine "must be weaned from an initially mistaken male object of desire by a second, more responsible wooer, who, as her mentor figure, provides a model of the correct behavior to which she herself needs to aspire in order to become an autonomous adult" (Boone 75). Whereas in the traditional courtship plot the heroine's developing maturity is gauged by her relationship to the rival lovers—one being regarded as socially responsible and the other as irresponsible—*The Edible Woman* makes the asocial, self-absorbed Duncan into Peter's rival and Marian's mentor.

An interpretation actively promoted by the text—and embraced by numerous critics—is that Duncan represents a hidden aspect of Marian's self. Occurring in a gap in the novel's realistic surface, Duncan suddenly materializes as if in response to Marian's unacknowledged needs. Suggestively, he tells her that he is "not human at all," that he comes "from the underground" (144). When Marian puts on Duncan's dressing gown, he says to her, "you look sort of like me in that" (148). To explain why he broke his bathroom mirror, he tells her, "I got tired of being afraid I'd walk in there some morning and wouldn't be able to see my own reflection in it. . . . [I]t was a perfectly understandable symbolic narcissistic gesture . . ." (143). Responding to Duncan's confusing speech, Marian fears that "if she said the wrong thing, took the wrong turning, she would suddenly find herself face to face with something she could not cope with" (144).

As if intent on rescuing Marian from her anorexia, the text does not depict her as becoming dangerously thin. Instead, this threat to Marian's body-self becomes figured in Duncan's "long famished body" (263). Duncan is "cadaverously thin," his ribs "stuck out like those of an emaciated figure in a medieval woodcut" (48). When Marian kisses him, she has the "impression of thinness and dryness" as though his body and face "were really made of tissue paper or parchment stretched on a frame of wire coathangers" (103). Later she imagines that if she were to reach out and touch him, "he would begin to crumble" (192). Similarly, in Duncan's "womb-symbol"—the skeleton found in the museum's ancient Egyptian exhibit room—the text provides yet another monitory image of Marian's endangered self. Marian finds the "stunted figure pathetic: with its jutting ribs and frail legs and starved shoulder-blades it looked like the photographs of people from underprivileged countries or concentration camps" (192, 193). Partially displacing Marian's fears onto the enigmatic Duncan—a character readers are forced to decode—the narrative temporarily deflects attention away from the anxiety subtending the description of Marian's self-starvation.

Unlike Duncan, who declares that he wants to be "an amoeba" to avoid the complications of personhood, Marian is afraid of "losing her shape, spreading out, not being able to contain herself" (207, 225). Presented with Marian's anorexic disorder, the reader is prompted to offer a diagnosis. If Marian's self-starvation concretizes her growing sense of self-fragility and diminishment, it also reflects her resistance to the cultural constructions of femininity. For in the text's code, the anorexic body can be read not only as a dissent from the body-identified, sargasso-sea femininity found in the amorphous, uncontainable "mature" figure or the pregnant female form, but also as a protest against the "slender laughing" women depicted in advertisements or the image of womanly fragility found in the "translucent perfume-advertisement" brand of femininity (120, 35). Remarking on the "continuum between female disorder and 'normal' feminine practice" observable in "a close reading of those disorders to which women have been particularly vulnerable," Susan Bordo comments that the "bodies of disordered women . . . offer themselves as an aggressively graphic text for the interpreter—a text that insists, actually demands, it be read as a cultural statement, a statement about gender" (16). In a disorder like anorexia, "the woman's body" can be viewed "as a surface on which conventional constructions of femininity are exposed starkly to view" (20). Describing the "painfully literal inscription, on the anorexic's body, of the rules governing the construction of contemporary femininity," Bordo posits that the "control of female appetite for food" provides a "concrete expression" of the general rule which governs the construction of femininity in our culture: "that female hunger—for public power, for independence, for sexual gratification—be contained, and the public space that women be allowed to take up be circumscribed, limited." Required to develop "a totally other-oriented emotional economy," women "learn to feed others, not the self, and to construe any desires for self-nurturance and self-feeding as greedy and excessive" (18). As Duncan tells Marian, "[H]unger is more basic than love. Florence Nightingale was a cannibal, you know" (102). What subtends the "other-oriented" ideal of femininity—embodied in the cultural representation of the self-sacrificing nurse—is a deep and all-consuming female hunger. Through the anorexic's "long famished body," then, *The Edible Woman* protests the contained, other-oriented femininity embodied in the slender female form.

Warning against the dangers inherent in women's acquiescence to masculine expectations, *The Edible Woman* depicts Marian's transformation into the consumable female object that Peter desires. During her preparations for Peter's engagement party, Marian goes to the hairdresser's where she is operated on "like a slab of flesh, an object," while her hair is "carefully iced and ornamented" like a cake (215, 214). Her body "curiously paralysed," she passively gazes at her "draped figure prisoned in the filigreed gold oval of the mirror." Surveying the "totally inert" women sitting under mushroom-shaped hairdryers, their heads "metal domes," she wonders if she, too, is being pushed toward this semimechanical existence, "this compound of the simply vegetable and the simply mechanical" (215–16). In the hairdresser's scene, *The Edible Woman* dramatizes what Catharine MacKinnon describes as the "thingification of women who have been pampered and pacified into nonpersonhood" (520). Later, when Marian sees her reflection in the silver globes of the bathtub taps, she perceives herself as a "curiously-sprawling pink thing," for her "waterlogged body" appears "bulging and distorted." And when she looks down at her body, it seems "somehow no longer quite her own. All at once she was afraid that she was dissolving, coming apart layer by layer like a piece of cardboard in a gutter puddle" (224).

Metamorphosed into the object of Peter's desire—an artificial doll in a red dress—Marian surveys herself in the mirror after make-up is applied to her face and finds herself staring "into the egyptian-lidded and outlined and thickly-fringed eyes of a person she had never seen before" (228). Later, when she inspects herself in Peter's mirror, she perceives herself as fragmented, not whole. Unable to grasp the "total effect" created by the assorted details of her new appearance, she wonders what "lay beneath the surface these pieces were floating on, holding them all together?" When she gazes at her arms in the mirror, the only part of her without some artificial covering, they appear doll-like and "fake" to her, "like soft pinkish-white rubber or plastic, boneless, flexible" (235). In her "finely-adjusted veneers" and with her "huge billboard smile, peeling away in flaps and patches" (236, 251), Marian feels unreal. Anticipating *Surfacing*'s paranoid vision of people turning into machines, Marian, who earlier imagined that she had a "chrome-plated smile," fantasizes that as her billboard smile peels away, the "metal surface beneath" shows through (90, 251). But, predictably, Peter admires her new appearance, which fulfills the male ideal of a glamorized and sexualized femininity. When he tells her that she looks "absolutely marvellous," the "implication" is "that it would be most pleasant if she could arrange to look like that all the time" (235). Duncan, in contrast, is appalled when he sees her. "You didn't tell me it was a masquerade. . . . Who the hell are you supposed to be?" he asks Marian (245).

Femininity, as Atwood dramatizes in *The Edible Woman*, is a male-assigned role, an act and an acting out of feminine scripts, a masquerade. Indeed, femininity has been compared to transvestism, since, for a woman as for a transvestite, femininity is a role requiring "make-up, costumes, and well-rehearsed lines . . . in order to be properly performed" (Berman 124). According to Luce Irigaray, when women perform the masquerade, they "participate in man's desire, but at the price of renouncing their own," and "they submit to the dominant economy of desire in an attempt to remain 'on the market' in spite of everything"

(*This Sex* 133). But even as Atwood shows Marian submitting to the masquerade, she constructs a feminist reading position by focusing attention on femininity-as-masquerade. As Mary Ann Doane observes in her analysis of female spectatorship and film, the foregrounding of the masquerade "constitutes an acknowledgement that it is femininity itself which is constructed as mask" (81). Thus masquerade has the potential "to manufacture a distance from the image, to generate a problematic within which the image is manipulable, producible, and readable by the woman" (87).

Attracting Peter's gaze as she performs the feminine masquerade at his party, Marian becomes increasingly aware of her object status. Thus she panics when Peter asks to take her photograph, for to be photographed, she imagines, is to be "stopped, fixed indissolubly in that gesture, that single stance, unable to move or change" (252). As her sense of self-unreality grows, she envisions herself as a "two-dimensional small figure in a red dress, posed like a paper woman in a mail-order catalogue, turning and smiling, fluttering in the white empty space" (250). Anticipating *Surfacing*'s critique of women like Anna, who become imitations of imitations as they try to conform to the commercialized images of women presented in glossy magazines, Marian assumes a billboard smile and the pose of a woman in a mail-order catalogue. All but overwhelmed by her persecutory fears, she imagines that Peter, with his camera/gun aimed at her, is a dangerous predator. "That dark intent marksman with his aiming eye had been there all the time, hidden by the other layers, waiting for her at the dead centre: a homicidal maniac with a lethal weapon in his hands" (253). If, in the text's code, the camera/gun is a signifier of the voyeuristic male gaze which fixates woman as sexual object, to be "shot" by the camera/gun is to undergo a terrifying loss of self.

Marian's persecutory fears also erupt in her fantasies about her future life with Peter. At first she imagines that the "real Peter, the one underneath," is a "bungalow-and-double-bed man," a "charcoal-cooking-in-the-backyard man," a "home-movie man." But when she searches through time's corridors and rooms and finds the middle-aged, balding Peter standing beside a barbecue, she discovers that he is holding a large cleaver in one of his hands. That Marian has no real subjective presence in the masculine plot of desire is signaled in her chilling recognition that Peter is alone, that she isn't "there" (249–50). Caught up in a sinister Gothic plot, Marian fantasizes that her husband-to-be is a potential murderer, a Gothic fear that will continue to preoccupy Atwood's novels.

"[M]aybe you want me to rescue you? What from?" Duncan asks Marian after she escapes from Peter before he can photograph her (254). In the complex scene that follows, in which Marian and Duncan have sex in a cheap hotel room, Atwood uses the conventional love triangle plot both as a weapon and as a device to rescue Marian from her relationship with Peter. Invoking and parodying the male fantasy of the split good/ bad woman, the text casts Marian, who has shunned the culturally scripted roles of wife and mother, as a prostitute. In her red party dress, which Peter admired and which she felt made her "a perfect target" for his camera/gun, she is the "Scarlet Woman" (251, 254). "[I]f I'm dressed like one and acting like one, why on earth shouldn't he think I really am one?" Marian says to herself when the night clerk at the hotel leers at her (258). Assigning Marian yet another role—that of the rescuing noble nurse who is intent on curing Duncan's sexual problem—the narrative enacts a fantasy of female sexual empowerment. Marian recognizes the lure of the mass-culture nurse fantasy, for she is aware of the "embryonic noble nurse that is supposed to be curled, efficient and self-sacrificing, in the heart of every true woman" (111). Using and subverting the culturally sanctioned nurse fantasy—which is associated with the traditional feminine virtues of pleasing and serving others—the text reveals what is latent in this collective fantasy of womanly self-sacrifice: the wish to take control.

"I can tell you're admiring my febrility. I know it's appealing, I practice at it; every woman loves an invalid. I bring out the Florence Nightingale in them," Duncan had earlier told Marian (102). In a deliberate reversal of roles, Marian is the sexual aggressor as she assumes the "starched nurse-like" role (271) in the lovemaking scene and Duncan is the passive (and temporarily impotent) recipient. When Marian orders Duncan to remove his clothes and get into bed, he hangs his head "like a rebuked child." Unlike Peter who threatens Marian with his destructive male gaze, Duncan goggles at her in "a frog-like manner." As she walks "doggedly" toward the bed, she thinks that what she is undertaking will demand "perseverance" on her part. "If she had had any sleeves on she would have rolled them up." And indeed she does find it difficult to evoke any response from the "seemingly-passive surface, the blank white formless thing lying insubstantial in the darkness before her." Duncan echoes Marian's revulsion at the "mature" female body when he tells her that he feels "like some kind of little stunted creature crawling over the surface of a huge mass of flesh. . . . There's just altogether too much flesh around here. It's suffocating" (259–61). Reversing the gender hierarchy by assigning Duncan the role of the passive sex object, *The Edible Woman* acts out a fantasy of female sexual domination and male subordination.

Even more telling, the predatory, sexually aggressive Len Slank, who is "a seducer of young girls" (32), is openly punished by the narrative. Using parody to provide a feminist-dialogic commentary on the traditional seduction plot, the narrative depicts Len Slank's unwitting seduction by Marian's roommate, Ainsley, who, despite her "young and inexperienced" demeanor, is "in reality a scheming superfemale carrying out a foul plot against him, using him in effect as an inexpensive substitute for artificial insemination with a devastating lack of concern for his individuality" (125). That women are defined by their culture as passive objects for male consumption is one of the central premises of *The Edible Woman*. But Atwood's narrative also expresses a subversive female anger through its elaboration on a male myth voiced by Peter: that women are "predatory and malicious" (65).

Forced to assume a "pink-gingham purity" (121) to attract Len Slank, Ainsley resembles "one of the large plump dolls in the stores . . . with washable rubber-smooth skin and glassy eyes and gleaming artificial hair" (69–70). But despite her doll-like appearance as she performs the feminine masquerade, she is a female predator. "[I]t doesn't seem ethical," Marian says of Ainsley's campaign to get impregnated by Len Slank. "It's like bird-liming, or spearing fish by lantern or something." As Ainsley plays the little girl role designed to appeal to Len Slank's desire for sexual conquest, her "inert patience" resembles that of a "pitcher-plant in a swamp . . . waiting for some insect to be attracted, drowned, and digested" (71–72, 76).

When he later learns that Ainsley is pregnant, Len is "crushed." Marian compares his behavior to that of "a white grub suddenly unearthed from its burrow and exposed to the light of day. A repulsive blinded writhing. It amazed her though that it had taken so little, really, to reduce him to that state" (165, 164–65). In a reversal of the narrative's dominant plot—in which Peter preys on Marian—in this peripheral drama the woman preys upon and sexually uses the man. "All along you've only been *using* me. . . . Oh, they're all the same. You weren't interested in me at all. The only thing you wanted from me was my body!" Len complains to Ainsley. When Len expresses his anxieties about being "mentally tangled up in Birth. Fecundity. Gestation," which he finds physically disgusting, Ainsley angrily accuses him of "uterus envy" (163–64). As in the description of Marian's seduction of Duncan, the Ainsley/Len seduction plot reverses the gender hierarchy and acts out female desires for power and revenge. Indeed, Len Slank is not only emasculated by the text, he is also infantilized, reduced to sharing a room with Clara's infant son, Arthur.

In a strategic subversion of the traditional closure of the romance plot, *The Edible Woman* resolves Ainsley's plot through her marriage to Fish. Ainsley, who initially makes pronouncements against marriage, determines to find a husband when she learns that psychological studies "scientifically" prove that a child needs "a strong Father Image in the home" (186). When Len Slank refuses to marry her, she marries Fish, who views her not as a person but instead as an embodiment of the womb symbolism which so fascinates him. "I think I already know who you are," Fish says to Ainsley when he first meets her, "patting her belly tenderly . . . his voice heavy with symbolic meaning" (248). "In traditional comedy, boy meets girl, there are complications, the complications are resolved and the couple is united," Atwood remarks. "In my book the couple is not united and the wrong couple gets married. The complications are resolved, but not in a way that reaffirms the social order" (Sandler 13).

Determined, in *The Edible Woman,* to tell the "other side of the story," Atwood also provides a postromantic critique of the conventional resolutions of the love story. In the view of Rachel DuPlessis, "One of the great moments of ideological negotiation in any work occurs in the choice of a resolution. . . ." Describing the romance plot as a "trope for the sex-gender system as a whole," DuPlessis explains how traditional romance plot resolutions—the happy ending which rewards the heroine with marriage and the unhappy ending which punishes her with death—are part of the "cultural practice of romance." Whereas marriage "celebrates the ability to negotiate with sexuality and kinship," death results from "inabilities or improprieties in this negotiation" (3, 5, 4). Joseph Boone, in his discussion of the "privileged role played by modes of closure in the traditional love-plot," observes that "the impetus toward concluding stasis" works to "cut short any serious or prolonged inquiry into the ideological framework informing the fictional construct. For by leaving the reader in a state of unquestioning repose and acceptance, the self-contained or 'classic' text inculcates a vision of a coherence or stability underlying social reality and cultural convention alike . . ." (78). In contrast, *The Edible Woman* refuses to reaffirm the social order or provide the traditional "closed" ending of the marriage resolution. Instead, it incorporates elements of female protest and revenge in the novel's final—and controversial—cake-woman scene.

Interestingly, before reaching this final "resolution" to Marian's problems, the narrative invokes the inherited closure in which the price for the heroine's failure to successfully negotiate the romance plot is death. When Marian finds herself totally unable to eat—"Her body had cut itself off. The food circle had dwindled to a point, a black dot, closing everything outside"—she faces the prospect of "starving to death" (264, 271). In the displaced drama of Duncan, who is the very image of suicidal depression as he sits "crouched on the edge" of the snow-covered ravine cliff "gazing into the empty pit" (272), the text enacts the traditional tragic closure. The state Duncan is attracted to is "absolute zero." "[I]n the snow," he tells Marian, "you're as near as possible to nothing" (271). Refusing to offer Marian advice when she tells him she does not want to go back to Peter, Duncan remarks, "[I]t's your own personal cul-de-sac, you invented it, you'll have to think of your own way out" (272). Invoking but then discrediting the tragic ending of the failed love plot, the narrative finds a "way out" for Marian in the cake-woman scene, which is designed to puzzle readers and force them to interpret. Both using and refusing the master narrative of the traditional romance plot in *The Edible Woman,* Atwood is aware of what Joanne Frye describes as the "power of a male-dominant sexual ideology" to entrap "women characters and women novelists within outworn plots," but also of the ability of fictional narrative to resist "fixity" and to respond to its "social context through interaction rather than simple ideological miming" (5, 6).

When Marian creates the cake-lady as "a test, simple and direct as litmus-paper," she wants to avoid words and entanglement in a discussion. Although she has a "sudden desire" to tell Peter "the whole story," she also asks "what good" that would do (274). Marian, who recognizes the power of masculine discourse to silence the female voice, finds another way to communicate meaning. Through the cake-woman "text," she signifies her own transformation into a consumable object. Asserting active mastery over passive suffering, Marian does to the cake-woman what was done to her. She begins "to operate" on the cake-woman, just as she was operated on at the hairdresser's; she scoops out part of the cake and makes a head with it, repeating her feeling that the contents of her head had been "scooped out" after she became engaged to Peter; and she uses icing to draw "masses of intricate baroque scrolls and swirls" of hair on her creation, reenacting what was done to her when her hair was decorated like a cake (276, 277).

After Marian completes the cake-woman, she offers it to Peter. "You've been trying to destroy me, haven't you," she says to him. "You've been trying to assimilate me. But I've made you a substitute . . ." (279). Refusing to devour the cake, Peter flees, and then Marian, finding herself suddenly hungry, begins to eat the cake herself. When Marian subsequently tells Duncan that Peter was trying to destroy her, he replies that in actuality she was "trying to destroy" Peter. "What does it matter," he tells her. "[Y]ou're back to so-called reality, you're a consumer" (287). What the culture's official story of women as passive objects of male consumption leaves out, the text suggests, is the consuming female hunger for power and revenge. The fact that Peter's eyes widen "in alarm" and he leaves "quite rapidly" when Marian presents him with the cake-woman and accuses him of trying to destroy her is also suggestive (279). For as Dale Bauer remarks, "When women step out of their traditional function as sign; when they refuse the imposition of the gaze; when they exchange their sign-status for that of manipulator of signs, they do so through dialogic polemics. And, at that moment of refusal, they become threatening to the disciplinary culture which appears naturalized" (3).

A novel that makes a negative statement about society as it focuses on Marian's initial consent to and ultimate dissent from femininity, *The Edible Woman* is also potentially anxiety-provoking as it involves readers in the troubling plight of Atwood's character. Finding *The Edible Woman* a "perplexing book" that has an "uneasy appeal," T. D. Mac Lulich describes the narrative as "a series of haunting images, a sequence of dreamlike hallucinations which flicker through the mind" of Atwood's heroine. "Where, in this stream of subjective images," asks MacLulich, "can the reader find a firm point of reference? Is there any way of seeing past the obviously distorted perceptions of the central character?" (111). Sherrill Grace similarly comments that the reader becomes "enmeshed" in the novel's "increasing improbability" and is "locked within" Marian's perceptions (*Violent* 91, 94). If, as these comments suggest, reader proximity to Atwood's character can be unsettling, Atwood also uses novelistic form and design to provide a "firm point of reference" for her reader and to defensively aestheticize the persecutory fears and disintegration anxiety that impel the narrative.

In an oft-discussed passage that, at once, parodies academic discourse, thematizes the text, and indirectly focuses attention on the artistic design of *The Edible Woman*, Fish—a graduate student in English prone to long-winded discourses on literary symbolism—discusses *Alice in Wonderland*. "Of course everybody knows *Alice* is a sexual-identity-crisis book that's old stuff, it's been around for a long time . . . ," insists Fish, who indulges in grandiose displays of his intellectual mastery of the text. In Fish's analysis, Alice is "trying to find her role" as a woman. "Yes, well that's clear enough. These patterns emerge. Patterns emerge. One sexual role after another is presented to her but she seems unable to accept any of them, I mean she's really blocked" (199). This embedded passage provides an interpretive key to *The Edible Woman*, indicating that what happens to Marian can be understood as a "sexual-identity crisis." Pointing to a pattern of signification within *The Edible Woman*, the *Alice* passage specifies the kinds of details and descriptions that can be isolated and connected together. The *Alice* passage also anticipates a common critical interest in the emerging patterns of signification within *The Edible Woman*. Critics, for example, have traced the novel's *Alice in Wonderland* parallels (see, e.g., Harkness, Nodelman, Rigney, Stow) or have found analogues to Atwood's narrative in Conrad or in the fairy tale (see Carrington, "'I'm Stuck'"; MacLulich; Wilson, "Fairy-Tale Cannibalism"). In a similar vein, Linda Hutcheon, who sees the novel as "highly structured," claims that *The Edible Woman* "is as tightly knit as a lyric poem" and that the narrative's "thematic configurations . . . can actually be mapped out" ("From Poetic to Narrative Structures" 17, 20).

A carefully designed narrative, *The Edible Woman* promotes, at least in part, a defensive reading strategy as it draws attention away from the female anxieties dramatized in the text and onto the controlling authorial presence behind the text. It is, nonetheless, a book that has an "uneasy appeal," and the novel's ending seems designed to add to the reader's sense of uneasiness.

"One of us has to be the sympathetic listener and the other one gets to be tortured and confused," Duncan tells Marian in the final section of the novel (284), just as Atwood both invites her readers to sympathize with Marian and confuses them about the meaning of the closure. The cake-woman scene, with its enactment of female revenge, does serve to rescue Marian from her immediate problems. For after making the cake-woman and offering it to Peter, Marian is cured of her eating disorder, her engagement to Peter is broken, and she is able to think of herself "in the first person singular again" (284). Yet the ending remains puzzling. In a maneuver meant to entice and frustrate literary interpreters, the closure indicates that the cake is a "symbol" and insists that it is "only a cake" (279, 280). Because the closure both tells and refuses to tell what it knows, readers are left with the uneasy sense that they have not mastered the text but rather that the text has mastered them. "Duncan sheds more darkness than light on the symbolic significance of the cake, and on the meaning of the novel as a whole," writes one critic who seems frustrated with the novel's closure (MacLulich 127–28). "Perhaps there are as many interpretations of Marian's symbolic cake and of the ending of *The Edible Woman* as there are readers," writes another (Rigney 33). Ironically, Marian's nonverbal communication—her desire to avoid words and escape becoming "tangled up in a discussion" (274)—has provoked a seemingly endless critical conversation as critic/readers have felt compelled to insert themselves into and to supplement the text as they attempt to make sense of the novel's conclusion.

As a reader of her own novel, Atwood, too, has felt compelled to join the debate about *The Edible Woman*'s closure. In a positive reading of the cake-woman scene, Atwood comments that Marian is "acting, she's doing an action. Up until that point she has been evading, avoiding, running away, retreating, withdrawing" (Gibson 25). And yet, in another, more pessimistic reading, Atwood—describing the narrative as a "circle"—comments that Marian ends where she began (Sandler 14). Moreover, Fish's comment on the conclusion of *Alice*—"you can't say that by the end of the book she has reached anything that can be definitely called maturity" (199)—seems designed as an authorial gloss on the closure of *The Edible Woman*. Mirroring Atwood's conflicting readings of the closing scene, critics are divided in their interpretations of the ending.

Responding to Duncan's assertion that Marian has returned to "so-called reality" by becoming "a consumer," Robert Lecker feels that "Duncan's words suggest that Marian's plight is not resolved, and that the plot of *The Edible Woman* is metaphorically circular." According to Lecker, in offering Duncan and Peter the cake and in consuming it herself, Marian "re-enacts her female as food role" (179). For Gayle Greene, Duncan's words are similarly troubling, suggesting that Marian "resumes her place in a system that threatens her life." And while Marian's cake-woman "is a gesture of defiance, a way of saying 'no' to a system that defines women as commodities and devours them," Greene still finds it "difficult to see what Marian *will* be when she grows up, what she will do—what, in the terms of the novel, she will 'turn into'" ("Margaret Atwood's *The Edible Woman*" 111). Describing the "politics" of Marian's act of eating the cake-woman, Pamela Bromberg argues that in consuming the cake-woman, Marian "is quite literally joining her subject and object selves. . . . She has become active again, an agent, a subject, a consumer, rather than a consumable object of exchange traded on the marriage market" (18). But Bromberg is also bothered by the novel's closing description of Duncan finishing the cake. "[S]ince Marian has not been able to put her understanding into words, the reader is left to wonder whether he will then devour her." Marian "is more self-assertive and healthy, but for how long?" Bromberg asks (20). Also bothered by the ending, Jerome Rosenberg feels that while the experiences undergone by Marian "suggest the possibility of a positive transformation in her life," she, nevertheless, appears to have "changed very little" by the novel's conclusion (101).

Other critics are more positive in their reading of the closure. Responding to Atwood's comment that Marian's "choices remain much the same at the end of the book as they are at the beginning: a career going nowhere, or marriage as an exit from it" ("Introduction" 370), Barbara Rigney is "tempted to argue with Atwood about the ending" of the novel. "[S]urely Marian knows more than she did in the beginning . . . ," writes Rigney. "[A]t least she has come to terms with something, has objectified her situation and apprehended it more realistically. The cake thus serves as a reflection, a way of seeing herself as in a mirror, and it expresses a truth not before perceived" (34). In the view of Jayne Patterson, Marian's "fashioning and eating of the cake signifies her recognition and rejection of her former compliant self, culminating in her new ability to respond to her own inner feelings" (152). "[B]y demolishing society's synthetic stereotype of femininity through the ingenious mirroring-device of the cake," argues Nora Stovel, "Marian frees herself to realize her own true identity" (53). For Catherine McLay, the cake "feast" signals "the celebration of Marian's new freedom and even rebirth." At the end, according to McLay, Marian "has gained a sense of identity and a new knowledge of self" ("The Dark Voyage" 138, 126). In the view of T. D. MacLulich, at the novel's end Marian "is a whole person again" and while her "fate is uncertain . . . she will face it squarely instead of trying to escape" (128). And for Perry Nodelman, who finds Marian a "sympathetic" character, *The Edible Woman* is "a convincing narrative of personal growth" (82, 81). It is revealing that so many critics seem intent on rescuing Marian. For in the structured, controlled art of literary interpretation, critic/readers can reconstruct and rework the novel's closure and thus act out the rescue wish that the text generates but refuses to wholly gratify.

Although Atwood refuses to provide a definitive rescue in the closing scene of her novel, she does rescue her character from the traditional romantic and novelistic ideology that insists on marriage as the endpoint of the story of female maturation. "Feminist writers must engage with, and contradict, traditional narrative patterning in order to (re)construct texts capable of articulating their marginalized, oppositional positioning—both inside, described by, patriarchal ideology (as the idealist construct, Woman) and outside that discourse, experiential witnesses to its contradictions, its mystifications (as women) . . . ," writes Anne Cranny-Francis (15). Constructing a feminist reading position by both using and contradicting the conventional romance plot, *The Edible Woman* dismantles and demystifies the marriage ideal by laying bare what has long been naturalized—and hence ignored—in the traditional romance scenario: the painful objectification and self-diminishment of women in a male-defined order.

3

Cultural Feminism, Female Madness, and Rage in *Surfacing*

A novel that has been "[r]apidly incorporated into the standard feminist literary canon" (Hirsch 140), *Surfacing* is designed to appeal to a very special interpretive community—the cultural feminists—in its construction of a feminist reading position. " '[C]ultural feminists,' " as Rita Felski explains, "espouse a dualistic vision which counterposes a conception of a holistic, harmonious, and organic 'femininity' against an alienated, rationalist, and aggressive masculinity. These dichotomies constitute a significant dimension within feminist ideology, which in turn finds its expression in numerous fictional texts, in which the heroine discovers her true 'feminine' self beyond male-defined social roles, a subjectivity frequently described in strongly neo-Romantic terms as a form of mystical, intuitive empathy with nature." This brand of feminism is related to "widespread manifestations of cultural pessimism in contemporary Western societies, as expressed in the current reactions against industrialism and technology and the increased prevalence of ecological and back to nature movements." But because this approach views feminism as "a mystical secret knowledge residing in the inner worlds of women," Felski finds the political implications of cultural feminism troubling, for it "brings with it all the attendant dangers of quietism" (76). Felski is also troubled by cultural feminism's "mystification of femininity" and its "uncritical celebration of irrationalism." But although problematic because of its essentialism and its apoliticism, cultural feminism "as a poetic discourse . . . gives voice to a powerful experience of cultural dislocation." For Felski, the "Romantic feminist vision" derives from "a psychological and aesthetic (rather than political) conception of liberation" (149, 148).

"Every binary split creates a temptation to merely reverse its terms, to elevate what has been devalued and denigrate what has been overvalued," remarks Jessica Benjamin (9). Using this tactic, *Surfacing* reverses the hierarchical binary oppositions undergirding patriarchal ideology by valorizing femininity, nature, and the irrational and by devaluing masculinity, culture, and the rational. A novel premised on the ideology of cultural feminism, *Surfacing* rejects the masculinist culture—which is depicted as both rationalistic and dangerously aggressive—and idealizes a nature-identified femininity. But if *Surfacing* "has been read as a paradigmatic feminist tale of mythic dimensions" (Hirsch 140), it is also a "terrorist text," to borrow Patricia Yaeger's phrase (*Honey-Mad Women* 3), designed to enmesh readers in the female fears and angry fantasies it dramatizes. Described as "a remarkable, and remarkably misunderstandable" work and as a novel that "has to be read and experienced" (Schaeffer 319; Laurence 45), *Surfacing* does self-consciously evoke a world of myth and mysticism. But it also undercuts its own romantic feminism through its troubling depictions of female madness and rage.

Set in an era of sexual liberation—somewhere in the early 1970s—Atwood's novel exposes the sexist precepts that undergird the ideology of sexual emancipation. Drawing attention to the power politics of gender relations, it shows how women, in an age of supposed sexual freedom, remain bound in a social formation that assigns man the role of sexual aggressor and woman that of passive victim and sexual object. "*[W]hat* sexuality are women to be liberated to enjoy?" as Susan Sontag asks. "Merely to remove the onus placed on the sexual expressiveness of women is a hollow victory if the sexuality they become freer to enjoy remains the old one that converts women into objects" (188). "As the sexism underlying the putatively 'emancipated' 1960s reminds us," remarks Joseph Boone, "the historical substitution of sexual freedom for conjugal relationship does not automatically transform the transhistorical 'rules' of sexual hierarchy, of dichotomization into mutually exclusive and hierarchical roles, or of the exploitation encoded in institutionalized marriage" (135). Through its angry descriptions of permissive sexuality, *Surfacing* reveals the attempted male coercion of sexually "liberated" women. And through its repeated depictions of couples locked in domestic and sexual warfare, *Surfacing* continues and expands *The Edible Woman*'s critique of the ideology of romantic fulfillment. Following the devolving trajectory of the Surfacer's failure at love and her collapse into madness, Atwood's novel simultaneously highlights the power of, and carries on a literary revolt against, the traditional romance plot.

"I've been married before and it didn't work out. I had a baby too. . . .

I don't want to go through that again," the narrator of *Surfacing* claims. Having "tried and failed," she sees herself as "inoculated, exempt, classified as wounded" (104, 105). To catch unawares the unwary reader, *Surfacing* uses deceptive plotting to destabilize the very notion of the linear movement and totalizing function of narrative. For when the seemingly "realistic" and initially convincing story of the Surfacer's failure at marriage and motherhood—which she compulsively tells and retells—is revealed to be pure fabrication, what has appeared to be narrative "truth" is exposed as an elaborate fictional construct. Indeed, *Surfacing* has been described as "anti-fiction, or at least [as] closer to it than 'straight' or traditional fiction" because it parodies "reader expectations and 'straight' novel conventions" (Wilson, "Deconstructing Text" 60). That *Surfacing* redundantly circles around the text's central lie—the fact of the Surfacer's affair (not marriage) and abortion (not the loss of the custody of her child through divorce)—and deceptively embeds it in layer upon layer of traditional romantic discourse points to Atwood's desire to radically disrupt the romance convention and make visible its constructed, scripted nature. Atwood also contests the discourse of "liberated" sexuality in *Surfacing* by exposing the exploitive male scripts encoded in the 1960s and 1970s ideology of sexual emancipation.

Framed as both a wilderness quest and detective story—which are traditional masculine formats—*Surfacing* recounts the narrator's journey into the Canadian north to search for her missing father. Like the narrator who, detective-like, must attempt to unravel the "clues" of her father's "puzzle," critic/readers must decipher clues in order to piece together the complex puzzle of the Surfacer's narrative history and to make sense of her highly defended personality. "I'd reasoned it out, unraveled the clues in his puzzle the way he taught us and they'd led nowhere. I felt as though he'd lied to me" (150), the narrator says at one point. So, too, readers may feel in some way deceived by the text with its "undependable, perhaps mad" narrator (Rigney 39). Readers may also feel bewildered and anxious as they become caught up in a web of denials and falsehoods and as they are subjected to the lethal emotions that erupt from the subsurfaces of the text. But if the absorbed reader of Atwood's novel shares the Surfacer's feeling of powerlessness, the detached critic can gain a sense of power over the text and some control over its disruptive emotions through a retrospective reconstruction of the suppressed narrative events surrounding the "lie."

In the psycho-logic of the novel, it is significant that the sense-making activity of unraveling the lie and reconstructing the narrative is initiated at the moment the narrator's affective storm begins. By involving readers in this sense-making process and making them aware of the constructed nature of narration, Atwood partially defends her readers against the dangerous—and potentially contagious—emotional energies unleashed in the narrative. And although readers may find proximity to Atwood's "shockingly deviant" narrator (Pratt 154) unsettling as she undergoes an experience of internal fragmentation, Atwood also erects novelistic defenses against the dreadful inner world she dramatizes by aestheticizing her character's perceptions and experiences. Indeed, while *Surfacing* deals with intensely painful emotions and while it subjects readers to the narrator's frightening collapse into madness, it is, nevertheless, a "cerebral work" and a "self-consciously mythic novel" (Harrison 74; Arnold and Cathy Davidson, "Anatomy" 38). By focusing attention on the novel's intricate design, on its mythological journey pattern of descent and return, and on its recurrent motifs, symbols, and images, Atwood invites critic/readers to participate in the narrative's defensive aestheticizing of the paranoid fears and female rage it inscribes. Thus, as the Surfacer's self-crisis unfolds, critic/readers can shift their identification from the increasingly out-of-control character to the totally in-control authorial presence behind the text. Such an identificatory bond is betrayed in the observation that while the Surfacer "may be confused . . . Atwood is not" (Rosenberg 110).

"I thought it would happen without my doing anything about it, I'd turn into part of a couple, two people linked together and balancing each other, like the wooden man and woman in the barometer house at Paul's," the narrator initially reflects when she imagines that David and Anna are happily married, that they have "some special method, formula, some knowledge" that she has "missed out on" (46). Wanting to learn if there is a "secret trick" to sustaining a marriage, she asks Anna for advice. "She talked to me then, or not to me exactly but to an invisible microphone suspended above her head: people's voices go radio when they give advice. She said you just had to make an emotional commitment, it was like skiing, you couldn't see in advance what would happen but you had to let go" (55). As Anna repeats the message given to her by the official culture, she speaks in an artificial "radio" voice. Encoded in her feminine "advice" on making an "emotional commitment" is the male command that women must "let go": that is, be passive recipients and not active agents. In dialogic conflict with the feminine voice of Anna, the Surfacer internally resists Anna's advice. "Let go of what, I wanted to ask her; I was measuring myself against what she was saying.

Maybe that was why I failed, because I didn't know what I had to let go of. For me it hadn't been like skiing, it was more like jumping off a cliff." In a description later repeated in *The Handmaid's Tale* (292) and *Cat's Eye* (282), the Surfacer recalls the anxious feeling she had when she was "married": that she was "in the air, going down, waiting for the smash at the bottom" (55).

An openly angry novel, *Surfacing* constructs a feminist reading position in its powerful critique of the ideology of romance. Contesting the myths of romantic love as the attraction of opposites or the balance of complements, *Surfacing* draws attention to the oppression of women in a male-defined order of hierarchical and oppositional roles that empower men at the expense of women. And it replaces the romantic fantasy of marriage as a blissful union of opposites or complements with a condemning picture of marriage as sexual manipulation and warfare. David claims that he is "all for the equality of women" but that Anna "just doesn't happen to be equal and that's not my fault, is it? What I married was a pair of boobs, she manipulated me into it. . . ." Recalling Anna's comment about the need for an emotional commitment in marriage, the narrator thinks that David and Anna have made such a commitment, for they "hate each other; that must be almost as absorbing as love." And she compares them to her "ideal" barometer couple, except that they are "glued there, condemned to oscillate back and forth . . . without escape" (163).

David is the potentially dangerous male, a figure that repeatedly appears in Atwood's fiction. Like other Atwoodian split-male characters, David has an innocuous facade: he performs a "quick skit" with Anna, using the narrator and Joe as an audience; he softshoes out the door "like the end of a vaudeville act"; he affects a yokel dialect (52, 120, 32). But David also has a "Murderer's Thumb," according to Anna, who is an amateur palm reader (117). Elaborating on this textual clue, the narrative depicts David as a male predator. Preying upon Anna and seeming to delight in it, David forces her to comply with his "little set of rules." As Anna tells the narrator, "If I break one of them I get punished, except he keeps changing them so I'm never sure" (145). Anna is also subject to David's rage. "He's crazy, there's something missing in him. . . . He likes to make me cry because he can't do it himself," Anna comments. "Sometimes I think he'd like me to die. . . . I have dreams about it" (145, 146). When the narrator overhears Anna and David having sex, she likens the sound Anna makes to that of "an animal's at the moment the trap closes" (99). Using her body, which is her "only weapon," Anna is "desperate" as she fights "for her life, he was her life, her life was the fight." Anna perpetuates her "fight" with David because if she were to surrender, "the balance of power would be broken" and David "would go elsewhere" in order to "continue the war" (180).

A woman who experiences marriage as an unremitting battle for survival, Anna, when she was growing up, thought she was "really a princess" and that she would "end up living in a castle" (67). Now a "captive princess in someone's head," the aging Anna "takes her clothes off or puts them on, paper-doll wardrobe," and she compulsively uses cosmetics, "the only magic left to her" (194). Wanting to remain attractive to her husband, Anna attempts to conform to the eroticized and commodified images of women promulgated in the mass culture. What Marian MacAlpin fears will happen to her has already happened to Anna, who colludes in the fixation and thus destruction of her identity. Her "soul," as the narrator comes to see it, is "closed in the gold compact" (205) she so frequently stares into. Without the makeup she wears as a kind of protective camouflage, "shorn of the pink cheeks and heightened eyes," Anna's face is "curiously battered, a worn doll's, her artificial face is the natural one" (50–51).

A female commodity and the artificial woman, Anna is "a seamed and folded imitation of a magazine picture that is itself an imitation of a woman who is also an imitation, the original nowhere." In a description that recalls the sargasso-sea passage in *The Edible Woman,* Anna is described not as a liquid, amorphous other, but as a woman who is "locked in," who "isn't allowed to eat or shit or cry or give birth, nothing goes in, nothing comes out" (194). Her sexuality exploited and her body put on public display, Anna is presented as a pornographic object when she is coerced into playing the naked lady role in her husband's film, *Random Samples.* Imagining that Anna has been fixated by the camera/ eye so feared by Marian MacAlpin—a signifier of the voyeuristic, objectifying male gaze—the narrator, when she later destroys the *Random Samples* film, envisions it as the "release" of "bottled and shelved" images of Anna (195).

"The only defense was flight, invisibility," the Surfacer thinks to herself when she witnesses David's intentional humiliation of Anna (160). Repressing the trauma of her affair with a married man and her subsequent abortion, the Surfacer repeatedly and defensively tells herself the story of her "marriage" and how, after the "divorce," her "husband" took custody of their "child." Describing herself as "the offending party, the one who left," she claims that he "wanted a child, that's normal, he wanted us to be married" (55). But in a passage that looks back to fears expressed in *The Edible Woman* and that anticipates the concerns of *The Handmaid's Tale,* the narrator expresses her own censored feelings about being pregnant. "[H]e imposed it on me, all the time it was growing in me I felt like an incubator. He measured everything he would let me eat, he was feeding it on me, he wanted a replica of himself; after it was born I was no more use" (39). Similarly, when Joe asks her if she loves him, she thinks that Joe doesn't love her but that he, too, is making narcissistic use of her: "it was an idea of himself he loved and he wanted someone to join him, anyone would do" (131).

"He said he loved me, the magic word, it was supposed to make everything light up, I'll never trust that word again," the Surfacer says of the married man she had an affair with (55). Betrayed by her lover and by her naive belief in the romantic ideal, she has learned to distrust "love, the ritual word" (192), and to view language as a masculine tool, an instrument of betrayal and coercion. That women, as Dale Bauer remarks, can find it difficult to assert a voice "contrary to the bourgeois authoritative one which seeks to reduce all voices to the same" (x) is revealed in *Surfacing.* For when Joe asks the narrator if she loves him, she finds it difficult to answer. "It was the language again, I couldn't use it because it wasn't mine. He must have known what he meant but it [love] was an imprecise word; the Eskimos had fifty-two names for snow because it was important to them, there ought to be as many for love" (127). Despite her inner resistance to the monolithic voice and finalizing speech of bourgeois culture, the Surfacer—not unlike Anna who speaks in a "radio" voice—finds herself responding to Joe in an inauthentic feminine voice. Demanding a "straight answer" to his question of whether or not she loves him, Joe insists that she just say "yes or no." When the Surfacer replies that she is "trying to tell the truth," she feels that her voice isn't hers: "it came from someone dressed as me, imitating me" (126, 127). Similarly when Joe asks if she will marry him and she refuses, claiming that she has already been married, the words come out of her "like the mechanical words from a talking doll, the kind with the pull tape at the back; the whole speech was unwinding, everything in order, a spool" (105). Describing what happens when women speak "as men have spoken for centuries," Luce Irigaray comments how words make women "disappear," how they "become machines that are spoken, machines that speak" as they flee "into proper names" ("When Our Lips Speak" 69).

In her attempt to avoid the betrayals and coercions of the romantic relationship, the narrator refuses to overvalue love. She says that her decision to live with Joe "wasn't even a real decision, it was more like buying a goldfish or a potted cactus plant, not because you want one in advance but because you happen to be in the store and you see them lined up on the counter" (49). And she compares marriage to "playing Monopoly or doing crossword puzzles, either your mind worked that way . . . or it didn't; and I'd proved mine didn't" (105). Yet she, like Anna, becomes caught up in a "contest" of wills as Joe tries to compel her to "[g]ive in" (130–31). "Prove your love, they say," the narrator reflects when Joe asks her to marry him. Opposing the monolithic voice of official culture, the Surfacer opens up this masculine injunction to a feminist critique. "You really want to marry me, let me fuck you instead. You really want to fuck, let me marry you instead. As long as there's a victory, some flag I can wave, parade I can have in my head" (104). Through her internal, dialogic commentary, the Surfacer resists masculine discourse. But she remains painfully aware of the power of men to abuse and subjugate women. When she rebuffs Joe at one point, she fears he will hit her (148); at another point, he angrily pins her down, "hands manacles, teeth against my lips, censoring me, he was shoving against me, his body insistent as one side of an argument" and she imagines that he is "one of the killers" (173, 172). Later, after she urges Joe to make love to her so that she, unbeknownst to him, can get pregnant, she feels that Joe "thinks he has won, act of his flesh a rope noosed round my neck, leash, he will lead me back to the city and tie me to fences, doorknobs" (192). "[W]omen *must either* consent *or* be seduced into consenting to femininity," remarks Teresa de Lauretis. "This is the sense in which sadism demands a story or story demands sadism . . ." (134).

As if intent on containing the anxiety associated with the threat of male violence against and sexual mastery of women, the text not only pushes Joe to the periphery of the narrative, it also renders him essentially mute, depicting him as a man to whom "speech . . . was a task, a battle" (92). "Everything I value about him seems to be physical . . . ," the narrator comments (65–66). Insistently, the Surfacer depicts Joe as animal-like: he has hair on his back and his shaggy, blunt-snouted face resembles that of a buffalo (65, 10). Read in terms of the text's evolving distrust of language and its valorization of nature over civilization, these descriptions are meant to be read in a positive way. But in a broader sense Atwood's novel—in backgrounding and silencing Joe, in reducing him to a mere physical presence, and in associating him with nature—

overturns literary and cultural expectations by doing to him what traditionally has been done to female characters in literary texts.

The text similarly asserts mastery over David. "It'll be great, it's good for you, keeps you healthy," David tells the Surfacer as he attempts to involve her in "[t]it for tat," "[g]eometrical sex" to retaliate against Anna and Joe (177, 178). "[D]on't tell me you don't know where Joe is; he's not so noble, he's off in the bushes somewhere with that cunt on four legs, right about now he's shoving it into her" (177). That the narrator must "concentrate in order to talk" to David because the "English words" seem "imported, foreign" reveals her inner resistance to, and alienation from, his coercive "American" speech (176). "'Do you love me,' I asked in case I hadn't understood him, 'is that why you want me to?'" Searching for a workable "phrase" or "vocabulary," she tells him that he does not "turn" her "on." Momentarily losing control, David calls her a "tight-ass bitch" and "third-rate cold tail," but then, following a standard male script, he tells her that he respects her for resisting his overtures (178, 179). Asserting active mastery over passive suffering by staging a fantasy of female empowerment, the text depicts the Surfacer's ability to see through David and resist his sexist, "American" speech with the help of the "power." As the "power" flows into her eyes and she can "see into him," she recognizes him for what he is. A product of the dominant discourse, David is "an impostor, a pastiche" of worn-out catchphrases and slogans. Indeed, she envisions him to have "verbs and nouns glued on to him and shredding away" as "[s]econdhand American" spreads over him, making him "infested, garbled" (178–79). In this scene, *Surfacing* shows the power of a feminist-dialogic strategy to unmask and dethrone masculine discourse. And through its depiction of David, *Surfacing* dramatizes the central paradox of male power. "Feminism," remarks Catharine MacKinnon, "has unmasked maleness as a form of power that is both omnipotent and nonexistent, an unreal thing with very real consequences." Male power is both "real" and "a myth that makes itself true"; it is "total" and "a delusion" (543, 542).

Perceiving the sexual relationship as a form of entrapment, and distrusting the language of romantic love and sexual emancipation, the Surfacer chooses "flight, invisibility" as she attempts to defend her fragile self. To protect herself from further narcissistic injury, she has learned the "technique" of "[a]nesthesia": "if it hurts invent a different pain" (15). Emotionally blocked, she realizes that she has not felt "much of anything" for a "long time." "At some point my neck must have closed over, pond freezing or a wound, shutting me into my head; since then everything had been glancing off me, it was like being in a vase . . ." (126). While the Surfacer's sense that there is "something essential missing" in her and her description of herself as "cut in two" (161, 129) are coded references to the abortion, they also depict her self-state. Again and again, the text emphasizes the narrator's vulnerable selfhood: her sense of body-self fragmentation, self-unreality, and subjective emptiness. "The trouble is all in the knob at the top of our bodies," she comments at one point. "I'm not against the body or the head either: only the neck, which creates the illusion that they are separate." This separation, she feels, allows people to "look down at their bodies and move them around as if they were robots or puppets" (91). Similarly, she likens herself to a "[w]oman sawn apart in a wooden crate . . . smiling, a trick done with mirrors . . . only with me there had been an accident and I came apart." She feels "detached, terminal," that she is "nothing but a head, or, no, something minor like a severed thumb; numb" (129). "[I]f the head is detached from the body," she recognizes, "both of them will die" (91).

And yet although the Surfacer claims that she has not felt "much of anything" for a "long time," her response to the "Americans" tells another story. Delivering a blistering critique of the male supremist ideology of the "Americans," *Surfacing* makes visible the pervasiveness of male power. The Americans, who stand in the text as an embodiment of the masculine principle of conquest and wanton destruction, want power: "Straight power, they mainlined it. . . . The innocents get slaughtered because they exist . . . there is nothing inside the happy killers to restrain them, no conscience or piety . . ." (151). Observing the body of a heron strung up "like a lynch victim" in a tree, the narrator finds this a telling example of the need of Americans to "prove they could do it, they had the power to kill" (138). When she subsequently learns that the men she thought were Americans are actually Canadians, she feels that despite the country they come from, "they're still Americans, they're what's in store for us, what we are turning into. They spread themselves like a virus, they get into the brain and take over the cells and the cells change from inside and the ones that have the disease can't tell the difference" (152). Identifying with the heron as her persecutory fears surface, the narrator imagines that the men who come to the island to search for her might be Americans and that they will shoot her or "bludgeon in" her skull and hang her up "by the feet from a tree" (214). But while she fears being victimized, she also secretly identifies with the victimizers. "I wished evil toward them: Let them suffer, I prayed . . . burn them, rip them open," she thinks of the Canadian men she mistakenly believes are Americans (147). "My arm wanted to swing the paddle sideways, blade into his head: his eyes would blossom outward, his skull shatter like an egg" (151). Erecting defenses against the angry feelings it evokes, the text thematizes and validates the Surfacer's killing rage against the Americans. For even though the narrator later admits that she has participated in what she condemns—that she, too, is one of the killers—the narrative, in ultimately aligning the Surfacer with nature and against the Americans, legitimizes her anger and thus diffuses its potentially destructive, and textually disruptive, energies.

"People who experience conventionally unacceptable, or what I call 'outlaw,' emotions," writes Alison Jaggar, "often are subordinated individuals who pay a disproportionately high price for maintaining the status quo" (160). That "women's subversive insights owe much to women's outlaw emotions, themselves appropriate responses to the situations of women's subordination" (164), is dramatized in *Surfacing* when Atwood's narrator begins to experience her long-suppressed, outlawed anger. Indeed, rage marks the Surfacer's perceptions as her fabricated story about her failed marriage unravels and her socially constructed feminine identity disintegrates. Recalling *The Edible Woman*'s disgust at consumption, the narrator describes how animals die so that people may live. Although "eaters of death," people "refuse to worship; the body worships with blood and muscle but the thing in the knob head will not, wills not to, the head is greedy, it consumes but does not give thanks" (165). Equally repulsive in the narrator's view is the sexual act. "[T]wo people making love with paper bags over their heads, not even any eyeholes. Would that be good or bad?" she asks at one point (78). When David attempts to involve her in his game of "[g]eometrical sex," she thinks that "it would be enough for him if our genitals could be detached like two kitchen appliances and copulate in mid-air, that would complete his equation" (178). This, in turn, recalls the narrator's childhood memory of the tugboatmen's drawings of genitalia and her shock that body parts could be "cut off like that from the bodies that ought to have gone with them, as though they could detach themselves and crawl around on their own like snails" (142). Similarly, she imagines Anna copulating "under strobe lights with the man's torso while his brain watches from its glassed-in control cubicle at the other end of the room" (194–95). While the "themes and images" of *Surfacing* "acquire increasing poetic and mythic intensity" in the novel's middle and final sections

(Rubenstein, "*Surfacing*" 393), the narrative also increasingly assaults the reader's sensibilities as it expresses indignation at the masculinist culture which reduces woman to a voyeuristic, pornographic spectacle and to fetishized, fragmented body parts.

"I'm not sure when I began to suspect the truth, about myself and about them, what I was and what they were turning into," the Surfacer comments at one point as she imagines that her friends are transforming into "robots or puppets" (91). "The machine is gradual, it takes a little of you at a time, it leaves the shell" (195). As her self-crisis unfolds and she projects her sense of self-unreality onto others, she increasingly inhabits a dislocated, paranoid world in which people seem part-human and part-machine. When she overhears her friends laughing, she perceives it as "[c]anned laughter, they carry it with them, the midget reels of tape and the On switch concealed somewhere in their chests, instant playback" (92). In the narrator's imagination both Anna and David are "already turning to metal, skins galvanizing, heads congealing to brass knobs, components and intricate wires ripening inside" (186). If, on the one hand, the narrator's perceptions are meant to be read as delusional—as a projection onto others of her own disturbed state of mind—Atwood also, in effect, affirms the Surfacer's distorted perceptions by positioning her character against the dehumanizing forces of Americanism condemned by the text. Thus a commentator like Robert Kroetsch can romanticize the Surfacer's madness and claim that the "terror resides not in her going insane but in her going sane" (43).

Inviting readers to interpret the pivotal scene of the Surfacer's underwater dive psychoanalytically—as a sudden lifting of the repression barrier and the uncovering of buried trauma—*Surfacing* also prompts readers to locate and reconstruct the lost connections between the narrator's fragmented memories. "It was below me, drifting towards me . . . a dark oval trailing limbs. . . . I turned, fear gushing out of my mouth in silver, panic closing my throat, the scream kept in and choking me." As successive veils of concealment are lifted, the narrator comes to recognize the psychic significance of what she has just seen. "It formed again in my head: at first I thought it was my drowned brother. . . . Then I recognized it: it wasn't ever my brother I'd been remembering, that had been a disguise. I knew when it was, it was in a bottle curled up, staring out at me like a cat pickled. . . . It wasn't a child but it could have been one, I didn't allow it. . . . That was wrong, I never saw it" (167–68). While this scene involves the reader emotionally, it also promotes the process of sense-making and consistency-building as images that have recurred in the text—those of the drowned brother and jarred animals—take on a new significance and are incorporated into the narrative's evolving design.

"The trouble some people have being German . . . I have being human," the Surfacer thinks to herself after she sees the dead heron and feels a "sickening complicity" as if she had watched the torture of the bird and done nothing to stop it (155, 154). This provokes a memory of how, as a child, she allowed the animals trapped and jarred by her brother to die because she was afraid she would incur his wrath if she freed them. "Because of my fear they were killed," as she puts it (155). "He said I should do it, he made me do it . . . ," she similarly thinks as she remembers her abortion, admitting not only her own culpability but also her sense of coercion. "He said it wasn't a person, only an animal. . . . I could have said No but I didn't; that made me one of them too, a killer" (170). As her long-denied emotions surface, her rage intensifies. Just as the foetus vanished—"They scraped it into a bucket and threw it wherever they throw them . . . I stretched my hand up to it and it vanished" (168)—so she wants the hated Americans to vanish. "I wanted there to be a machine that could make them vanish, a button I could press that would evaporate them without disturbing anything else, that way there would be more room for the animals, they would be rescued" (181). At once the text depicts the narrator's increasing paranoia and dissociation—she sees, for example, that Joe is "human . . . one of the killers," that David is "an impostor," that David and Anna are "already turning to metal" (172, 178, 186)—and legitimizes her renunciation of the masculinist ethos, which the narrative finds epitomized in Americanism and its dehumanizing, killing technology.

Thus despite the Surfacer's paranoia, readers can and do validate her perceptions. We find a telling example of this in Arnold and Cathy Davidson's response to the narrator's fantasy that Joe, Anna, and David are standing in judgment of her: "A ring of eyes, tribunal; in a minute they would join hands and dance around me, and after that the rope and the pyre, cure for heresy" (180). Taking on the text-directed role of advocate, the Davidsons accuse the Surfacer's imagined accusers. In their view, while the "execution" the narrator anticipates is "an obvious exaggeration . . . the verdict is not. She is guilty of the heresy of failing to think and act according to the dictates of others. They cannot tolerate that and try to negate her identity" ("Anatomy" 46). In a similar vein, critics commonly endorse the narrator's perceptions by claiming, for example, that by the end of the novel David and Anna have become "sexual robots" (St. Andrews 91) or that they are "robots like the Americans" (Ewell 194). "Uncritical involvement with our technologies will turn us into zombies and robots," writes one commentator. "But with the help of the power, the narrator has brought the 'evil grail' of technological America to the surface of her consciousness where she can take steps to cope with it" (Catherine Ross 17).

Through its articulation of an oppositional discourse and its construction of a feminist reading position, *Surfacing* provides an effective critique of masculinist ideology. And in deviating from the novel's original trajectory—the search for the father which promises to take the form of a linear quest—*Surfacing* also challenges the privileging of masculinity as the site of power and knowledge. Unlike the Surfacer's father, who is associated with a rationalist mindset that measures and maps the world and explains "everything" (86), her mother, who is essentially silenced in the narrative, comes to represent the wordless, body-identified knowledge the narrator comes to find salvific. Desiring more than her father's knowledge—for his gods are "the gods of the head" (179)—the Surfacer searches for and finds, in one of her own childhood drawings saved by her mother, her mother's "gift" of knowledge. "On the left was a woman with a round moon stomach: the baby was sitting up inside her gazing out. Opposite her was a man with horns on his head like cow horns and a barbed tail" (185).

Immersing herself in "the other language," reading the meaning of the pictograph left by her mother with "the help of the power" (185), the narrator urges Joe to impregnate her. "I lie down, keeping the moon on my left hand and the absent sun on my right. . . . I'm impatient, pleasure is redundant, the animals don't have pleasure. I guide him into me, it's the right season, I hurry" (190–91). Repeating what it condemns, the text depicts this ritual mating as an act of copulation in which the woman makes sexual use of the man. Perhaps to deflect attention away from this assertion of female power and sexual mastery, the text involves the reader in the process of pattern-building. For the mother's gift—the crayon drawing of the child gazing out of the womb—is associated with other images in the text: the narrator's memory of bottled animals and her fabricated memory of the bottled foetus. Moreover, by including in this scene the symmetrical sun/moon design found in the narrator's childhood drawings (109), the narrative partially aestheticizes this potentially disturbing depiction of the sexual act as biologically driven.

Recalling her lover's description of the foetus as "only an animal," the narrator imagines her "lost child surfacing" within her, "its eyes and teeth phosphorescent." She envisions it as a "plant-animal" that "sends out filaments" in her body and as a "fur god with tail and horns, already forming"; and she fantasizes giving birth to a creature "covered with shining fur, a god" (191, 197, 212, 191). Read in light of the text's evolving distrust of American civilization and its killing technology—in particular, the "death machine, emptiness machine" of the abortionist (191)—these descriptions are meant as positive. Yet the notion of a child-creature is unnerving, and similar images surface in later Atwood novels as open expressions of female anxiety about pregnancy. Implicit in the Surfacer's fantasy of the symbiotic union of mother and foetus—again, evoking a childhood drawing, she imagines the child inside her "showing through the green webs" of her flesh—is the associated fear that the foetus will assimilate her, drain her of substance, for she imagines that if she does not feed the foetus, it will, predator-like, "absorb" her teeth and bones (212).

Thus, although the text consciously depicts pregnancy as rescue—indeed, Atwood's "controversial baby" has been described as a symbol of the "narrator's reconception of a powerful female self" (Grace, "In Search of Demeter" 42)—it also communicates the opposite message: that pregnancy endangers the fragile self of the Surfacer. This may help explain why, although pregnancy ultimately appears to heal the narrator's mind/body split, it initially "engenders a deeper separation" (McLay, "Divided Self" 93). Ostensibly, the critical controversy over the novel's pregnancy resolution derives from Atwood's enactment in *Surfacing* of what she herself condemns in the work of other Canadian writers: the use of "the Baby Ex Machina" at the conclusion of a book "to solve problems for the characters which they obviously can't solve for themselves" (*Survival* 207). But if Atwood makes use of this traditional closure, she also deliberately problematizes this pregnancy-as-rescue scenario and thereby adds to the ambiguities and uncertainties surrounding the novel's closing scene.

"[L]ogic is a wall, I built it, on the other side is terror"; "he was seeing the way I had seen, true vision; at the end, after the failure of logic" (205, 171). Through these announcements by the Surfacer, Atwood provides an interpretive key to her character's plunge into the world of madness, a world depicted as mystical and regressive, beautiful and menacing, awesome and horrific. It is telling that the narrator's mad world is bound by rules she must learn. Repeating the narrator's gesture, the critic/reader must follow the rules of the text to decipher these scenes. If her father's pictographs appear "unintelligible" (69) until the narrator finds an explanatory article on Indian rock painting and shamanism among her father's papers, so, too, the text may appear "unintelligible" until the reader-detective masters its hermeneutic code. As Barbara Rigney observes, in *Surfacing* Atwood makes conscious reference to initiation rites "which incorporate such patterns as the temporary withdrawal from society, the removal of the old clothing, the eating of new food, the symbolic arrival into adulthood" (52). Significantly, in the passage describing the rock paintings, Atwood not only provides an overt explanation of the shamanic aspects of the mad scenes which follow, but she also, in focusing attention on the "aesthetic qualities" of the Indian art (122), makes covert reference to the text's aestheticizing of madness and its use of structure and pattern to contain the psychic terrors it inscribes.

Aligned with the narrator's viewpoint, readers are invited to involve themselves in her "turmoil" and to experience her "confusion and struggle" (Rosenberg 108, 109). To the extent that "the prose" of *Surfacing* "calls forth" from readers "an extraordinary degree of empathy with the narrator" and urges them to "participate" in the Surfacer's madness (Larkin 50), it can evoke in readers feelings of bewilderment and anxiety. In her analysis of the emotions "inherent in psychotic phenomena" that develop when one is reading psychopathographic literature, Evelyne Keitel remarks that "the reader experiences the same ambivalent or negative emotions that accompany psychotic attacks: pleasure as well as oppression, paralysis and anxiety" (13, 2). While personality dissolutions "cannot be fully communicated in their subjective and emotional dimensions," writes Keitel, the "very impossibility of communicating such experiences adequately arouses a desire to know more about them. Realms beyond human experience exercise a fascination, a strange mixture of curiosity, anxiety and aversion, on those not afflicted by them . . ." (30). And yet although *Surfacing* is potentially anxiety-provoking as it invites readers to enter the narrator's delusional world and involves them emotionally in her madness, it also promotes the processes of sense-making, pattern-finding, and consistency-building. Despite the irrationality of the novel's final scenes, critic/readers can also trace the "inner logic" of the narrative (Rosenberg 110) and thus form an identificatory bond with the author-designer behind the text.

Indeed, because *Surfacing* is premised on the ideology of cultural feminism and because its romantic feminism openly invites mythical or archetypal interpretations, a number of critics have focused on these aspects of the narrative. They show, for example, how the novel can be linked to Mircea Eliade's account of shamanic rites or to Amerindian themes (Catherine Ross, Sullivan, Guédon) or to Joseph Campbell's description of the hero's mythological journey (Campbell, Donaldson) or to Northrop Frye's analysis of the pattern of the romance quest (Arnold and Cathy Davidson, "Anatomy"). "The only cure," writes Roberta Rubenstein, "is the journey of self-discovery: down and through the darkness of the divided self to the undifferentiated wholeness of archaic consciousness—and back" ("*Surfacing*" 399). In another common interpretation, which grows out of the "late-1970s feminist celebration of women's suddenly reclaimed, transformed, empowering religious and archetypal energies" (McCombs, "Introduction" 13), Atwood's novel has been read as a female mythic or spiritual quest novel. Such an interpretation, which the text does foster, similarly reclaims the character from her madness and effectively transforms psychotic breakdown into visionary breakthrough. Thus critics can claim, as does Annis Pratt, that the narrator "goes 'crazy' deliberately in order to empower herself" (154). But such readings also serve to domesticate the terrifying emotional energies that erupt in the novel's final sections, energies the narrative attempts to contain through its carefully constructed design. Because the narrator's visions "crystallize the parallel themes which Atwood has consistently developed" throughout the narrative (Rubenstein, "*Surfacing*" 397), critic/readers can thematize, and thus partially stave off, the negative emotions that threaten to disrupt the carefully patterned surface of this "grim, desperate novel" (Piercy 54).

Yearning to overcome the "barrier" separating her from her dead parents, sensing that they are "waiting," the Surfacer wants to "make them come out, from wherever it is they are hiding" (202, 203). And yet when she wakes up in the middle of the night, she is afraid to let her parents' spirits into the cabin. "The fear arrives like waves, like footfalls, it has no center; it encloses me like armor, it's my skin that is afraid, rigid." Because she has "willed" her parents' return by calling to them, it is "logical" that they should "arrive," but on the other side of logic's "wall" there is "terror" (204, 205).

"There must be rules: places I'm permitted to be, other places I'm not. I'll have to listen carefully, if I trust them they will tell me what is állowed" (206). Determined to perform the sacrifices required of her, she destroys the contents of her parents' cabin and then cleans herself in the water of the lake, leaving behind the "false body" of her clothes (208) and wrapping her naked body in a blanket until her fur grows. Recognizing that the food in the cabin is forbidden—"tin cans and jars are forbidden; they are glass and metal" (209)—she eats the vegetables found in her father's garden. Animal-like, she leaves her droppings on the ground, and because she is not permitted to return to the "cage, wooden rectangle" of her parents' cabin—for her parents' ghosts are against "marked out, enclosed" spaces—she sleeps in a lair that she hollows out near the woodpile (209, 211). In order to "talk" to her parents, as she comes to believe, she "must approach the condition they themselves have entered" (211).

Becoming "ice-clear, transparent" when something happens to her eyes and her feet are "released, they alternate, several inches from the ground," the Surfacer momentarily exists in a world of motion and fluid energy. "The forest leaps upward, enormous, the way it was before they cut it, columns of sunlight frozen; the boulders float, melt, everything is made of water, even the rocks" (212). She realizes that animals "have no need for speech, why talk when you are a word I lean against a tree, I am a tree leaning. . . . I am not an animal or a tree, I am the thing in which the trees and animals move and grow, I am a place" (212–13). Given the Surfacer's distrust of language, which she associates with the coercive sexual and power politics of patriarchy, it is appropriate that her resistance to the dominant culture takes the form it does, forcing her into a temporary existence outside the bounds not only of masculinist logic and discourse but also of conventional plot constructions.

Finally, the Surfacer sees the ghosts of her dead parents. Providing clues for the vigilant reader to piece together, the text associates the narrator's visions with her childhood memories, fears, and fantasies. When the Surfacer sees the ghost of her dead mother feeding the jays, something her mother often did when she was alive, she reenacts her childhood relationship with her emotionally remote mother. For the ghost of her mother "looks at" and "past" her, "as though she knows something is there but she can't quite see it" (213). Similarly, the Surfacer's vision of her father as a wolf-man gazing at her "with its yellow eyes" (218) has its source in her childhood world. This vision recalls her childhood persecutory fear—when she played hide-and-seek with her father in the twilight—that what might emerge from behind the tree where he was hiding "would be someone else." The wolf-man image is also associated with a remembered conversation she had with her brother as a child in which she learned of the Catholic folk belief that people who did not go to Mass changed into wolves (58, 65). Adding to the complexity of the Surfacer's encounter with the ghost of her father, the wolf-man is also a self-reflection: a projection of her own dangerous, outlawed feelings. Thus, when she later finds footprints in the place where she saw her father standing, she discovers that they are her own footprints. Indeed, Atwood explains that one of her aims in *Surfacing* was to write a ghost story—"an interesting area which is too often done just as pulp." For Atwood, the "most interesting" kind of ghost story and the "tradition" she followed in *Surfacing* was "the Henry James kind, in which the ghost that one sees is in fact a fragment of one's own self which has split off" (Gibson 30, 29).

Despite the fact that some commentators seem to take comfort in the narrative's "carefully controlled, artistically simulated descent" into the world of madness (Onley 80), the text's graphic depiction of the narrator's regression to an irrational, paranoid state is also meant to discomfort readers. Rejecting the male construction of the "feminine" woman, the Surfacer changes into a "natural woman." But despite her desire to escape the male plot of desire, she remains a female victim. When men come to the island to search for her, she imagines they will "mistake" her "for a human being, a naked woman wrapped in a blanket: possibly that's what they've come here for, if it's running around loose, ownerless, why not take it" (214). To her the men appear distorted, grotesque. "Their skins are red, green in squares, blue in lines, and it's a minute before I remember that these are fake skins, flags. Their real skins above the collars are white and plucked, with tufts of hair on top, piebald blend of fur and no fur like moldy sausages or the rumps of baboons. They are evolving, they are halfway to machine, the leftover flesh atrophied and diseased, porous like an appendix." Grouping together to talk, the men "chitter and sizzle like a speeded-up tape, the forks and spoons on the ends of their arms waving excitedly" (215). When she laughs out loud— "laughter extrudes" from her, as she puts it (215)—and the men, hearing her, give chase, she perceives them as ominous presences. "Behind me they crash, their boots crash, language ululating, electronic signals thrown back and forth between them, hooo, hooo, they talk in numbers, the voice of reason. They clank, heavy with weapons and iron plating" (216). After they leave, she wonders if they have set traps. "Caught animals gnaw off their arms and legs to get free, could I do that," she asks herself (217).

In this paranoid fantasy of the "natural woman" being hunted down by male adversaries, the novel's preoccupation with female persecution takes on a nightmarish quality. Despite the narrator's famous proclamation—"This above all, to refuse to be a victim" (222)—the novel's predominant message is one of female victimization. And while the text directs us to read the Surfacer's immersion in nature as a kind of break-

through, it also describes her experience as a terrifying kind of breakdown. Her attempt to escape the coercions of patriarchal discourse—the
"electronic signals" of the men who hunt her, men who "talk in numbers, the voice of reason"—leads her to the other side of logic's wall, to
the horrifying, alinguistic world of madness.

When the Surfacer destroys the contents of her parents' cabin, shuns
"marked out, enclosed" spaces, and becomes transformed into the "natural woman," she both rebels against the masculine mindset that maps
and delimits the world and enacts her secret desire to escape from the
contained, domestic sphere of femininity. But although she escapes
masculine logic and domestic confinement in her merger with nature,
and although the text insistently privileges nature over civilization, the
Surfacer's transformation into the "natural woman" is still unsettling.
For when she later looks in the mirror, she sees "a creature neither animal
nor human, furless, only a dirty blanket, shoulders huddled over into a
crouch, eyes staring blue as ice from the deep sockets; the lips move
by themselves." Recognizing that she fits the stereotype of the madwoman—"straws in the hair, talking nonsense or not talking at all"—she
feels that the "real danger" she confronts is "the hospital or the zoo,"
places where people are put when they "can no longer cope." With her
"face dirt-caked and streaked, skin grimed and scabby, hair like a frayed
bathmat stuck with leaves and twigs," she imagines herself as a "new
kind of centerfold" (222). Through this troubling image of the natural
woman, the novel deliberately subverts the cultural construction of an
eroticized, commodified femininity promoted by and circulated in the
men's magazines: the glossy magazine centerfold woman who is, like
Anna, an imitation of an imitation. But the image of the natural woman
conjured up by the text, while it registers protest, is also one of negation
and identity-loss. Indeed, it provides a graphic depiction of the female
self-in-crisis, the self as angry monster, the self in desperate need of
rescue.

Promoting and acting out a rescue fantasy—albeit an ambiguous
rescue which is typical of Atwood's fiction—the text does provide some
way out for the Surfacer as she reenters her "own time" (223). Although
she believes that she "saw" her parents and that they spoke to her "in the
other language," the gods also become "questionable once more" as they
recede "back to the past, inside the skull." Her parents "dwindle, grow,
become what they were, human," and she admits that the foetus she
imagines she is carrying is "[n]o god and perhaps not real" (220, 221,
223). As she prepares to go back to the city with Joe, she questions what

he will offer her: "captivity in any of its forms, a new freedom?" (224). Perhaps, she thinks, he has been "sent as a trick" but because he "isn't anything, he is only half formed," she feels she can "trust him." And yet her anxieties about the coercions and manipulations of the heterosexual relationship persist. "I tense forward, toward the demands and questions, though my feet do not move yet." As Joe waits for her, his voice sounding "annoyed," she tellingly pauses: "The lake is quiet, the trees surround me, asking and giving nothing" (224).

The emotional storm has passed. But if there is a muted hope in this closure, there is also a feeling of isolation and empty despair. Despite the conscious optimism of the closure, voiced in the narrator's famous refusal to be a victim, an unconscious pessimism also underlies the novel's final scene. This narrative split is reflected in the critical disagreement about the narrator's madness—some critics reading it as breakthrough and others describing it as breakdown—and in the "continuing debates on the Surfacer's transformation or powerlessness" (McCombs, "Introduction" 17).

Some readers are optimistic about the fate of Atwood's character. In Barbara Ewell's view, the Surfacer's visions "restore her to herself" and although she "must return to her own time," she also knows that "she can no longer live by the old prescriptions of self as a shadow of conformity" (201). For Charlotte Mendez, the narrator has "regained both self and power" (93). In the view of Mara Donaldson, the Surfacer journeys from "self-submission and passivity to self-awareness and celebration" and "emerges a female hero" (106). Nora Stovel claims that the narrator achieves "not merely survival, but also salvation" (56). For Carol Christ, the Surfacer's experience is "a revelation from great powers" that results in "the achievement of authentic selfhood and power" (46, 53). And Annis Pratt asserts that the narrator "has been so empowered by her fusion of spiritual or psychic and natural energies that she has brought about an implosion of her own world, a shifting of her selfhood from its stance on the margins of male society to a state of being in which her own feminine personality is central and patriarchy has itself moved to her margins" (156).

Other critics, in contrast, are troubled by the implications of Atwood's closure. Observing that Atwood's character "requires to be saved," Keith Garebian feels that despite the Surfacer's "refusal to be a victim, she is powerless to resist the implication of her defeat," nor can she ever "stop describing herself or her world as victimizing" (5, 7, 8). In the words of Robert Lecker, the final pages of the novel "bring the narrator full circle back to an uncertain beginning"; in his view "the ending of the novel is inconsistent with the narrator's ostensible affirmation of nature over culture" (186, 188). The merging of "positive elements of survival and acceptance" in the final chapter, writes Joan Harcourt, "is not easy to credit after having been confronted for so long with nothing but the evidence of disintegration" (281). Sally Robinson, who observes that the novel ends with the narrator's return to Joe and thus to "what has been represented as a relationship that suppresses *her* desire," feels that *Surfacing* "ends on a note of resignation" (113). And according to Rosemary Sullivan, "Atwood leaves her character in the ironic world and even though her intent seems to have been to expose the perfect circle of the mind as demonic, we end in the tautology of self" (40). "It's nice that she [the Surfacer] doesn't want to be a victim," says Atwood as she joins the critical conversation concerning the closure of *Surfacing,* "but if you examine her situation and her society in the cold light of reason, how is she going to avoid it? I'd say the ending is ambiguous" (Sandler 12). In yet another comment on the novel's closure, Atwood remarks, "I think that people have overestimated the amount to which the protagonist in *Surfacing* really has developed in understanding" (Struthers 25).

Given the persistence of this critical disagreement, it is not surprising that critic after critic has attempted to resolve the questions surrounding the novel's closure and thus, by proxy as it were, provide some form of resolution to Atwood's narrative. "[T]o overlook the affirmative resolution of *Surfacing,*" it has been argued, "is perhaps to have succumbed to the mentality of losing and victimization to a degree even beyond anything Atwood herself could have imagined" (William James 180). In this view those readers who "overlook" the narrative's "affirmative" ending have misread the closure. Another strategy is to see the hopelessness of the closure as a sign of the narrator's heroism: if the closure lacks hope, it is because "the narrator has gone beyond that recourse of the weak" (Woodcock 27). Another is to argue that there is "something heroic" about the Surfacer's "return to normality" and that "[i]f the ending is uncertain it is because the protagonist, who has confronted and solved the riddles that she set herself, has no society in which to report back her success" (Arnold and Cathy Davidson, "Anatomy" 51). And yet another strategy is to focus, not on the feelings engendered by the novel's ending, but on its artistic merits. In this view the closure of *Surfacing* is "tentative, indeterminate, and aesthetically correct" (Bartlett 27).

Although reading *Surfacing* is a potentially destabilizing experience, critic/readers can partially fend off the emotional energies unleashed in

the novel's depiction of female paranoia and madness by focusing attention on the text's intricate structure and its cultural feminist schema. For
the text is designed as a series of binary oppositions which the vigilant
reader is invited to map: female (nature) and male (civilization) with
their associated chain of signifiers—body and head, animal and human,
victim and victimizer. If the narrator's madness threatens to rupture the
patterned "reality" represented in the text, her madness itself is aesthet-
icized. Because it, too, can be read against the text's organizing grid of
opposites, the reader can schematize and thereby stabilize what is a
potentially destabilizing, anxiety-provoking experience: the description
of the Surfacer's psychotic breakdown. While Atwood's character experiences a frightening loss of self-cohesion, the text itself is a cohesive
whole. "Theme, image, and character blend in the aesthetic structuring
of *Surfacing,* bound together as they are by the mythical patterns of the
novel" (Bartlett 26–27). Thus, despite the narrator's terrifying loss of
control, readers can take comfort in the authorial presence behind the
text who maintains a careful artistic control over the narrative's emerging patterns of signification.

Unlike *Random Samples,* which stands in the text as a form of antiart,
Surfacing is highly ordered and carefully designed. But like *Random
Samples,* Atwood's novel focuses audience attention on images of degradation and violence. In the view of one commentator, *Surfacing* is "not a
pleasant book to read" with its "obscene, often perverse" language, its
"degrading" descriptions of sexual intercourse, and its "repulsive descriptions of violations of nature" (Quigley 86). Despite this, readers are
aware of the artistry of Atwood's novel, of "its subtly haunting patterns
of interlocking imagery" (Carrington, "Margaret Atwood" 53). "It is
part of the power of the novel that the descriptions and the events
immediately take on significance in the reader's mind," writes one commentator (King 24). "Rarely," writes another, "does one find a work of
fiction which is as conceptual as this one and yet as fictionally, aesthetically alive" (Mendez 89). Premised on the ideology of cultural feminism
and providing a powerful exposé of the power politics of gender relations—a concern that will continue to preoccupy Atwood's novels—
Surfacing depicts the terrifying world of the female self-in-crisis in a
highly patterned text, one that demands the intercession of words as
critic/readers repeatedly attempt to grapple with its affective intensities
and cognitive challenges.

4
Lady Oracle's Plot against the Gothic Romance Plot

■

n a radical departure from the high seriousness of *Surfacing,* Atwood's next novel, *Lady Oracle,* turns to high comedy in its critique of the romance plot. Narrative with a vengeance, *Lady Oracle* uses a devastatingly effective oppositional strategy as it appropriates and intervenes in the formulas and formats of traditional Gothic romance fiction. "Feminist romantic fiction seems to be a contradiction in terms, a parody in practice," remarks Anne Cranny-Francis (28). Bent on a feminist "parody in practice," *Lady Oracle* exploits and undermines the inherited mass-culture fictions which, in transmitting a conservative literary and cultural message, help perpetuate women's consent to femininity.

Interested in the female readership of mass-culture romance fiction, Atwood comments that one of the appeals of popular literature is that it hooks into "the reality" of the readers' lives in some way. Whereas the Harlequin romance centers on the fantasy that "there is a Mr. Wonderful who does exist," the Gothic form, in contrast, enacts the paranoid fantasy that "'My husband is trying to kill me.'" Depicting her protagonist, Joan Foster, as a woman who attempts "to act out a romantic myth we're all handed as women in a non-romantic world" (Hammond, "Margaret Atwood" 81, 80), Atwood deliberately debunks the romantic ideal through her comic descriptions of the mundane world of married life; and she provides a feminist-dialogic commentary on Gothic fiction through her self-conscious parody of the Gothic in the embedded novel-in-progress. But Atwood also recognizes the dangerous and persisting mass-culture fantasies contained in Gothic literature, which inscribes the female heroine as the potential victim of male violence, and she is intent, in her "anti-gothic," on "examining the perils of gothic thinking" (Struthers 23). Accordingly, one of her primary tasks in *Lady Oracle* is to construct a feminist reading position by exposing and resisting the romantic ideology that attempts to fix women in a rigid, culturally established order and literary structure.

Evidence of Atwood's resistance to the conventional romance format and closural strategy is found in her description of her original conception of the novel. She recalls how "*Lady Oracle* was more tragic to begin with—it was going to start with a fake suicide and end with a real one" (Sandler 14). Commenting on the classic tragic plot trajectory found in "examples of the female bildungsroman that end in the independently minded heroine's death," Joseph Boone observes how "the female rebel against the prescribed destiny and rules of her sex, no matter her degree of inner integrity, is demonstrated to have no place, literally, in the contained fictional world of the hierarchically structured novel, or in the hypothetical order it reproduces" (99). It is significant that, as Atwood recalls, she "set out to write a book that was all tangents" (Rosenberg 112). Plotting against the deadly and closed masterplot that insists on a tragic outcome for female rebellion against cultural—and novelistic—laws, *Lady Oracle* flaunts the classic romance convention in a deliberately diffuse and open-ended structure. A complex narrative, *Lady Oracle* contains multiple plots: the central mother/daughter plot, a series of proliferating romance plots, the embedded novel-in-progress Gothic plot, and the subversive female-as-artist plot. Like Joan's life, the plot of *Lady Oracle* tends "to scroll and festoon," to meander along "from one thing to another" (3) and thus resists closure. In *Lady Oracle* Atwood also makes use of the feminist strategy of mimeticism. "To play with mimesis," in the words of Luce Irigaray, "is . . . for a woman, to try to recover the place of her exploitation by discourse, without allowing herself to be simply reduced to it" (*This Sex* 76). Playing with mimesis, Atwood provides a self-conscious imitation of traditional literary discourses in order to subvert their authority and expose the ways in which they exploit women.

That family relations are "the principal conduits between cultural ideology and the individual unconscious" (Wyatt 104) becomes apparent in Atwood's exploration of the power relations within the traditional family with its overpresent, and domestically powerful but socially devalued, mother, and its absent, but socially powerful, father. If the myth of romantic love finds its source in the patterns of desire shaped by the patriarchal family in which the daughter is taught to idealize the father, *Lady Oracle* reveals the dark underside of this idealization in its depictions of the split male, who is perceived both as a savior and as potentially dangerous. And if, as we have observed in *The Edible Woman* and *Surfacing,* a diminished or fragile sense of self is the female legacy and condition in a male-ordered culture, *Lady Oracle* also reveals how the mother colludes in phallocentrism's plot against the female self by acting as a "cultural agent who transmits social mythology—fictional constructs into which the child is expected to fit" (Rosowski 89).

Joan's mother dutifully enacts the cultural script assigned to women. But although she does "the right thing" by devoting "her life" to her family and making "her family her career as she had been told to do," she is an unhappy woman burdened with an unwanted child and stranded in a house, a "plastic-shrouded tomb from which there was no exit" (200, 201). Despite this, she urges her daughter to consent to femininity. Acting as an agent of masculine culture, Joan's mother represents the repressive social forces that have traditionally crippled women. She also embodies, in Atwood's words, the "mother-monster" (Martens 46).

"[I]f a man has a bad mother it is not so destructive, because the mother is not the version of what he himself could become," Atwood remarks. Because the mother is "the model" on which the daughter is "supposed to form" herself, the mother-monster poses a threat to the developing girl. "What can the daughter do? She somehow ceases to exist. The girl-child somehow has to cease to exist in some rather important way, unless she can find a good mother substitute" (Martens 47). Like *The Edible Woman,* *Lady Oracle* reflects the daughter's definition of the self through a denial of the mother within. In the view of Jean Wyatt, the fact that "matrophobia"—that is, the fear of becoming the mother— has been labeled as a "specific pathology" reveals how familiar women are with the process of defining the self "through hostile opposition to the mother" (113; see also Rich 235). In *Lady Oracle* the mother-monster is not only punished by the text, she is also strategically killed off so that Joan Foster—a "foster" child whose mother has not "fostered," but thwarted, her daughter's development of a healthy sense of self—can survive. This follows the traditional pattern of maternal repression in women's novels described by Marianne Hirsch, in which the monstrous mother—who serves as a negative force in the daughter's development and threatens to impede the daughter's plot—is punished by and/or eliminated from the narrative (see 46–50).

The preestablished plot Joan acts out finds its source in her mother-controlled and tormented childhood, a world in which the "huge but ill-defined figure" of her mother blocks "the foreground," while her father is essentially an "absence" (134, 73). Cast in the role of the sympathetic listener, the reader is encouraged to take Joan's side in the mother-daughter conflict. Her mother is "the manager, the creator, the agent," and she "the product," says Joan as she reconstructs her childhood relationship with her mother (70). Motherly "concern" in Joan's childhood is equated with "pain" (121), her mother's anger barely camouflaged by her public pose as the concerned mother. "On her hands, in her hair," these are the metaphors Joan's mother uses to describe her, even though she "seldom" touches her (95). A primary force in the process of social construction and identity formation, Joan's mother attempts to teach Joan to be a proper little girl and to consent to femininity. Conspiring to curtail her daughter's development of feelings of self-worth and authenticity, she wants Joan to "change into someone else" (56), continually berates and finds fault with her, and always tries to teach her "some lesson or other" (85). Joan's anxiety about the mother-monster is expressed in a dream in which a memory of her mother putting on make-up in front of a three-sided mirror surfaces as a nightmare in which her mother metamorphoses into a three-headed monster and only Joan is aware of her "secret" monstrousness (70).

With her childhood contemporaries, her companion Brownies who persecute her for deviating from prescribed feminine behavior, Joan replays her troubled relationship with her mother. In brief scenes that anticipate *Cat's Eye*'s exploration of the potential coercions of girlhood friendship, *Lady Oracle* describes how Joan is tormented by her so-called friends who order her to walk ahead of them so they can "keep an eye" on her "from behind," and who take special delight in punishing her for failures in female decorum—for skipping "too heavily," for not standing "straight enough," for having dirty fingernails, or for being fat (63, 61).

Joan is similarly punished for deviating from the girlhood ideal of femininity in her experiences as an overweight, would-be ballet dancer. Although Joan aspires to the feminine ideal represented in the china music-box figurines of delicate ballerinas, she is denied the role of the butterfly in "The Butterfly Frolic," her favorite dance in the school recital. For in her butterfly costume with its short pink skirt and cellophane wings, she looks "grotesque": "with my jiggly thighs and the bulges of fat where breasts would later be and my plump upper arms and floppy waist, I must have looked obscene, senile almost, indecent" (47). Forced to don a teddy-bear suit and assume a new role in the dance—that of the mothball—she throws herself into the part. "[I]t was a dance of rage and destruction, tears rolled down my cheeks behind the fur, the butterflies would die. . . ." As she expresses her rage against the slender, graceful butterflies, she acts out her rebellion against the rules of femininity that dictate acceptable body shape and movements. But she also feels "naked and exposed, as if this ridiculous dance was the truth about me and everyone could see it" (51–52).

In open conflict with her mother during adolescence, Joan becomes obese. "The war between myself and my mother was on in earnest; the disputed territory was my body" (73). "Eat, eat, that's all you ever do," Joan recalls her mother saying. "You're disgusting, you really are, if I were you I'd be ashamed to show my face outside the house" (136). Consuming food "steadily, doggedly, stubbornly," Joan uses eating as a weapon. "I swelled visibly, relentlessly, before her very eyes, I rose like dough, my body advanced inch by inch towards her across the dining-room table, in this at least I was undefeated" (73). Eating to "defy" her mother, Joan also eats from "panic." Suffering from a diminished sense of self, sometimes she is "afraid" that she isn't "really there," that she is "an accident," for she has heard her mother call her an accident. "Did I want to become solid, solid as a stone so she wouldn't be able to get rid of me?" (82–83).

When Joan becomes overweight, she becomes a "reproach" to her mother, the "embodiment" of her mother's "failure and depression, a huge edgeless cloud of inchoate matter which refused to be shaped into anything" for which her mother "could get a prize" (71). As a "fat mongoloid idiot," Joan is a "defective," a "throwback, the walking contradiction of her [mother's] pretensions to status and elegance" (202). Determined not to be "diminished, neutralized" by the nondescript clothes her mother wants her to wear, she chooses outfits of "a peculiar and offensive hideousness, violently colored, horizontally striped" (94). Her confidence undercut when she recognizes that others view her obesity as an "unfortunate handicap," Joan comes to derive a "morose pleasure" from her weight "only in relation" to her mother. In particular, she enjoys her ability to clutter up her mother's "gracious-hostess act" (78). Putting on her fashion shows "in reverse," she calls attention to herself by "clomping silently but very visibly" through the rooms where her mother sits. "[I]t was a display, I wanted her to see and recognize what little effect her nagging and pleas were having" (75).

Through her obesity Joan not only gets back at her mother, she also signals her oppositional identity: her rebellion against the social construction of femininity. "I wouldn't ever let her make me over in her image, thin and beautiful," as Joan puts it (94). If, as we have observed in our analysis of *The Edible Woman,* the anorexic body can be read as a cultural text which inscribes the rules governing the construction of femininity—that women feed others, not the self, and that they severely limit their hunger for power and autonomy (see Bordo 18)—then the obese body can be read as a refusal to conform to these rules. "Through the pursuit of an ever-changing, homogenizing, elusive ideal of femininity . . . female bodies become what Foucault calls 'docile bodies,'— bodies whose forces and energies are habituated to external regulation, subjection, transformation, 'improvement,'" observes Susan Bordo. "Viewed historically, the discipline and normalization of the female body . . . has to be acknowledged as an amazingly durable and flexible strategy of social control" (14).

Protesting the social control of the female body, *Lady Oracle* dissents from the traditional construction of femininity—and its restrictions on female power and autonomy—in its initial focus on the obese female body. "She may be a *large* woman, but what powers!" Joan imagines people saying of her after Leda Sprott tells her that she has "great powers" (124, 123). In a recurring Fat Lady fantasy, Joan imagines a fat woman in a ballerina costume walking the high wire, proceeding inch by inch across Canada, "past the lumbering enterprises of the West Coast, over the wheatlands of the prairies, walking high above the mines and smoke stacks of Ontario, appearing in the clouds like a pink vision to the poor farmers of the St. Lawrence Valley and the mackerel fishermen of the Maritimes." Concentrating "all her forces on this perilous crossing, for a fall meant death," she wins the admiration of the watching crowds, their initial jeers turning to a roar of applause as she completes her death-defying feat (111–12).

Joan's obesity, then, is a signifier of her hidden desire for power. It also serves as a "magic cloak of blubber and invisibility" (157) that allows her, as an adolescent, to elude the sexual attentions—and thus the social control—of men. An "insulation, a cocoon," a "disguise," her obesity shields her from the voyeuristic male gaze, "a speculative look, like a dog eyeing a fire hydrant" (157, 135). Among the "untouchables" with her "halo of flesh," she does not experience men "as aggressive lechers but as bashful, elusive creatures who could think of nothing to say to me and who faded away at my approach" (168, 155). In a comic revenge fantasy that reveals her passive obesity to be a hidden form of female aggression, Joan—although she treasures "images" of herself "exuding melting femininity and soft surrender"—knows that she "would be able to squash any potential molester against a wall merely by breathing out" (156). Similarly, her fantasies about the foreign cook at Bite-A-Bit express female desires for power and revenge. Imagining their marriage ceremony after the cook proposes to her, she sees herself looming down the aisle dressed in white satin, "with this tiny foreign man slung over my arm like a purse." And when she daydreams about having sex with him, she envisions him "scurrying" over her body like a friendly animal, her body as "enormous to him as a peninsula" (109, 110).

Through its focus on female obesity, then, *Lady Oracle* rebels against the social discipline and male control of the female body. But it also depicts the unregulated and undisciplined female body as a grotesque spectacle. In a passage that recalls *The Edible Woman*'s repulsion at the uncontrollable and body-identified femininity represented in the mature female figure, Joan is overwhelmed at the sight of her enormous thigh: "it was gross, it was like a diseased limb, the kind you see in pictures of jungle natives; it spread on forever, like a prairie photographed from a plane" (133). After Joan loses weight, she fantasizes that she will be "absorbed" and "[o]bliterated" by the flesh she has shed. The "Fat Lady," the monstrous form that engulfs her, is featureless: "smooth as a potato, pale as starch," it resembles "a big thigh" and has a face "like a breast minus the nipple" (353). In a variation on her Fat Lady fantasy, Joan envisions a fat woman on a stage in a harem costume doing a striptease. "[S]he'd start taking off her clothes, while I watched, power-less to stop her. She'd wobble her hips, removing her veils, one after another, but no one would whistle, no one would yell *Take it off baby*. I tried to turn off these out-of-control fantasies, but couldn't, I had to watch them through to the end" (279–80). In a related fantasy, Joan imagines that Mr. Vitroni will keep her in a cage, fatten her up, dress her in black satin underwear, and then charge admission to the village men who want to see her. Imagining herself turning into "one of those Fellini whores, gigantic and shapeless," she envisions herself spending the rest of her life "in a cage, as a fat whore, a captive Earth Mother for whom somebody else collected the admission tickets" (361–62). Evoking the traditional cultural association of the fleshy female body with sexual promiscuity, this passage also voices concern about the male contain-ment and commodification of the female body. The obese female body, then, is a complex psychocultural symbol used by the narrative not only to register protest against the social construction of femininity, but also to express anxiety about the uncontained femininity that becomes sub-ject to social control.

If Joan, as an adolescent, used her obesity as a weapon against her mother, as a young adult she discovers that she can successfully battle her mother by appearing to follow the rules of femininity. Left two thousand dollars by her Aunt Lou on condition that she lose one hundred pounds, Joan begins to shed her fat. At first she expects that her mother will be pleased to see "her will being done." Instead, her mother becomes "frantic," for as Joan loses weight, her mother loses control over her. "About the only explanation I could think of for this behavior of hers was that making me thin was her last available project. She'd finished all the houses, there was nothing left for her to do, and she had counted on me to last her forever" (136). As Joan becomes attractive to men and thus threatens to usurp her mother's role, her mother becomes increasingly "distraught and uncertain" (135). It is revealing that her mother dies not long after Joan leaves home and that Joan imagines that her father may have murdered her. In the oedipal logic of this drama, not only does Joan replace her mother but, in the energic exchange between mother and daughter, Joan's female power exists at the expense of her mother's. And yet the dead mother remains a potent force in Joan's life.

When Joan receives a telegram announcing her mother's death, she thinks it might be a trap, her mother's attempt to bring her "back within striking distance" (195). Subsequently, she imagines that she somehow has killed her mother, for unconsciously she perceives her angry thoughts as lethal. Strategically "killed off" and banished from the text, the mother-figure resurfaces in a potentially more dangerous form. Twice after her mother's death Joan encounters what she thinks is her mother's astral body. Married to Arthur, she remains a partial prisoner of her noxious past. "All this time," she recalls, "I carried my mother around my neck like a rotting albatross. I dreamed about her often, my three-headed mother, menacing and cold" (238). Not unlike the Gothic heroine who, in a repetition of the "primal fear of being lost in the mother," has the sensation of being "possessed" and "suffocated" (Modleski, *Loving* 71, 70), Joan fears she will be engulfed by the mother. During her experiments with automatic writing, she gets trapped in the world of the mirror and feels as if she is "suffocating" (249). And in a nightmare in which she seems about to be sucked into the "vortex," the "dark vacuum" of her mother, Joan reexperiences the power of the lethal, interiorized mother, who, as Joan comes to realize, is also her own "reflection" (363). "[W]here a mother is hated to the point of matrophobia," as Adrienne Rich observes, "there may also be a deep underlying pull toward her, a dread that if one relaxes one's guard one will identify with her completely" (235). Describing the daughter's "ongoing battle" to escape enmeshment with the mother, "a mirror image who is both self and other," Claire Kahane links this to Gothic anxieties. For Kahane, the "dead or displaced" mothers figured in the Gothic point to "the spectral presence of a dead-undead mother, archaic and all-encompassing, a ghost signifying the problematics of femininity which the heroine must confront" (337, 335, 336).

Given the text's obsession with the bad mother, it is significant that Joan makes up a story, which she tells Arthur, about her good but dead mother, whom she characterizes as "a kind, placid woman who died of a rare disease" (41). This points to the recurrent pattern of splitting found in Atwood's fictional representation of the mother. As psychoanalysis explains the phenomenon of the good/bad mother, the splitting of the mother derives from the infant's perception of the mother as "good" (that is, as the source of pleasure) and "bad" (that is, as the source of frustration). The "conflict between love and hate," remarks Melanie Klein, "plays an important role" in the mother-infant relationship (271). To preserve the good mother, the infant projects both the internalized frustrating aspects of the mother and its own destructive feelings of anger and aggression onto the external "bad" mother, who is thus perceived as a persecutory figure. According to Klein, splitting "is one way of preserving the good object and the good impulses against the dangerous and frightening destructive impulses which create retaliatory objects" (273). Splitting, then, is a defense mechanism that arises from the infant's conflicting perceptions of and feelings about the mother. In the "complex" relationship with the mother "where feelings of love and hate, frustration and gratification coexist," splitting functions to keep dangerous feelings separate from gratifying ones. Through splitting the infant "protects the ideal, good relationship with the mother from contamination with the frustrating and bad"; splitting also protects "the good mother image" from the child's "destructive anger" (St. Clair 40, 132–33; Mahler 99). Keeping "incompatible feelings apart and separate," splitting is an important "developmental and defensive process" (St. Clair 190).

In *Lady Oracle,* as in other Atwoodian representations of the split mother, the "bad" mother is overpresent and powerful while the "good" mother is physically absent or dead. According to Atwood, Joan has two "good mothers" to choose from: Aunt Lou and Leda Sprott (Martens 46). But neither of these positive mother figures has the kind of lasting impact on Joan—or the narrative—as does the "bad" mother. Following the pattern found in other Atwood novels, Aunt Lou dies and is quickly ushered out of the text, while Leda Sprott is both physically and emotionally absent from Joan's life and plays a minor role in the narrative. Interestingly, the split mother also occurs in the contrast between *Surfacing,* which depicts the death of the good but remote mother, and *Lady Oracle,* which focuses on the bad mother figure.

Damaged in her relationship with her mother, Joan looks to men for rescue. That the romantic love scenario repeats significant features of the father-daughter relationship becomes apparent in *Lady Oracle.* Remarking on "women's tendency to recreate in their adult lives the structures of power and desire they first experienced in their father's houses," Jean Wyatt observes how the "girl's relation to her father trains her to idealize a distant and mysterious figure" and how romantic love encourages women "to find again the excitement of desire in games that manipulate illusion based on a man who is in important ways not there" (24, 27, 31). Fitting this paradigm, Joan's father is a man who "wasn't there" through much of Joan's childhood, and in one of her dreams he appears as a "mysterious man" standing outside the door (80, 70). Although he is essentially silent and emotionally unexpressive, Joan pretends, when he listens to the opera on the radio, that his voice is the "kindly and informed" voice of Milton Cross and that he is conversing to her "about lovers being stabbed or abandoned or betrayed, about jealousy and madness, about unending love triumphing over the grave" (81).

Like her father, the men in Joan's life seem—at least at first glance—distant and mysterious. Casting these men in a familiar fictional role, she sees them as Gothic heroes. When she meets Paul, the Polish count, and listens to his story, she thinks she has met "a liar as compulsive and romantic" as herself (165). Arthur at first seems a "melancholy fighter for almost-lost causes, idealistic and doomed, sort of like Lord Byron" (184). And the Royal Porcupine has "something Byronic about him" (283). But Joan is also aware of what happens when the romance wears off: that these men become "gray and multidimensional and complicated like everyone else" (300).

Intent on exposing the cultural myths that bind and confine women, *Lady Oracle* transforms Joan into a female beauty to continue the strategic sabotage of the romance plot begun in Atwood's earlier novels. Attractive to men after she loses weight, Joan discovers that she is the "right shape" but has "the wrong past"; thus begins her lifelong habit of compulsive lying as she creates "a different" and "more agreeable" personal history for herself (157). Dialogically contesting the official voices of culture, Joan insists that the basis of heterosexual romance is not openness and honesty but secrecy and lies. In her view, "hidden depths should remain hidden" (219). To sustain her marriage to Arthur, she needs not "more honesty" but more "dishonesty"; for in her experience, "honesty and expressing your feelings could lead to only one thing. Disaster" (37). She does not want Arthur "to understand" her; instead, she goes "to great lengths to prevent this" and she resists "the impulse to confess" (240).

A "sorry assemblage of lies and alibis" (236), Joan is aware of the feminine roles she enacts in her relationships with men: the "easygoing art student manquée" (167), the "scullery maid" (190), the passive, sympathetic wife who functions as a "nourishing blob" for her moody husband (236), and the seductive mistress. And she is also savvy to the fictional constructs—adopted from Gothic romance fiction and the popular culture of women's magazines—that women place upon men. "They wanted their men to be strong, lustful, passionate and exciting, with hard rapacious mouths, but also tender and worshipful. They wanted men in mysterious cloaks who would rescue them from balconies, but they also wanted meaningful in-depth relationships and total openness. . . . They wanted multiple orgasms, they wanted the earth to move, but they also wanted help with the dishes" (241). Providing a comic deflation of and dialogic commentary on the romance plot, Joan describes the beginning of her love affair with the Polish count. Anything but an "erotic" experience, she recalls that his pajamas turned her off and that he looked strange without his glasses (167). While she initially finds Arthur's aloofness "intriguing, like a figurative cloak," for heroes are "supposed to be aloof" and cover their passionate nature with a feigned indifference, she later realizes that Arthur's indifference is real and she also learns that "passionate revelation scenes" should be avoided (219). Married to Arthur, she gives up expecting him to be "a cloaked, sinuous and faintly menacing stranger. He couldn't be that: I lived with him, and cloaked strangers didn't leave their socks on the floor or stick their fingers in their ears and gargle in the mornings to kill germs. I kept Arthur in our apartment and the strangers in their castles and mansions, where they belonged" (241). And although when she begins her affair with the Royal Porcupine she is pleased to finally have someone who will waltz with her, when she meets him in Simpson's Basement she finds his cape "a little incongruous," and her sexual fantasies about him droop "slightly" (283). "Was every Heathcliff a Linton in disguise?" she wonders when the Royal Porcupine tells her he wants to "live a normal life" with her (300).

Unlike other women who are "merely amateurs" about fantasy lives, Joan, in her identity as Louisa K. Delacourt, the middle-aged writer of costume Gothics, prides herself on being a "professional" (241). Describing the fate of Charlotte, the Gothic heroine in her novel-in-progress *Stalked by Love,* Joan describes how her "eternal virgin on the run," her "goddess of quick money" is "in peril," for not only is the house "after her" but also the master and maybe even the mistress (146). And yet ironically while Joan mocks the paranoia of her fictional heroine, she, too, is plagued by persecutory fears. Like her Gothic heroine, she feels vulnerable, exposed, haunted and hunted down by malevolent, spectral pursuers. Evidence of the childhood source of these feelings of helplessness and persecution is found in Joan's terrifying dream of her mother in which she feels "helpless" when she hears people on the other side of a door talking about her and realizes that "something very bad" is going to happen (239). But these fears are also a response to Joan's anxiety about men. Having entered the romance plot which destroyed her mother, Joan faces a new threat to her self. For what defines the female heroine in the Gothic romance is her passivity, helplessness, and potential victimization at the hands of men.

Joan's initiation into the potentially dangerous male begins in childhood. In tracing the origins of Joan's anxieties about men, *Lady Oracle* also highlights a significant cultural moment in the socialization of young girls. Because Joan's father is absent during the first five years of her life, he becomes a "story" told by her mother, a story that varies "considerably." In some versions he is a savior, a "nice man" who will come home and bring "all kinds of improvements and delightful surprises"; in others, he is "retribution personified" or a "heartless wretch." Consequently, Joan is left wondering if her father is "a bad man or a nice man." Taught to read the behavior of men according to a shared cultural code, Joan learns from her mother that there are "two categories" of men: "nice men did things for you, bad men did things to you" (72–73).

In her childhood confrontation with a "bad" man, a pattern begins which is repeated in Joan's subsequent relationships with men. After the "bad" man—an exhibitionist wearing a tweed coat—exposes himself to Joan, he gives her a bouquet of daffodils. Later, when her so-called friends tie her up and then abandon her, leaving her for the bad man, she is rescued by a man in a tweed coat, possibly the same man who had exposed himself to her. "Was the man who untied me a rescuer or a villain? Or, an even more baffling thought: was it possible for a man to be both at once?" (67). Similarly, as she is growing up, she learns that her father, who as an anesthetist brings people back to life, also killed people "[i]n cold blood" during the war (80); later she imagines that her father might have killed her mother. All the men she has been involved with, as she eventually realizes, have had "two selves" (325): the man in the tweed coat, her childhood rescuer but also possibly the daffodil man, a pervert; her father, a doctor-savior and wartime killer and possible murderer of her mother; Paul, an author of innocuous nurse novels and a man she suspects of having a secret sinister life; the Royal Porcupine, her fantasy lover and feared "homicidal maniac" (303); and Arthur, her loving husband and suspected madman, possibly the unknown tormentor sending her death threats. Splitting men into dual identities, Joan perceives the apparently good man as a lurking menace, a hidden pervert, a secret killer.

The fact that Joan perceives men as both protectors and persecutors reveals her intense ambivalence toward them and her defensive need to split the good and bad qualities of men. It also reveals her learned Gothic thinking, and thus reveals the way adult women may use the splitting mechanism to sort out their contradictory feelings about and experiences of men. Splitting the good qualities of men from the bad helps control the spread of anxiety about male persecution, but only in a temporary way, as the Gothic novel reveals. Remarking on the "tendency in women to divide men into two classes: the omnipotent, domineering, aloof male and the gentle, but passive and fairly ineffectual male," Tania Modleski observes that this "tendency has characterized the female Gothic since its inception." In the generic code of the Gothic novel, not only are men divided into two categories, but often the "kind, considerate, gentle male . . . turns out to be vicious, insane, and/or murderous" (*Loving with a Vengeance* 79; see also Russ). Atwood, who is fascinated with the mass-culture appeal of Gothic fiction—a "paranoid form of escape literature"—speculates that it "is consumed in such great quantities by women because secretly they think their husbands are trying to kill them" (Martens 49). Gothic fiction, then, inscribes the hidden fears of women, who fear the very men they look to for rescue. It also points to the need of women to constantly "read" the behavior of men as a strategy of survival.

Plotting against the male plot against women, Atwood describes Joan's discovery of her own "lethal energies" (242) and dialogic power when she experiments with automatic writing. The first word Joan writes—"*Bow*" (246)—is suggestive, pointing as it does not only to her anxiety about female submission to male authority but also to her secret desire to assume power over others. As Joan continues her automatic writing experiment, she collects other "bizarre and even threatening" words (248) when she, sitting in the dark in front of her triple mirror and staring at a candle, imagines herself journeying into the world of the mirror. "There was the sense of going along a narrow passage that led downward, the certainty that if I could only turn the next corner or the next—for these journeys became longer—I would find the thing, the truth or word or person that was mine, that was waiting for me" (247). On the trail of an elusive stranger, she discovers, in the subterranean world of the unconscious, a woman unlike anybody she's "ever imagined," a woman who, she feels, has "nothing to do" with her. "[S]he lived under the earth somewhere, or inside something, a cave or a huge building. . . . She was enormously powerful, almost like a goddess, but it was an unhappy power" (248).

At once powerful and unhappy, Joan's Lady Oracle, who evokes Rider Haggard's *She*—"she who must be obeyed"—and Tennyson's "Lady of Shalott," presents "emblematic figures in the nineteenth century iconography of women"; for while She "embodies the myth of ruling womanhood," Tennyson's character "proposes an image of the Victorian ideal of feminine self renunciation" (Rao 139). And in a description meant to recall Robert Graves's poetic muse, the White Goddess—the moon trinity who undergoes cyclic changes from the new moon/white goddess to the full moon/red goddess to the old moon/black goddess—Lady Oracle is depicted as a triple goddess (see Atwood, *Survival* 199–201; see also Sciff-Zamaro and Patton):

> She sits on the iron throne
> She is one and three
> The dark lady   the redgold lady
> the blank lady   oracle
> of blood, she who must be
> obeyed   forever
> Her glass wings are gone
> She floats down the river
> singing her last song. (252)

The fact that Atwood deliberately patterns Lady Oracle after Robert Graves's triple goddess points to her oppositional, dialogical intent in her dramatization of Joan's discovery of her artist's identity. In a comic description of the cultural myths of the woman artist that she confronted early in her own career, Atwood recalls how she was "terrified" when she read *The White Goddess*. For rather than dismissing women, Graves "placed them right at the center of his poetic theory," but as "inspirations rather than creators, and a funny sort of inspiration at that. They were to be incarnations of the White Goddess herself, alternately loving and destructive, and men who got involved with them ran the risk of disembowelment or worse. A woman just might—might, mind you—have a chance of becoming a decent poet, but only if she too took on the attributes of the White Goddess and spent her time seducing men and then doing them in" ("Great Unexpectations" xv). Mocking the myth of the destructive female poet in *Lady Oracle*, Atwood stages a scene in which Joan begins to cry—she oozes tears "like an orphan, like an onion, like a slug sprinkled with salt"—when confronted with the media portrayals of her as a "challenge to the male ego" and "a threat" (299, 298). An author who is aware that "cultural myths about women are very much a form of 'power politics'" (Patton 29), Atwood recognizes how easily women writers can be seduced by the texts of others and by the cultural and literary stereotypes presented in figures such as Graves's White Goddess, Rider Haggard's She, and Tennyson's Lady of Shalott. But she is also aware of the subversiveness of women's laughter and the dialogic potential of feminist parody. Commenting on the disruptive, dialogic power of parody, Mikhail Bakhtin observes how "the process of parodying forces us to experience those sides of the object that are not otherwise included in a given genre or a given style," and how parodic literature "introduces the permanent corrective of laughter, of a critique on the one-sided seriousness of the lofty direct word" (*Dialogic* 55).

Using the corrective of laughter as it sabotages and provides a dialogic, postromantic commentary on Gothic fiction and its cliché-ridden, overblown, stylized speech, *Lady Oracle* traces the evolution of Joan's novel-in-progress, *Stalked by Love*. At first, Joan follows the conventional Gothic code by depicting Charlotte as the good, innocent virgin and Felicia as the bad, angry wife and sexually dangerous woman. "*[R]avishingly beautiful*," the red-haired Felicia moves "*with the sensuousness of a predatory animal*" (30). In contrast, the orphaned Charlotte, who knows she will be "*doomed, fated to wander the polluted night streets of London or to find asylum only in a house of shame*" if she falls from virtue, perpetually defends herself from Redmond's advances, once by threatening to strike him with Boswell's *Life of Johnson* (143). But as Joan continues to plot her novel, she begins to identify more and more with the wife. Distraught at the thought that Redmond no longer loves her, Felicia fears she will be discarded. "*Perhaps she could foresee that life would be arranged for the convenience of Charlotte, after all, and that she herself would have to be disposed of*" (351). Although Joan realizes that sympathy for the wife is "against the rules" and "would foul up the plot," which demands wives to be "eventually either mad or dead, or both," she nevertheless balks at sacrificing Felicia for Charlotte. "I was getting tired of Charlotte, with her intact virtue and her tidy ways. . . . I wanted her to fall into a mud puddle, have menstrual cramps, sweat, burp, fart" (352). A deliberate parody in practice, *Lady Oracle* asserts the dialogic authority of the resisting feminist voice by mocking the traditional representations of the split good/bad woman found in Gothic literature and by protesting the Gothic formula that binds women in the victim's role, either as the "eternal virgin on the run" or as the bad or defective wife who must be gotten rid of so that the husband can "*replace her with . . . the next one, thin and flawless*" (146, 377).

It is ironic that Joan wants to inject some realism into her Gothic heroine by making her sweat and burp even as her own Gothic fears of male persecution intensify. Indeed, as Linda Hutcheon comments, "The plot of *Lady Oracle* both mirrors and contains that which it consistently parodies: the forms of popular art" (*Canadian Postmodern* 146). Describing parody as a form of "formal and ideological critique" that allows authors "to speak to their culture, from within, but without being totally co-opted by that culture," Hutcheon explains that the "irony and distance implied by parody allow for *separation*," while the "doubled structure" that results from the superimposition of two texts "demands recognition of *complicity*." Parody, then, "asserts and undercuts that which it contests" (*Canadian Postmodern* 7). Constructing a feminist reading position through its parody of the generic codes of Gothic romance fiction, *Lady Oracle* is written for the "ideal" reader of parody, the reader who, in Barbara Godard's description, "enjoys the recognition of the hidden irony and satire and exchanges a sideward glance in complicity with the writer" ("Telling It Over" 4). And yet the fact that some critic/readers have found themselves "caught up in the work-in-progress" (Vincent 158), or have experienced the "overlapping" of Joan's real and fantasy worlds as "unnerving" (MacLean 191), or have felt that Atwood's novel "evokes rising horror over the similarity between the two worlds" (Rosowski 89) suggests the ability of *Lady Oracle* not only to assert Gothic form but also to communicate Gothic fears to some readers.

As the narrative progresses and Atwood carries us deeper and deeper into Joan's fun-house, hall-of-mirrors world, a kind of infinite regression occurs as fantasy and reality coalesce. In her Gothic novel, *Stalked by*

Love, Joan's stand-in, Felicia, is compulsively drawn into the labyrinth's *"central plot"* where she meets four women who claim they are all Lady Redmond. *"[E]very man has more than one wife,"* Joan-Felicia learns. *"Sometimes all at once, sometimes one at a time, sometimes ones he doesn't even know about"* (375, 376). At the psychocenter of the novel, the "central plot" of the maze depicted in the inset Gothic text provides interpretive clues to the narrative plot of the text we are reading. For in the specular world of the maze's center, Joan-Felicia encounters not only the ubiquitous fat lady—her oppositional self—but also embodiments of the culturally scripted roles she has assumed: that of Louisa Delacourt, the middle-aged writer of Gothic novels, and the dual red-haired, green-eyed identities of Joan, the seductive mistress, and Joan, the self-effacing wife. And there behind the closed door which she imagines is her pathway to freedom, she discovers Redmond, who, like Bluebeard, is a wife-murderer. *"She was about to throw herself into his arms, weeping with relief, when she noticed an odd expression in his eyes. Then she knew. Redmond was the killer. He was a killer in disguise, he wanted to murder her as he had murdered his other wives. . . . Then she would always have to stay here with them, at the center of the maze . . ."* (376–77).

In this Gothic scene gone awry, Joan-Felicia backs away from Redmond-Bluebeard, who transforms sequentially into the men in Joan's life: her father, Paul, the Royal Porcupine, Arthur. But when Redmond, his mouth *"hard and rapacious"* and his eyes smoldering, offers to rescue Joan-Felicia, she almost yields to his promise that they will be together *"forever, always."* Although she once *"had wanted these words . . . had waited all her life for someone to say them,"* she refuses. *" 'No,' she said. 'I know who you are.' The flesh fell away from his face, revealing the skull behind it; he stepped towards her, reaching for her throat. . . ."* (377). Describing the repetition compulsion evident in Gothic plots, Michelle Massé remarks that the "originating trauma that prompts such repetition is the prohibition of female autonomy in the Gothic, in the families that people it, and in the society that reads it" (12). Narrative with a vengeance, *Lady Oracle* is aware of the power of romantic discourse to seduce women into consenting to femininity. To be "stalked by love," as Joan's novel-in-progress dramatizes, is to be trapped in the "maze" of the romance plot. When women seek rescue and self-fulfillment through romantic affiliation, they risk becoming subject to the smothering dominance of men, who unconsciously plot to obliterate the female self.

To be terrorized by love, as *Lady Oracle* reveals, is also to be crippled as an artist. In a passage that openly thematizes the woman artist's dilemma, Joan, her feet bloodied from dancing barefoot over broken glass, identifies with the female dancer in *The Red Shoes*. "The real red shoes, the feet punished for dancing. You could dance, or you could have the love of a good man. But you were afraid to dance, because you had this unnatural fear that if you danced they'd cut your feet off so you wouldn't be able to dance. Finally you overcame your fear and danced, and they cut your feet off. The good men went away too, because you wanted to dance" (368). "[T]here is some truth to the *Red Shoes* syndrome," Atwood comments in an essay ("Curse of Eve" 226). Evidence that Atwood experienced this dilemma in her own life is found in her description of how, when she first realized that she wanted to write, marriage seemed a "kind of death" to her. "The men who didn't want me to write—who felt threatened by it—entrenched me in my belief that I wanted to write," she recalls. "Nothing else had as much meaning for me" (Valerie Miner 181, 184).

"What? . . . A book? You?" Arthur responds when Joan tells him that her Lady Oracle poetry is about to be published (253). It is telling that Joan must hide her Gothic novel writing from Arthur and that he openly disapproves of her Lady Oracle poetry, for as Jean Wyatt observes, the "fantasy of erotic love nurturing creativity" is "rare among female artist novels" (109). In "a striking number of novels about female artists, a woman has to choose between husbanding all her energies for art and pouring all her energies into personal relationships" (18). Describing the crippling effects of erotic love, Wyatt describes how the romantic love script "confirms the central doctrine of patriarchy—the inferiority of women, the superiority of men—by making the man rather than the self the center of a woman's existence and subordinating her creative powers to the single task of ensnaring him into a permanent alliance" (162). Moreover, the cultural injunction that "a woman must choose between art and love functions as a powerful preserver of the status quo." For if women believe that "pursuing a career of writing or painting means giving up the traditional satisfactions of being a woman—love and family—all but the most independent and self-determining women will be deterred from entering the cultural sphere; that leaves male cultural hegemony intact, with men creating the art works that define cultural expectations and interpret human experience" (235, n. 1).

Protesting the Red Shoes myth of the woman artist, Atwood interrogates and interrupts yet another cultural myth: that of the self-destructive woman artist. In a comic description of her initiation into the cultural role of the woman author, Atwood responds dialogically to this negative stereotype. "It began to occur to me," she recalls, "that maybe Robert Graves didn't have the last word on women writers, and anyway I wanted to be a novelist as well as a poet, so perhaps that would let me off the homicide." But although "let off" homicide, she soon found herself asked when she was going to commit suicide as authors like Sylvia Plath and Anne Sexton set "new, high standards in self-destructiveness for female poets." Was it "really all that necessary for a woman writer to be doomed, any more than it was necessary for a male writer to be a drunk," she wondered. "Wasn't all of this just some sort of postromantic collective delusion?" ("Great Unexpectations" xv–xvi).

Debunking this "postromantic collective delusion" in *Lady Oracle*, Atwood describes Joan's popularity with the death cultists. When all the convoluted romance plots of Joan's life converge—her current lover, the Royal Porcupine, wants her to marry him; Paul, her former lover, finds her and wants her back; she imagines that Arthur is the persecutor sending her death threats—she determines to fake her death in order to escape from her life, which has become "a snarl, a rat's nest of dangling threads and loose ends" (326). After Joan's faked accidental death becomes a suspected suicide, she becomes attractive to "every necrophiliac in the country" and is "shoved into the ranks of those other unhappy ladies, scores of them apparently, who'd been killed by a surfeit of words" (346). As the elusive suicidal artist, she takes on the role of Tennyson's Lady of Shalott, a literary figure she was initially attracted to in grade nine, even though she came to think of her as "The Lady of Small Onion" after she looked up the word "shallott" in the dictionary. "I was a romantic despite myself," she recalls, "and I really wanted, then, to have someone, anyone, say that I had a lovely face, even if I had to turn into a corpse in a barge-bottom first" (159). After her faked death, Joan finds herself "on the bottom of the death barge" where she once "longed to be." Reading the media portrayals of her "morbid intensity" and "fits of depression," she begins to feel that even though she had not committed suicide, perhaps she should have, for they "made it sound so plausible" (346). Playing with mimesis, Atwood veers away from her original "tragic" conception of the novel—which would have led to the closure of suicide—through this parodic dismissal of the cultural myth of the suicidal woman artist.

Aware of how the romance script perpetually turns into a trap, and determined to create her own female plot of desire, Joan sees herself as "an artist, an escape artist. I'd sometimes talked about love and commitment, but the real romance of my life was that between Houdini and his ropes and locked trunk; entering the embrace of bondage, slithering out again" (367). In a comic dénouement and enactment of female revenge, Joan, fearing that her murderous pursuer is at the door, both refuses to be a victim and vents her anger by attacking the reporter who has come to interview her. "I've begun to feel," she comments, "he's the only person who knows anything about me. Maybe because I've never hit anyone else with a bottle, so they never got to see that part of me" (379–80). When she later plays nurse to the hospitalized reporter, she self-consciously assumes the identity of the Mavis Quilp nurse heroines. But side by side with this enactment of the culturally scripted role of the nurturing, self-sacrificing woman is Joan's fantasy of herself as a "female monster, larger than life . . . striding down the hill, her hair standing on end with electrical force, volts of malevolent energy shooting from her fingers" (370). A hidden menace to the men who menace her, Joan determines to stop writing Gothic novels and considers turning, instead, to science fiction, a process she has already begun by depicting herself as a female monster: that is, as a powerful, oppositional goddess-artist.

"I never know how a book is going to end when I begin it. If I knew how it was going to end, I probably would not continue on," Atwood states (Draine 375). Responding to the remark that the endings of her novels "toss the ball of yarn into the reader's lap," Atwood replies, "[w]here it should be" (Castro 220). The reader, in her view, "is actually participating in the creation of the book. Every time someone reads a book, a new book is being created in the reader's head. Reading is a creative activity" ("Conversation" 178). If some of Atwood's readers, like Joan, long for a conventional "happy" ending and "the feeling of release" that results from the resolution of conflict (352), *Lady Oracle* frustrates such desires with its inconclusive ending. Commenting on the classic linear plot trajectory that moves from "instability to equilibrium," Joseph Boone observes that the movement toward a final stasis functions "to cut short any serious or prolonged inquiry into the ideological framework informing the fictional construct" (78). In contrast, the open-ended narrative form, which is typical of twentieth-century fiction, actively disrupts "the reader's traditional expectation of repose and relaxation of tension." When "forced to engage with the text beyond its actual close, the reader loses the ability to recuperate, hence naturalize, the text's manifold possible meanings or contradictions into a centrally unifying statement and must therefore actively struggle to reach an even tentative judgment" (146).

Forestalling closure in *Lady Oracle*, Atwood piques reader curiosity and invites speculation on the unwritten future of her character. Atwood also initiates a lively exchange among critics, who are divided in their analyses of the novel's closure. Cathy and Arnold Davidson, for example, feel that Joan is "moving in the right direction" at the conclusion of the novel. In their view science fiction, unlike the Gothic romance, "looks forward and implies at least survival." Joan's decision to stop writing Gothic novels "entails a recognition that she need no longer be a victim and that she will no longer inflict the myth of the victimized woman onto herself and her readers" ("Margaret Atwood's *Lady Oracle*" 176). For Lucy Freibert, unlike Gothic novels, which "are somewhat passive and are based on hope," science fiction is "active": "[b]ased on vision and invention, it can make things happen" ("Artist as Picaro" 31). At the end of the novel, according to Ann McMillan, readers "can see better possibilities for Joan than the pattern of escape attempts," and even Joan's thought about writing science fiction rather than Gothics "can appear hopeful." For although science fiction "may represent another form of escape, it would at least allow her to create alternatives to the ideal of victimization" (63, 63–64). And Catherine Rainwater feels that although Joan's "successful future is not guaranteed," her interest in science fiction "suggests that she will invent a vision of the future to some extent free of the oppressive (victimizing) feminine stereotypes which Gothic novels perpetuate" (25).

Other critics express less optimism about Joan's future. Barbara Rigney feels that even though Joan resolves to abandon Gothic novel writing, the science fiction she considers adopting is "merely another kind of romance." The reader's "hopes" for Joan's "regeneration are not rewarded" (79). According to Sherrill Grace, "there is no way for the reader to be certain that anything has changed by the end of Joan's narration. Quite possibly she will begin to spin another plot, this time around the new man in her life" (*Violent Duality* 127). At the end, comments Susan MacLean, "the reader suspects that there are more Joans to come. Although no longer interested in writing Costume Gothics, Joan is toying with the idea of writing science-fiction, a literary genre which is even further removed from reality" (195–196). Susan Rosowski states that the reader watches "in helpless recognition as the narrator . . . assumes the role of the nurse in yet another thinly veiled Gothic myth. In doing so, she creates a new character that is, if anything, potentially more monstrous than her previous ones" (97). And in the view of Sybil Vincent, "Atwood's conclusion is too reassuring to be reassuring. We suspect that Joan is once again adopting a disguise to elude the realities of her psychic conflicts—this time the militant female" (163). As these responses to *Lady Oracle* reveal, whether the ending signals a positive development in Atwood's character or suggests the continuation of her life as an escape artist is deliberately left unclear.

Creating a plot like her character, one that is entangled and full of loose ends, Atwood is aware of what critic/readers of contemporary novels want, and she gives them—in her "meta-fictional exploration of a writer who writes about writing" (Lecker 197) and in her "open-ended, fluid structure" (Givner 144)—the paradoxes and puzzles, the mirror tricks and indeterminacies, that so intrigue them. Described by Atwood as the "most rewritten" of her books (Sandler 15), *Lady Oracle,* as critics have noted with delight, is full of autobiographical satire and asides. Grafting details of her life onto her art, Atwood pokes fun at the Canadian publishing industry, at her descriptions in *Survival* of Canadian male artists, and at her relationship with her publishers. For as Judith McCombs observes, "Joan's books obviously represent Harlequins," a "major publishing export" of Canada; and while the Polish Count is a parody of "*Survival*'s paralyzed male artist," the Royal Porcupine is a parody of Atwood's "Canadian male artist" and his con-create art of frozen dead animals "burlesques *Survival*'s colonial mentality, victims, dead animal and frozen Nature stories" ("Atwood's Fictive Portraits" 76, 77). In *Lady Oracle,* comments Sherrill Grace, "[e]verything from the snobbery of Toronto suburbs, nationalist fervor and empty rhetoric (*Resurgence*), to charlatans peddling spiritualism and Canadian publishing (Black Widow Press/Anansi, Morton and Sturgess/McClelland and Stewart), is fair game" (*Violent Duality* 123).

Similarly, Atwood mocks the media's treatment of her not only in her depiction of Joan's transformation by the press into a cult figure, but also in her description of Joan as a "female monster" who has "volts of malevolent energy shooting from her fingers" (370)—this female monster image recalling Atwood's description of the media's various characterizations of her as "Margaret the Magician, Margaret the Medusa, Margaret the Man-eater" ("The Curse of Eve" 227). Even Atwood's own references to her work find their way into the novel. For example, her oft-cited description of the difference between *Surfacing* and *The Edible Woman*—"*Edible Woman* is a circle and *Surfacing* is a spiral" (Sandler 14)—is echoed by Joan: "I was waiting for something to happen, the next turn of events (a circle? a spiral?)" (342). Atwood also wryly anticipates the critical discussion of the unresolved closure of her narrative by having the publisher that rejects Joan's Lady Oracle poetry describe it as "unresolved" (250). And in *Lady Oracle,* as critics frequently have observed, Atwood parodies her earlier novels. For example, she travesties the eating obsession and identity search in *The Edible Woman* and the underwater dive and consequent emergence of a new awareness in *Surfacing* (see, for example, Godard, "My (m)Other, My Self" 23–24); she also parodies the romantic feminism of *Surfacing* as the myth and mysticism of her earlier novel give way to *Lady Oracle's* comic depictions of spiritualism. Atwood also echoes critical approaches to her poetry and engages in self-parody as she deliberately ridicules the angry, oppositional rhetoric of her own verse. "[Y]ou could say it's about the male-female roles in our society," Joan tells Arthur when he asks about her Lady Oracle poems. "I was uneasy about this; I was thinking of Section Fourteen, which had the embrace between the Iron Maiden, smooth on the outside but filled with spikes, and the man in the inflated rubber suit" (253).

Confronting "her own image in a very complicated, sometimes self-indulgent, literary game" in *Lady Oracle* (Carrington, "Margaret Atwood" 66), Atwood employs a dialogic strategy not only as she contests the official voices of the culture—her media and academic commentators—but also as she subverts the lofty words of her own work. Also a feminist parody in practice, *Lady Oracle* sets out to travesty Gothic romance fiction and to expose the perils of Gothic thinking. But even as Atwood strategically intervenes in established literary practices in *Lady Oracle,* she also reveals the seductive power of inherited mass-culture romance fictions and their potentially damaging effect on women.

5
Domestic and Sexual Warfare in *Life Before Man*

———————————————————— ■ ————————————————————

nlike *Lady Oracle* which is, at times, outrageously comic in its plot against the romance plot, *Life Before Man* views the romance plot in deadly earnest as it describes the dismal and lonely love lives of the three main characters, Elizabeth, Lesje, and Nate. In her comments on *Life Before Man,* Atwood describes the novel, which is set in Toronto in the mid-1970s, as taking place "in the actual middle of a middling city, in the middle class, in the middle of their lives, and everything about it is right in the middle, and it's very claustrophobic" (Schreiber 209). Although limited in its focus on the power struggles occurring within the sexual and family relationships of the three protagonists, *Life Before Man* is much more than an "Atwoodian soap opera" (Rosenberg 126). Deliberately interrogating bourgeois and romantic illusions, *Life Before Man* depicts a claustrophobic but also frighteningly brutal world, for the love lives of Atwood's characters are marked by the violence of suicide and rape.

Responding to the complaint that a book like *Life Before Man* "only adds to the ennui of the present," Atwood remarks, "That's like saying everybody should write happy books." For Atwood, the novel "reflects society" and is a "social vehicle." "Serious writers these days don't write uplifting books because what they see around them is not uplifting. It would be hypocritical to say the world is inspirational. It's not. These days the world is a pretty dismal place" (Twigg 125–26). The question that Lesje asks herself early in the novel—if she cares "whether the human race survives or not" (24)—is a question the text indirectly poses to the reader. Incorporating the voices of science and politics, *Life Before Man* expresses a deep-seated cultural pessimism as it describes geologic and cosmic disasters and the long-range effects of environmental pollution, and, more particularly, as it enumerates the horrors human beings inflict upon each other in the name of politics. "Children tortured in front of their mothers. Sons disappearing, to surface months later, fingernails missing, skins covered with burns and abrasions, skulls crushed, tossed on roadsides. Old men in damp cells dying of kidney problems. Scientists drugged in Soviet lunatic asylums. South African blacks shot or kicked to death while 'escaping'" (41). Just as Nate finds these accounts from the Amnesty International newsletter "so overwhelmingly painful that he's no longer able to read them" (42), so the stories in the newspapers, which tell of child abuse and murders and explosions, come across to him as "one long blurred howl of rage and pain" (232).

It is against this backdrop of human brutality—this howl of rage and pain—that Atwood chooses to stage the individual dramas of her characters. Because the terrible sickness afflicting the body politic is mirrored in the lives of Atwood's characters, the social and political crises described in the text provide an appropriate background for the domestic and sexual warfare which is the primary focus of the narrative. Dealing with women's deeply embedded feelings of powerlessness and rage in its depictions of violent sex and rape, *Life Before Man* also offers a uniquely female pleasure of the text through its enactments of women's domestic and sexual revenge against men.

If Atwood depicts a world that is potentially disturbing to readers in *Life Before Man,* she also, as is characteristic of her fiction, draws attention to the careful design of the text. In the novel, Atwood uses a triple point of view and third-person narration in a series of brief, dated scenes to tell a story about shifting triangular relationships. Given this unusual narrative format, it is not surprising that some commentators have felt compelled to "establish a motivation for this narrative" and "propose an explanation of the structure" (Grace, "Time Present" 168). Through this tripartite perspectival structure, Atwood decenters the narrative as she follows the complicated rising and falling narrative lines of the three protagonists. And in presenting both the breakup of Elizabeth and Nate's marriage and the unfolding of Nate's affair with Lesje from the differing perspectives of the characters, Atwood effectively opens up her text to multiple—and, as we shall see, conflicting—interpretations.

Although some commentators have claimed that the "formal structure" of *Life Before Man* "ultimately dwarfs the characters" (Stone), or that Atwood, in this "functional, ordered, structurally sound" novel, can be accused of controlling her characters just as Elizabeth supervises Nate's affairs (Glendinning, "Survival"), others applaud the narrative's "control that is almost a form of dignity" (Brown 34). *Life Before Man* has been described as "a book meant to be heard as a disembodied voice, very nearly objective for all the intimate details it renders" and as "a mockup of a scientific treatise on the behavior of primates rapt in their ritual love-hate behavior" (Brown 35). Similarly, the novel's "series of dated and labelled scenarios" has been compared to "a collection of file cards, or even field notes, that attempts to sum up the species it purports to describe" (Grace, "Time Present" 168). But unlike the "impersonal and objective third-person narrator," who, "scientist-like," treats the characters as "the subjects of a report" (Rigney 84), critic/readers—despite the narrative's reportorial style—do react emotionally to the text and the characters who inhabit it.

Describing her desire "to have a structure" that presents "triangularly balanced" points of view, Atwood comments that with such a structure readers cannot side with Nate without thinking that the women are "doing him dirt and not understanding him," nor can they be on Elizabeth's side without thinking that the others are "being grossly inconsiderate." Her "aim," she explains, is "to present all those points of view with equal weight and fairness" so her readers cannot, "except through personal preference alone, choose one over the other" (Draine 376). According to Murray Bowen's and Michael Kerr's description of the process of triangling, "Once the emotional circuitry of a triangle is in place, it usually outlives the people who participate in it. . . . The actors come and go, but the play lives on through the generations" (Kerr 135). While Bowen and Kerr are referring to the intergenerational repetition of triangular relationships in families, their comment on the staying power and emotional force of the triangle may help explain some of the critical responses to Atwood's novel. For again and again, as we shall see, critic/readers of *Life Before Man* have become involved in the drama of side-taking. Although some critics assume the emotionally neutral position Atwood intended, others become "triangled into" the text as they openly side with one character against another. This underscores Atwood's ability to make emotional contact with her readers even in a work like *Life Before Man,* which uses a fragmented structure—the novel, with its "independent, discrete" chapters, has been likened to the "discontinuous stanzas" of poetry (Davey 82)—to diffuse the anxiety and anger that drive the narrative.

Like the other Atwood novels we have analyzed, *Life Before Man* acts out a literary revolt against the romance plot. Through its dominant plot of love triangles and marital infidelity and through its focus on the sadistic underside of the heterosexual relationship, Atwood's narrative contests the socially constructed myths of romanticized love and marital harmony. In an ironic reversal of traditional love plotting, the falling movement of Elizabeth's plot—her failure at love and marriage—evolves into a muted sense of triumph; at the same time, the rising movement of Lesje's rite of passage into adulthood through her love affair with Nate promises, as the narrative draws to a close, to recapitulate Elizabeth's initial devolving trajectory. Unlike the other novels we have examined in which the apparently passive heroine is revealed to have a deep hunger for power and revenge, *Life Before Man* represents this split through the contrasting behaviors and personalities of the two female protagonists: the passive, child-woman Lesje and the powerful, angry Elizabeth. That the narrative insistently draws attention to the hidden intersections and correspondences between these characters—in particular, to Elizabeth's sense of powerlessness and Lesje's secret rage and desire for revenge—points to the text's view of these characters as complementary figures.

"She is surely," wrote an early reviewer about Elizabeth, "among modern heroines, a woman who challenges the reader to decide whether characters need to be liked, or only . . . understood" (Brown 34). Elizabeth has been variously described by commentators: as both a "villainess" and a "tragic figure" for whom readers have "grudging respect and sympathy" (Jeannotte 77); as a "powerful but poignant figure" who is "cruel, monstrous, but perceptive to the point of genius" (French 26); and as a "survivor" and "fighter," a person who "endures and does so through an admirable strength that is more than the obverse of her bitchy calculation" (Arnold and Cathy Davidson, "Prospects" 217, 218). A character who is meant to provoke a strong response from readers, Elizabeth, as critics have noted, occupies a special place in Atwood's narrative. For not only is Elizabeth the sole character to be given, on several occasions, a first person voice in the novel, but her experiences are also prominently placed at the beginning and end of the novel and at the beginning of three and the ending of four of its five sections. If one can say that Elizabeth's experiences structure the novel, it is also the case that her narcissistic fears and anxieties both frame and infect it. And if Elizabeth functions as a site of female power in the text, the narrative also repeatedly calls attention to her diminished selfhood.

"I don't know how I should live. I don't know how anyone should live" (3). These opening words in the novel, voiced by Elizabeth, provide a thematic focus for the narrative with its recurring thoughts about

Chris's suicide: "No head left at all, to speak of. The headless horseman" (10); "A tantrum, smashing a doll, but what you smashed was your own head, your own body" (3). Both Nate's unempathic description of Chris's remains and Elizabeth's thoughts about the suicide provide early evidence of the novel's preoccupation with body-self fragmentation and rage. Elizabeth's fragility and rigid self-containment are also signaled early in the text. In a description that recurs in the novel, she is depicted as "lying on her back," her "[a]rms at her sides, feet together, eyes open" (4). Feeling exposed and vulnerable, she wants her "shell back," she wants "a shell like a sequined dress, made of silver nickels and dimes and dollars overlapping like the scales of an armadillo" (3). As she stares at the crack in the ceiling, she attempts to stave off her feeling of incipient self-dissolution. "[T]he crack will not widen and split and nothing will come through it," she insists. And yet, she is "not in," she is "somewhere between her body, which is lying sedately on the bed . . . and the ceiling with its hairline cracks" (4). Elizabeth "can see herself there, a thickening of the air, like albumin," and she "knows about the vacuum on the other side of the ceiling" into which "air is being sucked with a soft, barely audible whistle. She could be pulled up and into it like smoke" (4–5). Just as *Life Before Man* insists on Elizabeth's power in the social sphere, so it repeatedly emphasizes her inner powerlessness. A center of power and angry energy in the narrative, she is also the character most threatened by the void of her own fragmenting selfhood.

Despite Elizabeth's assertion that she is not "merely the sum" of her past (108), the narrative follows the psychoanalytic paradigm as it tells the story of her traumatic childhood in an attempt to explain the source of her powerful, oppositional, yet narcissistically fragile personality. Deserted by her father, then abandoned by her mother and raised by her aunt, Elizabeth is the product of the absent father and defective mothering. Repeating a familiar pattern in Atwood's fiction, the bad mother, Elizabeth's Auntie Muriel, has a powerful and lethal personality and is a harmful presence in Elizabeth's life, while Elizabeth's real mother is both emotionally and physically absent. An alcoholic, Elizabeth's mother "sold" (253) Elizabeth to Auntie Muriel and later died as the result of a rooming-house fire. Elizabeth's deep-seated rage at her mother is signaled in her sarcastic description of how her mother "finally succeeded in frying herself to a crisp" and then "finally died, after smoldering in the hospital bed for longer than anyone could have expected" (133, 201). Similarly, Elizabeth attempts to contain her angry feelings about her aunt by transforming her into a "droll story." But she also realizes that this tactic doesn't affect her aunt's "malignance" (154). Indeed, because Auntie Muriel once had dominance over her, Elizabeth remains vulnerable in her relationship with her aunt. "Elizabeth is an adult in much of her life, but when she's with Auntie Muriel she is still part child. Part prisoner, part orphan, part cripple, part insane; Auntie Muriel the implacable wardress" (136–37).

Anticipating *Cat's Eye*'s depiction of Mrs. Smeath, *Life Before Man* presents Auntie Muriel as a self-righteous and harshly judgmental woman, who speaks in the punishing, controlling voice of religious conservatism. *"This is God's punishment,"* she tells the twelve-year-old Elizabeth, who is suffering from her first menstrual cramps (132; see also *Cat's Eye* 191). Elizabeth, as an adult, uses a dialogic strategy to unmask and dethrone the disciplinary, judgmental speech of her aunt. Openly mocking her aunt's religion, she describes her aunt's Great Chain of Being: "First comes God. Then comes Auntie Muriel and the Queen, with Auntie Muriel having a slight edge. Then come about five members of the Timothy Eaton Memorial Church, which Auntie Muriel attends. After this there is a large gap. Then white, non-Jewish Canadians, Englishmen, and white, non-Jewish Americans, in that order. Then there's another large gap, followed by all other human beings on a descending scale, graded according to skin color and religion" (153–54). Sitting opposite her aunt, Elizabeth scrutinizes and condemns her aunt's appearance, observing how the "solid bulk" of her aunt's "torso [is] encased in two-way stretch elastic with plastic boning" and how the jersey of her aunt's tailored dress is stretched "across her soccer-player's thighs." Similarly, Elizabeth is aware of her aunt's hostile gaze. Her aunt's eyes, "like two pieces of gravel, cold and unreflecting, [are] directed at Elizabeth, taking in, Elizabeth knows, every disreputable detail of her own appearance. Her hair (too long, too loose), her sweater (should have been a dress), the absence of a lipstick-and-powder crust over her face, all, all are wrong. Auntie Muriel is gratified by this wrongness" (131–32).

Rehearsing the book and magazine explanations for her aunt's malignant behavior, Elizabeth reflects that "Auntie Muriel was thwarted in youth. She had a domineering father who stunted her and wouldn't let her go to college because college was for boys. . . . Auntie Muriel had a strong personality and a good mind and she was not pretty, and patriarchal society punished her." And yet Elizabeth—and indeed the text—"can forgive Auntie Muriel only in theory. Given her own sufferings, why has Auntie Muriel chosen to transfer them, whenever possible, to others?" Elizabeth asks (132). Punished by patriarchy, Auntie Muriel becomes, in turn, an embodiment of its repressive values. Moreover, because Auntie Muriel works at "developing" the parts of Elizabeth that most resemble herself and "suppressing or punishing the other parts" (153), she transfers not only her sufferings but also the negative aspects of her personality onto her niece. Her aunt, Elizabeth realizes, terrifies her because she does not "know where to stop"; unlike other people who have "lines they won't step over," these lines "do not exist" for her aunt. Similarly, Elizabeth fears that "these lines do not exist in herself, either" (205).

Encouraged by the text to respond with anger at Auntie Muriel's excessive behavior—indeed, she has been characterized as a "brontosaurus of a woman, immovably self-righteous in her ponderous certainty that she was always right" (Arnold and Cathy Davidson, "Prospects" 215)—readers are also prompted to find the connections between Elizabeth's and her aunt's personalities. As reflected in the eyes of the other characters, Elizabeth does resemble her powerful, repressive aunt. Nate, for example, feels stifled by Elizabeth's "rules, subrules, codicils, addenda, errata" (184). Although he once envisioned Elizabeth as the "lady with the lamp," he now sees her as the "lady with the axe" (50). During the divorce negotiations, he feels trapped, "caught in a vise, the handle . . . turning, slowly, inexorably" (300). According to Nate's lover, Martha, Elizabeth wants to *"supervise"* her affair with Nate "[l]ike some kind of playground organizer" (165). And to Lesje, Elizabeth is "a combination of the Dragon Lady and a vacuum cleaner" (284). Just as Elizabeth makes Martha, in her affair with Nate, feel like a "housemaid" who is doing the "dirty work," so she succeeds in giving Lesje the impression that she is "going to be tried out as a kind of governess" (30, 244). To Lesje, Elizabeth is a dangerous predator. "Today she classifies Elizabeth as a shark; on other days it's a huge Jurassic toad, primitive, squat, venomous; on other days a cephalopod, a giant squid, soft and tentacled, with a hidden beak" (307).

Invested with the social power of class and money that is the traditional male prerogative, Elizabeth makes use of her "haute Wasp" (106) upbringing and demeanor in her relationships with men. While her husband Nate, a lawyer turned toymaker, is economically dependent on Elizabeth, Chris, her lover, is her social inferior. Chris is attracted to her because she has what he wants—"power over a certain part of the world"—and although she lets him see and touch that power, she also lets him see that he is "deficient" (182). What haute Wasp men have traditionally done to socially inferior women, Elizabeth does to Chris.

She uses him sexually and then discards him, showing him that he is "only a vacation" and is a "dime a dozen" (182).

A woman who openly transgresses society's rules, Elizabeth has "two" vocabularies: an acquired "genteel chic," which is a useful "veneer," and an "older, harder" language "left over from those streets and schoolyards on the far edge of gentility where she fought it out" as a child (166). And yet despite her dialogic resistance to bourgeois culture and her ability to "speak from that other life" (168), Elizabeth also admits that she "has been doing imitations for years. If there is some reason for it she can imitate a wife, a mother, an employee, a dutiful relative" (251). While Elizabeth's self-consciousness about her role-playing points to her awareness of femininity-as-masquerade, it also reveals her own capitulation to cultural expectations, her own consent to femininity.

More significantly, despite Elizabeth's power in the social sphere—a power enhanced by her ability to do imitations—she, like other Atwood heroines we have encountered, suffers from a deficient sense of self. The fact that Auntie Muriel loves dressing Elizabeth and her sister Caroline "like twins" (93) while they are growing up provides an important textual clue to Elizabeth's narcissistically defective selfhood. Although backgrounded and rendered almost totally silent in the text, the insane Caroline represents Elizabeth's unacknowledged reflection, her psychic "twin." Caroline's appearance on the night of her collapse into madness—she lies on a blanket on the floor, "arms folded across her breasts, eyes open and fixed on the ceiling" (205)—resembles Elizabeth's familiar posture of depressive withdrawal. After Caroline is institutionalized, she does not talk, move, or feed herself. "I know you're in there," Elizabeth whispers to her sister but to no avail (95). Elizabeth's transient experiences of body/self fragmentation—at times she is "not in" but is somewhere "between her body . . . and the ceiling" (4)—is Caroline's permanent condition. While Elizabeth is "part insane" (137), her sister is totally mad. While Elizabeth feels "almost frozen" at times, her sister is rendered totally immobile within her "sealed body" (109, 95).

A contradictory character, Elizabeth has social power but a fragile self. Thus, when she suspects that Nate has a new lover, her ancient feelings of vulnerability surface. "[A]t the base of her skull the old chill begins, the old fear, of events, cataclysms preparing themselves without her, gathering like tidal waves at the other side of the world. Behind her back. Out of control" (156). "Stay in your place, Nate. I will not tolerate that void," she thinks to herself when she realizes that Nate is in love with Lesje (183). Eventually recognizing that Nate is preparing to desert her, she experiences momentary self-disintegration. "The cracks between the boards of the table are widening; grey light wells from them, cold. Dry ice, gas, she can hear it, a hushing sound, moving toward her face. It eats color" (236). Meditating on the meaning of All Souls day, Elizabeth thinks of "all souls" as those who have "come back, crying at the door, hungry, mourning their lost lives" (54–55). Later, when she—"discarded, invisible"—stands alone in the dark outside Nate and Lesje's house, she acts out the narcissistic drama of the lost, mourning child (291). Imagining that her own daughters are "preparing for flight, betrayal, they will leave her, she will become their background," she envisions herself as an old woman. "Her shoulders will sag, she will have difficulty with shopping bags, she will become *My Mother,* pronounced with a sigh" (289, 290). If Elizabeth provides an outlet in the text for women's desires for power and revenge, she also is an embodiment of feminine powerlessness and self-diminishment.

"Elizabeth has made herself into a victor, though she suffers more pain than we tend to attribute to the powerful," writes Rosellen Brown (34). For Marilyn French, although Elizabeth is "a soul freezing in agony," she survives, and "[g]iven her pain, her survival is a triumph—and the novelist's triumph as well" (26). In the view of Cathy and Arnold Davidson, Elizabeth—although initially presented in a "passive, helpless role"—is "not just a survivor," she is also a "fighter" and her "indomitable strength" distinguishes her from Atwood's "earlier heroines." But if she is shown originally as a "helpless victim," she is also "a most capable victimizer" ("Prospects" 217). Because, as the Davidsons remark, Atwood provides the "points of view of different observers, none of whom is the least bit objective," readers are compelled to "synthesize their own point of view" ("Prospects" 218). Similarly, Atwood seems intent on synthesizing her own view of Elizabeth's character. "As a creation, I think I probably did the best job on one of the most unpleasant characters, namely Elizabeth in *Life Before Man,*" Atwood comments ("Conversation" 176). "She's ruthless in her dealings with other people, but then people have been ruthless in their dealings with her. Violence begets violence," says Atwood as she provides a psychological explanation for—and thus provides an implicit authorial defense of—her character's "unpleasant" behavior (Twigg 125). Atwood also appears to admire Elizabeth for being a "strong character" and "very self-determined," despite the fact that she is "very single" and "very alone" (*Atlantis* interview 210).

Like Atwood, some critics seem to admire Elizabeth for her strength and for her ability to survive. And yet many critic/readers openly express their preference for Lesje. Although Lesje has been condemned for being one of Atwood's "perennial child/women" (Rigney 93)—and indeed Atwood has characterized her as "unrealistic and wimpish" (Brans 307)—a number of commentators act as Lesje's advocate and condemn Elizabeth as they, becoming triangled into the text, participate in the dialogic drama of side-taking. In this view, if Lesje exemplifies "flawed innocence," then "a good case can be made for Elizabeth as the 'villainess'" (Jeannotte 77). If Elizabeth is "cruel" and "monstrous," Lesje is "an endearing innocent stumbling around in a world booby-trapped by other people's opacities and ambivalences" and is "the most redeemable character of the novel" (French 26; Davey 92).

Because *Life Before Man* seems to invoke feminine stereotypes promoted by masculinist culture—that of the passive, innocent child-woman and her opposite, the aggressive, angry woman who transgresses social codes of feminine conduct—it is not surprising to find critic after critic coming to Lesje's defense. And yet despite the fact that Lesje and Elizabeth appear, at first glance, to be paired opposites in the text's design, there is also a deliberate "blurring" of characters in Atwood's novel (Carrington, "Demons, Doubles" 233). Although Elizabeth is clearly the primary carrier of the text's anger, Lesje takes on more and more of Elizabeth's negativity as the narrative progresses. Thus even as Lesje fantasizes Elizabeth as a dangerous predator, she herself becomes text-identified as a potential predator.

Through various coded descriptions, the contradiction in Lesje's personality—her overt passivity and covert aggression and anger—is made apparent. As commentators have observed, the novel deliberately associates Lesje with the child-heroine of *Alice in Wonderland:* first by indicating that the name 'Lesje' means 'Alice' in Ukrainian, and then by describing Lesje's fantasy of "Lesjeland," which she envisions as "tropical, rich and crawling with wondrous life forms" (99). This, in turn, suggests Lesje's kinship with Marian, the passive child-woman in *The Edible Woman,* who is similarly associated with Lewis Carroll's Alice. But although Lesje sees herself as "a timorous person, a herbivore," she also fears that her teeth are "too large for her face: they make her look skeletal, hungry" (14, 15). It is also suggestive that Lesje's fantasies about dinosaurs become increasingly violent and predatory as they shift from an innocent description of grazing stegosaurs and camptosaurs (12) to that of an attacking Gorgosaurus. "In a minute William Wasp and Lesje Litvak will be two lumps of gristle. The Gorgosaurus wants,

wants. It's a stomach on legs, it would swallow the world if it could" (27). Watching "from the immunity" of her treetop as the deinonychus uses its razor-sharp third claw to disembowel its prey, she is fascinated with this "innocent though bloody dance" (158). Like *The Edible Woman* and *Lady Oracle*, *Life Before Man* contests the social regulation and control of female appetite in masculinist culture, which provides a "concrete expression" of the "general rule" governing the construction of contemporary femininity: "that female hunger—for public power, for independence, for sexual gratification—be contained, and the public space that women be allowed to take up be circumscribed, limited" (Bordo 18).

At one point, Lesje thinks to herself that if she is not "careful," she will "turn into Elizabeth." While Nate expects that Lesje will assume the passive, nurturing role allotted to women—that she will be "serene, a refuge" and "kind"—she is not "like this at all," even though "she wants to be this beautiful phantom, this boneless wraith he's conjured up" (310). Indeed, despite Lesje's belief that she is "not a web-spinner, expert at the entrapment of husbands" (142), she becomes more and more manipulative in her relationship with Nate, ultimately trying to entrap him by deliberately getting pregnant. She also begins to openly express her anger. "Elizabeth needs support like a nun needs tits," she tells Nate. "To hell with the children" (338–39, 340). In their discussions of the children, which become more and more frequent, she feels "like a mean-minded ogre" (278).

Like Elizabeth, who was damaged by her childhood relationship with her aunt, Lesje has been adversely affected by her relationship with her Ukrainian and Jewish grandmothers. Embodiments of the bad mother, they "mourned over her as if she were in some way dead" because of her "damaged gene pool," each thinking that she "should scrap half her chromosomes, repair herself, by some miracle" (69). Anticipating *Cat's Eye*'s description of how Elaine Risley is ridiculed by her young girlfriends for her social awkwardness, Lesje recalls how, when she was in grade four, the older girls taunted her for being a "dirty foreigner": "Pee-ew, they said, holding their noses, while Lesje smiled weakly, appeasingly. Wipe that smirk off your face or we'll wipe it for you" (244; see *Cat's Eye* 183). If Lesje represents "in slightly disguised terms the religious and ethnic schisms of Canadian identity" (Rubenstein, *Boundaries* 75), she is also used by the narrative to critique the dominant bourgeois culture. Because Lesje "grants extra rungs" on the social ladder to people who have "an authentic British name," she feels socially

inferior to her lover, William. His behavior toward her serves to reinforce this feeling. For although William is "proud of her as a trophy and
as a testimony to his own wide-mindedness," he also finds her "impossi-
bly exotic" but not of "his own kind" (26). Lesje, then, is doubly
devalued—both as a woman and as a member of a marginal cultural
group. Lesje's dialogic resistance to the dominant culture becomes apparent in "the small raucous voice" that on occasion "makes itself heard"
behind her "studiously attentive face" (23). Deeply angry at William,
Lesje calls him William Wasp; she thinks of his brain as "pink-cheeked,
hairless"; and she imagines him with a woman of his own kind making
love "like two salmon, remotely, William fertilizing the cool silvery eggs
from a suitable distance" (24, 26). "[W]hich came first, man or venereal
disease?" she pointedly asks William. "I suppose hosts always have to
precede their parasites, but is that really true? Maybe man was invented
by viruses, to give them a convenient place to live" (27).

If, through such adversarial, feminist-dialogic speech, the text gives
voice to a female oppositional identity and if there is a spreading of anger
in the text, there is also a spreading of narcissistic anxiety. For Lesje, like
Elizabeth, suffers from a fragile sense of self. While Nate finds Lesje
remote and beautiful, she feels "awkward, as if the bones of her elbows
and knees aren't really touching but are attached to one another with
string. Gangling" (84). When Nate telephones home to Elizabeth and
uses the words "home," "love," and "mother," Lesje suffers temporary
self-dissolution. "A vacuum forms around her heart, spreads; it's as if she
doesn't exist" (143). At another point, Lesje thinks that she is "only a
pattern" and "not an immutable object" and that she will someday
"dissolve" (191–92). Like Elizabeth, Lesje contemplates suicide, her
desire to kill herself resulting from both her anger and her "fear of being
nothing" (340). And like Elizabeth, who feels a "black vacuum" sucking
at her and fears that "the past will yawn around her, a cavern filled with
menacing echoes" (350, 305), Lesje feels a "vacuum" form around her
heart and she associates childhood with "a hollow sound, like a cave
where there might be an echo" (143, 219). The fact that Lesje and
Elizabeth have similar perceptions and share imagery in the text serves to
reinforce their psychic kinship. Moreover, through this deliberate blurring of characters, Atwood focuses reader attention on the author-
designer behind the narrative.

Using the corresponding histories of Lesje and Elizabeth to under-
score feminine powerlessness and enact fantasies of power and revenge,
Life Before Man openly plots against the imbalance of power in the

heterosexual relationship through its depiction of Nate, a passive male. Both condemned as "a shallower character than any of the women in the novel" and lauded as "Atwood's first three-dimensional male character" (Greene, "*Life*" 79; McLay, "Triple Solitaire" 122), Nate has been the subject of critical speculation and debate. As a reader of her own novel, Atwood has felt compelled to publicly defend Nate against the type of complaint made by interviewer Jo Brans: that he is "wishy-washy" and "wimpy." The fact that Nate finds it difficult to decide whether or not to leave his children because his "marriage is rotten," Atwood comments, does not mean that he is "a wimpy man." When Brans responds that she is "glad" to hear Atwood "defend" Nate, Atwood makes a telling reply. "Now, notice what you did. You came after me for Nate, who's actually the nicest person in the book." When Brans then asks if Nate is "nicer" than Lesje, Atwood responds that he is "lots nicer" and that although Lesje is "a wimp," people never attack Lesje "for being unrealistic and wimpish and so on, because they expect girls to be like that" (307). While Atwood is correct in pointing out that Brans's objection to Nate invokes traditional gender expectations—namely, that men are strong and decisive, not wimpy—the fact that Atwood takes Nate's side also reveals that she, like others, has been triangled into the text and caught up in the dialogic drama of side-taking.

Despite Atwood's spirited defense of Nate and her complaint that people expect the male to be a kind of superman (Brans 308), Nate is depicted as essentially passive, as the object of female desire. In dialogic competition with traditional novelistic discourse, *Life Before Man* overturns the official cultural—and novelistic—notion of male agency. Instead, it depicts Nate's entrapment in the male masquerade as he performs assigned roles in a female-directed script. Under the control of the women in his life—first Elizabeth and Martha and later Lesje—he sometimes thinks of himself "as a lump of putty, helplessly molded by the relentless demands and flinty disapprovals of the women he can't help being involved with" (40). Having lived in the "perpetual spotlight" of his mother's approving gaze, "alone on the stage, the star performer" (149), he remains emotionally dependent on women. Elizabeth recognizes his desire to be "protected" by a woman. "He wanted a woman to be a door he could go through and shut behind him. . . . Earthmother, Nate her mole, snouting in darkness while she rocked him" (183). "Running away from Mother?" Martha accuses him. "Wanted some other nice lady to give you a cookie and a tumble in the sack?" (31). But he also finds women potentially threatening. Elizabeth, whom he once envisioned as "a Madonna in a shrine, shedding a quiet light," transforms into the frightening "lady with the axe" (50). And Martha, who, like Lesje, at first attracted him because of "her vagueness, her lack of focus, an absence of edges that gave her a nebulous shimmer," becomes "hard": "it's as if she's been dropped on the sidewalk from a great height and has frozen there, all splayed angles and splinters." He imagines Martha's embrace to be suffocating, engulfing. "She'll be on him in a minute, arms winding like seaweed around his neck . . ." (32). With Elizabeth he feels "*[c]ornered*" and "like a stick man" (11, 115); with Martha he feels "withered" and his body sags on his spine, "the flesh drooping like warm taffy on a sucker stick" (32, 29).

Inverting the sexual hierarchy that governs the cultural—and fictional—system of representations, *Life Before Man* casts Nate in the passive role in the perennial war for domestic and sexual mastery. What initially attracts Nate to Elizabeth is her haute Wasp demeanor. "At first she'd been remote and a little condescending, as if he was some sort of perverted halfwit she was being kind to. It knocked him out; that, and the impression she gave of knowing exactly what she was doing" (49–50). Supervising Nate's affair with Martha, Elizabeth, in effect, turns Nate into an object of female exchange, a sexual commodity. "We figured it out that Elizabeth really owns you, but I get fucking privileges one night a week," as Martha tells Nate (116). When, after their affair has ended, Martha thinks that Nate is trying to humiliate her by flirting with another woman, she physically attacks him. "Martha punches him in the face, then begins kicking him in the shins. She's hampered by the long skirt of her dress, so she slugs him, aiming for the belly, hitting him in the rib cage" (119). Looking to be rescued, he turns to Lesje, imagining her as "the bearer of healing wisdom" (76). "A woman hit me," he tells her when she asks about his bruised face. "Is he about to cry?" Lesje wonders as she comforts him. "No. He's making a gift of himself, handing himself over to her, mutely. Here I am. You may be able to do something with me" (128). Like the female characters in other Atwood novels, who experience men as potentially violent but also as possible rescuers, Nate similarly splits women into persecutors and rescuers.

Thus, *Life Before Man* deliberately presents a feminist-dialogic challenge to traditional novelistic discourse and transgresses the social and sexual order in its depiction of Nate's relationships with women. It also flaunts the myth of romantic attraction by revealing that Nate's notions of romance are derived from mass-culture fantasies. For example, Nate imagines himself falling to his knees before Lesje's veiled figure, only to recognize that he has borrowed this image from the movie *She,* which he saw "when he was an impressionable twelve and masturbating nightly" (76). Nate's vision of marital harmony is also derived from popular culture. When Elizabeth ends her affair with Chris, Nate thinks it might be possible to salvage their relationship. "This is what he wants, wants back. This image, of a shared harmonious life, left over from some Christmas card of the forties, a log fire, knitting in a basket, glued-on snow . . ." (269). Similarly, when Elizabeth lapses into depression after Chris's suicide, Nate remembers their former times together "as the olden days, like a bygone romantic era, like some Disneyland movie about knighthood" (8).

Contrasting the fantasies of popular romance with domestic realism, *Life Before Man* traces the devolving trajectory of Nate's affair with Lesje. What begins as an escape from his troubled marriage soon becomes a new trap. Aware of Lesje's growing depression when he finds it difficult to leave Elizabeth, he feels oppressed. "She hasn't been putting any pressure on him, any spoken pressure. Nevertheless he can scarcely breathe" (227). To keep Lesje from feeling "rejected and miserable," he makes love to her, or tries to, "[n]o matter how drained he is" (228). Torn between his obligations to both Elizabeth and Lesje, he realizes that he cannot "keep up his divided life much longer. He'll get an ulcer, he'll implode. An incoherent anger is growing in him, not only with Elizabeth but with the children: what right do they have to hook him, hold him back? Also with Lesje, who is forcing him to make painful decisions" (231). Even after he moves in with Lesje, Nate still finds it necessary to be "in two places at once." He feels that he "should have two sets of clothes, two identities, one for each house; i.'s the lack of this extra costume or body that is cracking him apart." In a wooden toy which he recalls making, he finds an emblem of his fragmented state. "This iŝ his body, stiff fragments held together by his spine and his screwtop head. Segmented man" (283).

And yet although Nate is depicted as the Atwoodian innocuous male, there is another side to his character. When Martha makes him angry, he wants "to take her by the shoulders and give her a good shake, throw her against the wall" (29). Similarly, during the divorce negotiations with Elizabeth, he has "a swift desire to stand up, lean over her [Elizabeth], put his hands around her neck and squeeze" (299). Although externally passive, Nate envisions himself as a wolflike predator when he begins his affair with Lesje (149–50). Projecting his violent feelings onto Chris at another point, Nate imagines Elizabeth in Chris's grasp, her "white flesh buckling under those fists, powerless, whimpering" (272). But although Nate has a potential for violence, he does not act on it.

The text's deliberate pairing of Nate and Chris offers yet another example of the split male in Atwood's art. Unlike Nate, the innocuous male who is essentially feminized in the text, Chris embodies a dangerous, and potentially sadistic, male sexuality. Attracted to violent sex—to "[v]iolence, metal on metal" (204)—as long as she can control it, Elizabeth has an affair with Chris. Her "demon lover," Chris is "a dangerous country, swarming with ambushes and guerrillas, the center of a whirlpool" (247). Sex with Chris is energizing. As she later reflects, should she have "[f]oregone that jag, energy flowing into her" (181). But Chris also assumes a kind of sexual power over her. Passing himself off as part French and part Indian, sneering at "the whiteness of her skin and presumably her blood," he makes love "as if exacting payment" and she allows herself to "be bullied" by him (181). "Backing her against the door, his arms clamping around her, shoulders massive when she tried to push him off, face heavily down on hers, force of gravity. Leaning on her. I won't let you go yet. She hates it when anyone has power over her. Nate doesn't have that kind of power, he never had" (18–19).

That the "desire to be taken by force," as Tania Modleski observes in her analysis of the fantasies encoded in mass-culture romance fiction, "conceals anxiety about rape and longings for power and revenge" (*Loving* 48) is dramatized in Atwood's narrative. For in *Life Before Man*, Chris is depicted as the sexually overmastering and threatening male, but he is also strategically absent from and ultimately mastered in the text. "I treated him the way men treat women. . . . He couldn't take it," Elizabeth thinks of Chris (182). The narrative repeatedly makes reference to Chris's power and potential for violence, describing him as a "massive man" and as someone who held back the "violence in his hands" (67, 19). But it also depicts his defeat by Elizabeth. Chris has a "bludgeoned" look after Elizabeth breaks off her relationship with him. "He looks so beaten; surely Elizabeth alone could not account for such wreckage," Nate thinks to himself (270, 271).

Also mastered in the text are the salesman, who forces sex on Elizabeth, and William, who rapes Lesje. Another example of the split male, the salesman—who at first appears "ordinary enough" (112)—rapes Elizabeth in the front seat of his car. Yet afterwards, "[s]adness radiates from him like heat" and she thinks that "he will probably cry" (266). Similarly, the innocuous William sadistically attacks Lesje after learning that she is having an affair with Nate. "His arm is against her throat, cutting off her wind. . . . She's always thought of rape as something the Russians did to the Ukrainians, something the Germans did, more furtively, to the Jews. . . . But not something William Wasp . . . would ever do to her" (212). And yet when Elizabeth engages in "a tit for a tat" sex with William (201), she finds copulation with him unmemorable. "It was like sleeping with a large and fairly active slab of Philadelphia cream cheese" (246). Revealing the underlying sadomasochistic structure of the culturally sanctioned ideal of romantic love based on male power and female powerlessness, *Life Before Man* deals with women's anxieties about rape and also acts out the need for active mastery over passive suffering, using Elizabeth to even up the score in the perennial male battle for sexual dominance over women.

Although Elizabeth's female power and rage seem to exist at the expense of the men over whom she assumes power, the vacuum that threatens her after Chris's suicide is a testament to the emotional force he still exerts on her life. Indeed, the narrative deliberately associates Chris with the black holes in space which Elizabeth learns about at the planetarium, those collapsed stars with enormous density that "suck energy in instead of giving it out" (83). Elizabeth fantasizes that somewhere in outer space, Chris's "collapsed body floats, no bigger than a fist, tugging at her with immense gravity. Irresistible. She falls towards it, space filling her ears" (237). In the energic exchange between Elizabeth and Chris, then, each individual is both enormously powerful and yet depleted: he becomes a collapsed body and she feels "devoid," as if she is "leaking electricity" (107). Similarly, Auntie Muriel is "both the spider and the fly, the sucker-out of life juice and the empty husk," and Elizabeth imagines Auntie Muriel feeding off her presumably dead but really "paralyzed but still alive" husband whom she keeps webbed in old lace tablecloths in a trunk in the attic so she can have "a little nip now and then" (131). The grotesque humor of this passage serves a defensive function as it partially diffuses the text's very real anxiety about the way individuals emotionally and vampiristically feed off others, absorbing their energy and power—an anxiety that also lies at the emotional center of *Cat's Eye,* as we shall see.

In the scene describing Elizabeth's dismissal of her aunt, we find yet another example of the text's fascination with the interpersonal system in which one person's power exists at the expense of the depleted or destroyed other. When Auntie Muriel suggests that Elizabeth and Nate patch up their marriage, Elizabeth becomes enraged. "You moldy old bitch!" she screams, her antagonistic, dialogic retort in open conflict with the bourgeois speech of her aunt. Although she longs to say "*cunt*," she imagines that if she "pronounces that ultimate magic word, surely Auntie Muriel will change into something else; will swell, blacken, bubble like burned sugar, giving off deadly fumes" (253). The fact that Elizabeth typecasts her aunt as a kind of evil fairy tale figure points to the archaic feelings attached to this relationship, for the evil stepmothers and witches of fairy tales are derivatives of the "bad" mother figure of childhood (see, e.g., Bettelheim 66–70 and Caper 175). Moreover, by imagining her aunt in fairy tale roles, Elizabeth—and the narrative—attempts to lessen or minimize the anxiety associated with this persecutory figure from the past. After throwing a bowl at her aunt, who is thus reduced to scuttling down the hall, Elizabeth "stamps her bare feet, exultant," believing that her aunt is "as good as dead." Elizabeth "feels savage, she could eat a heart" (253–54). As if to corroborate Elizabeth's fantasy that angry feelings are destructive, the narrative subsequently depicts Auntie Muriel as she lies dying in a hospital. While Elizabeth knows that her aunt has cancer and will die, she feels that "[s]uch malevolent vitality cannot die. Hitler lived on after the discovery of his smoldering teeth, and Auntie Muriel too is one of the immortals" (324). But Auntie Muriel, whom Elizabeth once described as having "[n]othing diminutive" about her, has now "shriveled" (131, 324). Elizabeth imagines that her aunt is "falling in on herself" and "melting, like the witch in *The Wizard of Oz*," and that what is left is "this husk, this old woman" (324, 327).

As if to neutralize the angry energies unleashed in the narrative's description of Elizabeth's relationship with her aunt and its enactment of revenge against the bad mother figure, *Life Before Man* depicts Elizabeth comforting her dying aunt. But although Elizabeth is able to provide Auntie Muriel with the soothing touch and word she craves, and although Elizabeth becomes aware, at her aunt's funeral, of her desire to "restructure" her aunt "closer to her own requirements" (348), she remains angry. Thus, while she finds it "difficult to believe that Auntie Muriel, now shriveled, boxed, dirted over and done with, actually did all the harmful, even devastating things she remembers her doing," she also realizes "she's got the scars" that prove how "awful" her aunt was and she does not want this terrible truth "diminished or glossed over" (349).

The description of Elizabeth's collapse at her aunt's funeral suggests that Elizabeth was paradoxically sustained by her adversarial relationship with her aunt and energized by her rage. As Atwood explains this scene, Elizabeth's hatred for her aunt has been a driving force in her life, so that when her aunt dies, she is "left without anything to push against" and consequently experiences "a great feeling of evaporation" (Draine 377). Feeling at her aunt's funeral that "there's nothing to push against, hold on to," Elizabeth blacks out. "A black vacuum sucks at her, there's a wind, a slow roar" and she "falls through space" (350). Asking herself "[h]ow close has she come, how many times, to doing what Chris did?" she feels the "horrified relief of someone who has stopped just in time to watch an opponent topple in slow motion over the edge." For Elizabeth the "miracle" is to make the world "solid" in spite of "the rushing of wind, the summoning voices she can hear from underground, the dissolving trees, the chasms that open at her feet; and will always from time to time open" (351). Because her self-cohesion is so fragile, readers are meant to applaud—as indeed they do—her ability to persist in the face of difficult odds. If Elizabeth's fainting and suicidal thoughts recall the tragic closure of the romance plot, which enacts the death of the heroine who fails at love, *Life Before Man,* even as it invokes this traditional ending, also contests it. For as Elizabeth thinks with "anticipation" of returning to her house, she feels a quiet satisfaction in realizing that she has "managed to accomplish a house. Despite the wreckage. She's built a dwelling over the abyss, but where else was there to build it? So far, it stands" (352).

While Elizabeth's declining trajectory moves toward a guarded sense of triumph, Lesje's rising expectations ironically lead toward a tragic resolution in death. Elaborating on what has always been implicit in the traditional representation of romantic marriage as a woman's point of entry into the adult world, *Life Before Man* depicts Lesje as a child-woman. During the divorce negotiations between Nate and Elizabeth, Lesje feels "[s]hut out, like a child whose parents have closed the door on important matters, things they consider too adult for her to hear" (307). "Perhaps," Lesje comes to speculate, "it wasn't even Nate himself that attracted her at first, but Elizabeth. Elizabeth and Chris. She'd looked at Elizabeth and seen an adult world where choices had consequences, significant, irreversible" (256). Initially believing the conventional romantic-marital ideology that insists that women achieve self-definition through marriage and motherhood, Lesje feels she is a "cipher" because her name is not Mrs. Schoenhof, that "officially she is nothing" because she "isn't the mother of anyone" (309, 310). But although Lesje appears to be rewarded for her feminine passivity—she gets the traditional prize for such behavior, the man—Elizabeth gives Lesje the impression that "Nate has been, or is about to be, fired for incompetence" and that Lesje "is therefore free to take him on" (244). Lesje knows that when Nate moves in with her, Elizabeth should feel "deserted and betrayed" and she should feel "if not victorious, at least conventionally smug"; it appears, instead, "to be the other way around" (276). Indeed, at times, Lesje thinks that Nate "is an obscure practical joke being played on her by Elizabeth" (310). When, after an argument with Nate, Lesje decides to kill herself, she is "amazed by this decision; she'd never considered anything remotely like it before." Long puzzled by Chris's suicide, she feels she now understands why he killed himself: because of his "anger" and his "fear of being nothing." "People like Elizabeth could do that to you, blot you out; people like Nate, merely by going about their own concerns. . . . Chris hadn't died for love. He wanted to be an event, and he'd been one" (340).

Deciding ultimately against suicide, Lesje instead throws away her birth control pills, intending to get pregnant. As in *Surfacing*, *Life Before Man* questions the pregnancy resolution found in conventional literature, what Atwood calls "the Baby Ex Machina" ending (*Survival* 207). "If children were the key, if having them was the only way she could stop being invisible, then she would goddamn well have some herself." Although Lesje knows she has "committed a wrong and vengeful act," she is "unrepentant" the next morning. "Surely no child conceived in such rage could come to much good," she thinks. "She would have a throwback, a reptile, a mutant of some kind with scales and a little horn on the snout" (341). This, in turn, recalls the pregnancy fears voiced earlier in the text in the scene in which William, describing the possible effects of DDT and radiation on childbearing, warns Lesje that she could give birth "to a two-headed child or to a lump of flesh the size of a grapefruit, containing hair and a fully developed set of teeth . . . or to a child with its eyes on one side of its face, like a flounder" (158–59). The image of the "lump of flesh" with teeth is akin to the text's depiction of the nursing child as a kind of "sucking, voracious" and "biting" predator (62). Looking back to *The Edible Woman* and *Surfacing* and anticipating *The Handmaid's Tale*, *Life Before Man* does not idealize but instead conveys an underlying anxiety about pregnancy.

Despite all this, a number of critic/readers insist on reading Lesje's attempt to get pregnant as a creative act, not as potentially destructive. In the view of Frank Davey, Lesje seeks pregnancy "to claim her future" and "to re-invent herself through giving birth to a child" (92). Similarly, Gayle Greene feels that Lesje's action is "a creative rather than a destructive 'event,' an acceptance of forward-looking processes, a going with time rather than regressing" ("*Life*" 78). "While Lesje's decision to have a child is partly a move in the game to hold Nate," writes Catherine McLay, "it is also . . . an affirmation of life" ("Triple Solitaire" 128). According to Carol Beran, Lesje's action is "an assertion of a basic human desire for individual survival, and, ultimately, survival of the species" (64). For Linda Hutcheon, the "truly creative act" of Lesje's pregnancy "becomes the real paradigm of the novelist's act of creation, an act of moral responsibility for the creation of life" ("From Poetic to Narrative" 29).

Conversely, Ildikó de Papp Carrington, who argues that Lesje throws away her birth control pills in order to "authorize her position," feels that this "self-serving trick" is not creative or responsible but is "merely a very bitchy act of survival" ("Demons, Doubles" 237). Cathy and Arnold Davidson are similarly troubled by the text's depiction of "suicide forestalled through prospective motherhood" ("Prospects" 214). And Barbara Rigney feels that childbirth "becomes an ironic commentary, a mockery of artistic and biological creativity" (97). Despite the claim that *Life Before Man* "begins with an emblem of death and concludes with a confirmation of life" and that Atwood suggests that "the source of the continuity of life is maternity" (Stovel 62–63), we find evidence, in the critical split on Lesje's decision to become pregnant, of Atwood's deliberate problematizing of the traditional pregnancy resolution.

"Every second a pulsebeat, countdown"; "time will flow on; soon everyone will be one day older"; "run . . . or time will overtake you, you too will be caught and frozen" (290, 88, 87). If Atwood's characters, as these repeated textual messages indicate, are caught in a temporal sequence—and, by extension, in the closed field of a devolving linear plot line—they also seem driven by the compulsion to repeat. Despite Elizabeth's insistence that she is not merely the "sum" of her past, she also knows that "[n]othing ever finishes" (108, 215). Similarly while Lesje realizes that she and Elizabeth may someday be grandmothers and that they "ought to stop" their warring behavior to spare the children, she also imagines the possibility that some twenty years hence the two of them will remain enemies, "never seeing each other, but each keeping the other locked in her head, a secret area of darkness like a tumor or the black vortex at the center of a target" (359). Just as Lesje and Elizabeth may reenact the drama of Lesje's warring grandmothers, so Nate's impending marriage to Lesje seems to promise to recapitulate his troubled relationship with Elizabeth.

That *Life Before Man* engenders in some readers a desire for rescue is reflected in the critical commentary surrounding the closure. Disagreeing with those critics who read the ending as "hopeless," Gayle Greene claims that "[a]gainst the determinism that Atwood evokes . . . the characters do attain a degree of freedom and dignity" (*"Life"* 81). Similarly, Atwood, as a reader of her own novel, holds out some hope for her characters, claiming that each character "makes a movement outwards": Lesje "by getting pregnant, even though it's for awful reasons"; Nate "by getting involved" with one of his mother's political causes; and Elizabeth "by reconnecting with her children and realizing that there is something outside herself" (Draine 378). According to Paul Goetsch, Atwood "sides" with her characters in their struggle for survival, but because they remain "ordinary people," it is "not unlikely that they will soon become creatures of habit again, trying to live on the surface of life." And yet since "they have not given in to despair and resignation," they "may perhaps leave some traces in the life of the next generation" (147, 148). For Carol Beran, the fact that Atwood's three protagonists "begin to connect with society and each other at the end of the novel allows for hope that life before man is not merely a bleak matter of the survival of isolated individuals" (70–71). While Cathy and Arnold Davidson describe the closure as providing "no hint of better or different things to come," they still find "glimmerings of hope" in the fact that the characters "exhibit an urge to order and create" ("Prospects" 220–21). Yet Sherrill Grace holds out little hope for Atwood's characters. In Grace's view, *"Life Before Man* has a final page, but no conclusion, no finality, no *anagnorisis*. Elizabeth, Nate and Lesje will simply go on, unable to feel and unaware that they are already museum pieces, gray dinosaurs" (*Violent Duality* 138).

The fact that the critical constructions of the novel's characters, the pregnancy resolution, and the closure vary so widely points to how difficult it is to interpret Atwood's narrative. Repeating the characters' varied and conflicting interpretations of each other's behavior, critics cast different constructions on the characters and events described in the novel as they, again and again, become "triangled into" the text. But although Atwood deliberately problematizes the process of interpretive reconstruction in *Life Before Man,* she also positions her readers as privileged witnesses to the inner lives of her characters. "[W]e were conspirators, we knew things about each other no one else will ever know," Elizabeth thinks to herself as she remembers Chris (21). Positioned as co-conspirators and empathic listeners, readers are made privy to the empty despair and radical disconnection of Atwood's troubled and troubling characters. Overturning the myths of romantic attraction and marital harmony, *Life Before Man* interrupts and undermines bourgeois and romantic illusions as it focuses attention on the rage and pain of sexual and domestic warfare.

6

The Brutal
Reality of
Power
and Sexual
Politics in
Bodily Harm

I f you think of a book as an experience, as almost the equivalent of having the experience," Atwood comments in an interview, "you're going to feel some sense of responsibility as to what kinds of experiences you're going to put people through. You're not going to put them through a lot of blood and gore for nothing, at least I'm not. I don't write pretty books, I know that" (Brans 314). Like *Life Before Man, Bodily Harm* is anything but a "pretty book." In it, Atwood deliberately attacks what she calls our "affluent way of thinking" (Brans 311) by transporting her protagonist, Toronto lifestyles journalist Rennie Wilford, to a politically unstable Caribbean island. An "eloquent, gnarled, ugly sermon" and an "overwhelming" work that "goes for the hands . . . and arrives at the throat" (Leonard 21; Fitzgerald), *Bodily Harm* focuses on the contrast between affluent thinking and the brutal reality of power and sexual politics.

Set early in the "postfeminist" 1980s, *Bodily Harm,* like Atwood's next novel *The Handmaid's Tale,* sounds a warning about the backlash against feminism which emerged in the 1980s. Postfeminism, as Gayle Greene observes, describes "an attitude and a phenomenon." It speaks "directly to a new generation of young women" who believe that feminism is irrelevant and who imagine themselves as " 'past all that.' " Such women are "the victims of contradictory messages." For although they "should achieve in the workplace and take control of their lives," they "should above all be sexy, seductive, deferential, dress fashionably, consume endlessly, and make themselves marketable" (*Changing the Story* 198, 39, 198). Side by side with the "postfeminism" of the 1980s is what Naomi Wolf describes as the "stupendous upsurge in violent sexual imagery" depicting the abuse of women (136). Explaining how the "conventions of high-class pornographic photography, such as *Playboy*'s, began to be used generally to sell products to women," Wolf observes that by the end of the 1970s, sadomasochist images "had ascended from street fashion to high fashion in the form of studded black leather, wristcuffs, and spikes," and that models "adopted from violent pornography the furious pouting glare of the violated woman" (135, 136). And via Hollywood, a new popular genre of " 'women in danger' " films entered mainstream culture (136). Taking "its energy from male anger and female guilt at women's access to power," such imagery serves a political purpose, according to Wolf, for it has arisen "to counterbalance women's recent self-assertion" (137, 142).

Providing a scathing exposé of the misogyny and power politics underlying masculine culture in the "postfeminist" 1980s, and reflecting on the social reality of women in an age of pornography, *Bodily Harm* spotlights the dark underside of contemporary Western life in its treatment of male violence against women. The male gaze that transforms women into sexual commodities and pornographic art forms, the text reveals, is malignant. If women are objectified and marginalized by masculine desire, they are also, as the narrative graphically depicts, bodily dissected and psychically damaged. Throughout the novel, anxiety about male power and violence returns obsessively in the narrative's repeated descriptions of the bodily and psychic harm done to women.

A novel that involves readers in a brutal and brutalizing experience, *Bodily Harm* is also a carefully constructed work that choreographs a particular reading strategy. Using a complicated narrative format, *Bodily Harm* interweaves present-tense and past-tense narrative and, in the closure, shifts to the future tense; it is narrated in both the first and third person; and it has two narrators, Rennie and Lora. Using repeating configurations within linearity, *Bodily Harm* prompts readers to locate the links between Rennie's past and present and between Rennie's and Lora's stories. Thus, the narrative, observes Denise Lynch, requires readers "to question" the assumption underlying the convention of linear narrative: "that *then* can be distinguished from *now*" (47). Directed by the text, readers of *Bodily Harm* are also invited to trace the narrative's recurring images, most notably hand and face imagery, and to decode and thematize the text. In Ildikó de Papp Carrington's description, for example, Atwood's protagonist "confronts a truth about herself, a truth that Atwood . . . shapes to its climax through a network of recurring images that evolve into thematic metaphors" ("Another Symbolic Descent" 52). For Mary Kirtz, the characters in the novel are assigned "thematic slots" and "often, even their movements, particularly those associated with hands, are similar, following a stylized choreography set up by the author" (129). In the view of Lorna Irvine, the novel "operates on a series of increasingly complicated levels that require decoding and that covertly appeal to an initiated reader" (39). To the extent that the "sense of buried information [is] persistent" (42), as Irvine comments, *Bodily Harm* resists critical formulation. But the fact that this novel has prompted overly subtle intellectual responses from some commentators also suggests the need of many readers to deflect attention away from the painful feelings that motivate and drive the narrative.

Described by Atwood as an "anti-thriller" (Draine 379), *Bodily Harm* plays with mimesis in its self-conscious manipulation of the conventions of a popular masculine form: the spy thriller. The "overtly traditional" narrative plot of *Bodily Harm,* remarks Lorna Irvine, "emphasizes the possibility of rescue, specifically the rescue of a female character by a male character." It is an "acceptable plot; a politicized romance; a story about victimized women, about strong men, about foreign places" (40, 41). Countering these conventions, *Bodily Harm* insists on the potential sadism of the male rescuer, who becomes text-identified with the faceless stranger that threatens Rennie and thus prompts her escape-motivated—not goal-directed—journey and narrative plot. And while *Bodily Harm* engenders in readers a wish to see Rennie rescued, it also refuses to provide a definitive rescue in its closing scenes, as we shall see.

That this novel will be at once gamelike—providing clues for the detective reader/critic—and sadistic is suggested in the novel's opening scene, which describes the faceless man's violent intrusion into Rennie's life. Yet another encoding of the split male who haunts Atwood's fiction, the faceless man with the rope is both sinister and innocuous. For after he breaks into Rennie's apartment, he makes himself a cup of Ovaltine as he waits for her, presumably intent on assaulting or even killing her. When the police show her the coiled rope the man has left behind, Rennie is reminded of a game she used to play called Clue. "You had to guess three things: Mr. Green, in the conservatory, with a pipewrench; Miss Plum, in the kitchen, with a knife. Only I couldn't remember whether the name in the envelope was supposed to be the murderer's or the victim's. *Miss Wilford, in the bedroom, with a rope*" (13–14). To Rennie, the man is "an ambassador" and the rope is a "message." Won-

dering what will "come up" if she pulls on the rope, she believes that
there is "someone" at the end of the rope, for everybody has a face; there
is "no such thing as a faceless stranger" (41).

The rope also becomes a "message" to the reader-detective as the
narrative deliberately manipulates detective novel conventions. In traditional detective fiction, as Anne Cranny-Francis observes, the detective
"conceals the nature of crime in bourgeois society even as s/he detects its
perpetrator." By identifying the criminal, the detective "eradicates a
threat to the social order." But because detective fiction individuates the
criminal "rather than identifying inimical social practices," it "conceals
the true nature of the social order." In such fiction, "the crime is an
aberrant act unrelated and inimical to the social order (not a product of
it) and the criminal is an aberrant individual (not a subject or product of
the social order)" (152, 159, 201). In *Bodily Harm,* however, the criminal—the man with the rope—is never specifically identified; instead, he
assumes a variety of identities, including not only the sadistic island
police but also the men Rennie is romantically involved with. Thus,
rather than representing a particular individual, the faceless stranger
comes to represent the latent potential in *all* men to brutalize women.
His crime is not an aberration but a direct consequence of patriarchal
ideology with its hierarchical—and pathological—system of male dominance and female subordination.

And thus, when the man with the rope violently inserts himself into
Rennie's life, he leaves her a message she has been given many times by
masculinist culture but has refused to recognize. In the epigraph to the
novel—taken from John Berger's *Ways of Seeing* (45–46) and addressed
specifically to women readers—Atwood directs attention to the novel's
focus on the potential sadism of the heterosexual relationship. "A man's
presence suggests what he is capable of doing to you or for you," writes
Berger. "By contrast, a woman's presence . . . defines what can and
cannot be done to her." A sexually liberated "postfeminist," Rennie
initially believes that sex is not "an issue": it is merely "a pleasant form of
exercise, better than jogging, a pleasant form of communication, like
gossip" (102). Unwittingly colluding in the male objectification and
devaluation of women, Rennie finds Jake's candor "refreshing" when he
tells her that he likes her body. "Most of the men she knew used the word
person, a little too much, a little too nervously. *A fine person.* It was a
burden, being a fine person. She knew she was not as fine a person as
they wanted her to be. It was a relief to have a man say, admit, confess,
that he thought she had a terrific ass" (104). Despite her dialogic

resistance to feminist speech, Rennie feels threatened by Jake and indeed experiences him as a sexual predator. This is revealed in her perception of his "narrow muzzle, grinning like a fox," and in her insistent focus on his teeth, which are "flawless except for the long canines" (103, 15). "I'm uncontrollable," Jake suggestively tells Rennie. "I'm an animal in the dark" (117).

"[T]he female body is constructed as object of the gaze and multiple site of male pleasure—and so internalized, for this is the meaning it bears: female equals the body, sexuality equals the female body" (de Lauretis 149–50). The pain and humiliation of being a woman trapped in the male construction of femininity is one of the central focuses of Atwood's narrative. Affected by what Naomi Wolf describes as the "new social forces of beauty pornography and beauty sadomasochism" (132), Rennie allows Jake to alter her appearance to fit the eroticized images of female sexuality favored by the culture of pornography. Although the things he buys her are in bad taste, she performs the feminine masquerade to please him. "Garters, merry widows, red bikini pants with gold spangles, wired half-cup hooker brassieres that squeezed and pushed up the breasts. The real you, he'd say, with irony and hope. Who'd ever guess? Black leather and whips, that's next" (20). In bed, he stage directs Rennie, arranging her body in erotic poses. "Put your arms over your head . . . it lifts the breasts. Move your legs apart, just a little. Raise your left knee. You look fantastic" (106). That pornography is "the representation of the eroticisation of relations of power between the sexes" (Assiter 103) is revealed in Atwood's novel. In the sexual economy of their relationship, Jake is the packager—aptly, he is a designer of packages by profession—and Rennie the product. "It took her more time than it should have to realize that she was one of the things Jake was packaging." After redoing her apartment, he starts working on her, telling her that she has "great cheekbones" and should "exploit them" and that she should "make the most" of her looks (104, 105). Contrary to Jake's claim that a man cannot "rape a woman's mind without her consent" (104), the narrative reveals the mind-rape of women like Rennie who, through their culturally induced passivity and desire to please men, become collaborators in their own sexual exploitation.

"Sometimes I feel like a blank sheet of paper. . . . For you to doodle on," Rennie tells Jake (105). As a blank sheet of paper, Rennie's body becomes a cultural text on which Jake inscribes the narrative of male desire. Reduced to an erotic object, she is both shaped and interpreted by the male gaze. "The determining male gaze," writes Laura Mulvey, "projects its fantasy onto the female figure, which is styled accordingly. In their traditional exhibitionist role women are simultaneously looked at and displayed, with their appearance coded for strong visual and erotic impact . . ." (436). Rennie's persecutory fears of the faceless man who leaves behind a coiled rope reveal just how threatening the male gaze is. Unable to "shake the feeling" that she is being watched, she begins to "see herself from the outside, as if she was a moving target in someone else's binoculars." And she feels "implicated, even though she had done nothing and nothing had been done to her. She had been seen, too intimately, her face blurred and distorted, damaged, owned in some way she couldn't define" (40). As a receiver of the voyeuristic male gaze that views woman as a sexual, exhibitionistic object, Rennie feels vulnerable, subject to the masculine desire to visually possess and control female sexuality.

What the male gaze does to women is figured in the two pictures Jake hangs in the bedroom. The first one, a Heather Cooper poster appropriately called *Enigma,* shows a brown-skinned woman bound in a piece of material that pins her arms to her sides while exposing her breasts, thighs, and buttocks (105). A mystery to be solved, *Enigma* depicts woman as pictorial, as arranged and fixed in a posture over which the male has hermeneutic control. Women's sexuality is an enigma of female sexual power and feminine powerlessness. Man's relationship to woman is one of voyeuristic removal and sadistic control. And in the other picture, which shows a woman lying feet-first on a 1940s sofa, her head at the other end of the sofa "tiny, featureless, and rounded like a door knob" (105–06), woman is represented as a replaceable object (a body) rather than as a subject (a head).

"At the very core of the pornographic mise-en-scène is the concept of woman as object," writes Susan Griffin. "Like a piece of furniture, she must be pictured from the side, and particular parts of her body, those intended for use—her breasts, her vulva, her ass—must be carefully examined. And yet at each turn of her body, at each face or curvature exposed, we see nothing. For there is no person there" (36). "What is a woman. . . . A head with a cunt attached or a cunt with a head attached? Depends which end you start at," Jake tells Rennie (235). That Rennie has internalized this male conception is suggested in her fantasy of Jake's lover as a "headless body," and in her perception, when Jake tries to have sex with her after the surgery, that she is watching him "from her head . . . at the other end of her body" (235, 199).

As the recipient of the male gaze that turns her into an object, Rennie is subject to the male use and control of her sexuality. In Jocasta's analysis of sexual politics, men "don't want love and understanding and meaningful relationships, they still want sex, but only if they can *take* it" (167). That story "demands sadism," that it depends on "forcing a change in another person, a battle of will and strength, victory/defeat," all of which is "to some extent, independent of women's consent" (de Lauretis 132–33) is an underlying premise of Atwood's narrative. Symptomatic of the male oppression of women the text is intent on exposing are Jake's "inventive" sexual games. To be the object of erotic desire is to suffer potential sexual abuse, for in Jake's staged sexual encounters, Rennie is cast as the submissive victim of forced sex. "Sometimes he would climb up the fire escape and in through the window instead of coming through the door, he'd send her ungrammatical and obscene letters composed of words snipped from newspapers, purporting to be from crazy men, he'd hide in closets and spring out at her, pretending to be a lurker" (27). "Pretend I just came through the window. Pretend you're being raped," he says to Rennie (117). Pinning down her hands, holding her so she cannot move, Jake likes "thinking of sex as something he could win at." And yet despite the fact that he sometimes hurts her—"once he put his arm across her throat and she really did stop breathing"—she tells herself that he is merely playing a game. "He would never do it if it was real, if she really was a beautiful stranger or a slave girl or whatever it was he wanted her to pretend. So she didn't have to be afraid of him" (207).

Insisting that she has no reason to be "afraid" of Jake, Rennie also initially sees no real harm in pornography. When she accepts an assignment to write an article on "pornography as an art form," her male editor tells her that antipornography feminists miss "the element of playfulness" in pornography. He wants Rennie to write a kind of response to the "anti-porno pieces in the more radical women's magazines," which he finds "heavy and humourless" (207). Rennie's assignment first takes her to a male artist who uses life-sized mannequins to make table and chair sculptures. "The women were dressed in half-cup bras and G-string panties, set on their hands and knees for the tables, locked into a sitting position for the chairs. One of the chairs was a woman on her knees, her back arched, her wrists tied to her thighs. The ropes and arms were the arms of the chair, her bum was the seat" (208). Next Rennie views the Metro Police collection of seized pornographic objects, the "raw material" for pornographic art (209). Rennie makes it through the whips and rubber appliances "without a qualm," and when she views the pornographic films seized by the police, she thinks that the sex-and-death films that show "women being strangled or bludgeoned or having their nipples cut off by men dressed up as Nazis" cannot be "real." Only when she sees the "grand finale" of the police exhibit—a film of a rat emerging from a woman's vagina—does Rennie experience "a large gap" in what she has been accustomed "to thinking of as reality" (209, 210). Afterwards, she has trouble "dismissing" Jake's sadistic sex as a mere game. "She didn't want him grabbing her from behind when she wasn't expecting it, she didn't like being thrown onto the bed or held so she couldn't move. . . . She now felt that in some way that had never been spelled out between them he thought of her as the enemy." While she does not want to be "afraid of men," she has the uneasy sense that she is being used as "[r]aw material" (211, 212). Focusing attention on the inherent misogyny of pornography, *Bodily Harm* emphasizes not only how pornography objectifies and exploits women, but also how, in eroticizing male domination and female subordination, it helps perpetuate acts of violence against women. Indeed, as Kathleen Barry has remarked, pornography not only embodies the "ideology of cultural sadism"—the belief that women enjoy sexual violence—it also disseminates this ideology into mainstream culture (see 205–52).

Focusing on the hierarchical relations of power that lead to the sexual humiliation and abuse of women, *Bodily Harm* graphically demonstrates the narcissistic suffering of women in masculine culture. Imagining that the man with the rope is watching her, Rennie feels narcissistically wounded, as if she has been "seen, too intimately, her face blurred and distorted, damaged." When she acquiesces in the presentation of her body as a sexual object and becomes a "blank sheet of paper" on which Jake inscribes his erotic desires, her sense of body-self wholeness is threatened. Attempting to make love to Jake after her surgery, she feels dissociated and fragmented as she watches "from her head . . . at the other end of her body." And she imagines that her diseased, cancerous breast, with its scarred and "nibbled flesh," bears the marks of the male "probers, the labellers and cutters" who violate the integrity of the female body-self (284, 101). Deliberately the text associates Rennie's breast surgery, which is described as a phallic-sadistic act that causes a severe narcissistic wound, with the violent attacks enacted on the female body—in particular on eroticized body parts like the female breast—in sadomasochistic pornography.

Reluctant to undergo her breast surgery, Rennie has "a horror of someone, anyone, putting a knife into her and cutting some of her off," for she dislikes "the idea of being buried one piece at a time instead of all at once, it was too much like those women they were always finding strewn about ravines or scattered here and there in green garbage bags" (23). After the mastectomy, Rennie does not want Jake to see her "damaged, amputated" body (198). A potent signifier of her feelings of narcissistic vulnerability and defectiveness, her diseased body is a "sinister twin." She feels "infested" and dreams that she is "full of white maggots" that eat away at her "from the inside" or that the scar on her breast will split open "like a diseased fruit" and some venomous-looking insect will crawl out of it. In her "resurrected" body, she feels that she is "not all that well glued together," that she will "vaporize," that her body is "only provisional" (82, 83, 60, 143). Intensely cathected, the contaminated, fragmented body part—the fetishized breast—is equated not only with female mutilation and narcissistic wounding by the phallic knife of the "probers" and "cutters," but also with the sexually contaminated and contaminating female body which is censored and punished by phallocentric culture.

"Enough with the voracious female animalistic desires. . . . You should all be locked in cages," Jake says at one point to Rennie (73). In the competing value systems described in the text—Griswold's repressive puritanism and Toronto's putative sexual freedom—women are similarly trapped and punished. If the sexually liberated, middle-class woman like Rennie is perceived as uncontrollable and voracious, she is also subject to the potential sadism of the male. And Rennie, despite her sexually emancipated lifestyle, retains a deep-seated awareness of Griswold's punishing attitude toward permissive female sexuality. In the displaced drama of Lora, the text acts out the fate of the lower-class, "bad"—that is, sexually promiscuous—woman who not only is locked in the cage of a prison cell but also is brutally and bodily punished for her uncontrolled sexuality. When Paul appears to take a sexual interest in Rennie, Rennie senses, in the disciplinary "lazer-beam gaze" of the Englishwoman at the hotel, the woman's "disapproval, automatic and self-righteous," and her "ill-wishing." Having grown up in Griswold, Rennie knows about the hostile attitudes of such women, for "it's part of her background. Whatever happens to Rennie the Englishwoman will say she was asking for it; as long as it's bad" (145).

In Griswold, where a high value is put on being decent, "[d]ecency was having your clothes on, in every way possible." According to Griswold's conservative code, there are two types of women: those who are "decent" and those who are "flashy or cheap" (55). Rennie's need to flaunt this value system, which is deeply ingrained in her, is dramatized in the novel's opening scene. When a policeman suggests that perhaps Rennie has enticed the man with the rope—"He wanted it to be my fault, just a little, some indiscretion, some provocation"—she exhibits her scarred breast (15). Despite Rennie's perverse acting out of the female exhibitionism she has been accused of, she nevertheless associates the rope with the punishment meted out to "bad" women. For she knows what Griswold would say about the rope on her bed. "This is what happens to women like you. What can you expect, you deserve it." In Griswold, people get "what they deserve" and what they deserve is "the worst" (18). The fact that people deserve "the worst," according to Griswold's social code, points to the underlying malignancy of Griswold's supposedly "decent" values. *If you can't say anything nice, don't say anything at all.* Not that its own maxims ever stopped Griswold," as Rennie thinks of Griswold (66).

Mocking the popular culture's idealization of family and cultural "roots," Rennie remarks that those people "who'd lately been clamouring for roots had never seen a root up close." But although she attempts to define herself "against" Griswold, she also knows that it is "not always so easy to get rid of Griswold" (18) or to free herself from the lasting effects of her defective upbringing. Repeating a familiar pattern in Atwood's fiction, Rennie's father is physically and emotionally absent from her life (109–10), while her grandfather, also like other Atwoodian father figures, is an object of reverence and fear. Taught as a child to idealize her grandfather, the town doctor, Rennie recalls how she wanted to be like him until she learned that "[m]en were doctors, women were nurses; men were heroes, and what were women? Women rolled the bandages and that was about all anyone ever said about that" (56). In the stories Rennie's grandmother tells about him, the grandfather is figured as both a doctor-savior and a sadistic mutilator, for he hazards blizzards "to tear babies out through holes he cut in women's stomachs" and he amputates a man's leg "with an ordinary saw" (55). Depicted as a hero in the official version of the family history, the grandfather is also described as a man with a "violent temper," according to the subversive stories that Rennie's mother and aunts circulate about him. And yet although he is a potentially dangerous man, he is also tamed and domesticated. For Rennie recalls her grandfather as a fragile old man under the "control" of her mother and grandmother, a man "who had to be protected like the clocks and figurines" (56).

If in the grandfather we find yet another representation of the split male, in the grandmother we find another Atwoodian bad mother. Rigidly self-contained, the grandmother acts as a guardian of Griswold's repressive social code, a system of censorship and social conditioning that teaches the developing girl to maintain, at all costs, restraint and control. For as a child Rennie learns "three things well: how to be quiet, what not to say, and how to look at things without touching them" (54). The grandmother, a deeply angry woman who is "proud" of the fact that she never loses her temper (53), subscribes to the conventional values that punish and thwart, rather than nourish, the female self. Rennie's story about one of her earliest memories of her grandmother—her grandmother punished her for doing something wrong and then shut her in the cellar—significantly prefigures the novel's closure in which Rennie is incarcerated in a basement cell of a prison for an unknown crime. Focusing on the relationship between Rennie's alienating past and her paralyzing present, *Bodily Harm* shows that Rennie, in effect, ends where she began and thus suggests that women are condemned in advance to the cultural—and literary—role of victim.

An embedded story which the narrative both tries to tell and suppress, the story of Rennie's grandmother and the symbolic loss of her hands obsessively repeats and circulates in the text. Plotting against the grandmother who victimized Rennie, the novel finds an appropriate punishment for this unfeeling woman. Having unempathically pried away the hands of her frightened granddaughter, the grandmother comes to suffer in her old age from the delusion that she has lost her hands, the good ones, the ones she touches things with. It is telling that the grandmother's symptomatic loss of hands becomes transferred to Rennie who dreams that she, too, has misplaced her hands. Emotionally victimized early in life, Rennie has learned to shut off her feelings and thus avoid involvement with others. "Massive involvement. . . . It's never been my thing," Rennie comments at one point (34).

Becoming "a quick expert on surfaces" after moving from Griswold, Rennie initially looks at others "in order to copy"; later she looks "in order not to copy," and then she just looks (26). Deliberately standing "off to the side," she chooses "neutrality," "[i]nvisibility" (26, 15). And because during her youth she perceived her mother as "trapped," as sentenced to a life term of enforced domesticity, she becomes determined to avoid her mother's fate. "I didn't want to be like her in any way," Rennie recalls. "I didn't want to have a family or be anyone's mother, ever . . ." (58).

Consciously shunning the romance plot, Rennie wants "no mess, no *in love"* when she begins her relationship with Jake. In a description that recalls the scene in *Lady Oracle* in which Joan Foster dances on broken glass—and that evokes the *Red Shoes* motif which recurs in Atwood's fiction—Rennie thinks that she does not much like being in love. "Being in love was like running barefoot along a street covered with broken bottles. It was foolhardy, and if you got through it without damage it was only by sheer luck." To be in love is to give others "power over you" and to become "visible, soft, penetrable" (102). Despite this, Rennie falls in love with her surgeon, Daniel, a man who, because he has looked inside her while she "lay on the table unconscious as a slit fish," has privileged knowledge about her. "[H]e knows something about her she doesn't know, he knows what she's like inside" (80–81).

The fact that Rennie succumbs to the lure of romantic fulfillment points to the staying power of the romance plot. But while *Bodily Harm* incorporates the romance plot, it also undercuts it, using a feminist-dialogic strategy to contradict and parody romantic discourse. Mocking the official belief that the emotional center of a woman's life is her involvement with a man, Rennie, in one of her articles, discusses how women can combat boredom in the romantic relationship. Claiming that two people are involved in boredom, "the borer and the boree," Rennie assumes that "the active principle, the source of the powerful ergs of boredom" is the man, while the "passive recipient" is the woman. *"Study his tie . . . ,"* she advises her women readers. *"If you're stuck, make an imaginary earlobe collection and add his"* (19). At lunch with Daniel, Rennie, as is her wont, translates her experience into a journalistic headline—"Romance Makes a Comeback"—even though she finds talking to him "a good deal like waltzing with a wall" (142). And in the makeover game she plays with Jocasta, Rennie subversively views men as commodities and imagines herself altering the appearance of men just as Jake altered her appearance. "Pick a man, any man, and find the distinguishing features. The eyebrows? The nose? The body? If this man were yours, how would you do him over?" (44).

Serving an important function in the narrative, Rennie's flamboyant woman friend, Jocasta, openly challenges the masculinist code and she also voices the female desire for revenge. Although Jocasta affects "drain-chain" jewelry, which gives a "slave-girl effect" (23–24), she does this in a blatant mockery of the male enchainment of women in the role of sexual slave. She also subverts sexual stereotypes in her description of men as replaceable objects and sexual commodities. Describing her thwarted desire to have sex with a man who is having an identity crisis and "wants to be valued for himself," she asks, "Why do we have to start respecting their *minds?* . . . What do they *want?*" (167). "I think it would be a great idea if all the men were turned into women and all the women were turned into men, even just for a day," Jocasta tells Rennie. "Then they'd all know exactly how the other ones would like to be treated." When Rennie repeats Jocasta's remark to Jake, he recognizes the latent hostility of this fantasy. "The women would say, Now I've got you, you prick. Now it's my turn," he tells Rennie. "They'd all become rapists" (156, 157).

Through her feminist appropriation of male speech and her dialogic opposition to romantic discourse, Jocasta is a resisting reader of the popular romance culture. "I can't seem to get it up for love any more. It's such an effort," Jocasta tells Rennie at one point. "So it's walking-on-air time, a little pitty-pat of the heart, steamy dreams, a little how-you-say purple passion? Spots on the neck, wet pits?" Jocasta remarks when Rennie tells her about Daniel. The fact that Daniel is a married man, in Jocasta's view, can hold special advantages. "They've got their own lives, they don't need to muck up yours. You can do it in the afternoon, have a nice fuck, hear all about how important you are in their life, listen to their little troubles, their mortgage, the way their kid grinds chewed-up caramels into the shag, how they had to get the clutch on the Volvo replaced, and then you can go out with someone fun at night" (153–54).

Rennie, who is determined not to overvalue love, explains her romantic thralldom to Daniel as an instance of imprinting. She theorizes that she "imprinted" on him "like a duckling, like a baby chick" because he was the "first thing she saw after her life had been saved" (33, 32). To Rennie, "[f]alling in love with your doctor was something middle-aged married women did, women in the soaps, women in nurse novels and in sex-and-scalpel epics with titles like *Surgery* and nurses with big tits and doctors who looked like Dr. Kildare on the covers. . . . Rennie could not stand being guilty of such a banality" (33). Feeling that she is caught up in the outmoded doctor-romance plot, Rennie also finds Daniel hopelessly out of date. When he uses the word "corny," she thinks she is "caught in a time warp, it's nineteen fifty-five again. He's from another planet" (85). And when, after the surgery, Daniel tells Rennie that she should think of her life "as a clean page," she wonders if he got this "facile crap" from *The Reader's Digest* (84). "[A] dutiful husband, a dutiful parent, a dutiful son," Daniel is "a lot like Griswold, not as it was but as it would like to be. Ordinary human decency, a fine decent man they would say, with a list of things you just couldn't do" (142, 196).

Daniel is "normal, that was what she'd fallen in love with, the absolutely ordinary raised to the degree of X" (196–97).

Unlike Jake, who represents the threatening male predator, Daniel, the doctor-savior, is initially presented as the male protector. As Rennie regains consciousness after her mastectomy, she is aware of Daniel's reassuring presence. "He was telling her that he had saved her life, for the time being anyway, and now he was dragging her back into it. . . . By the hand" (32). "I want you to save my life. . . . You've done it once, you can do it again" (144), Rennie thinks of Daniel. Using the recurring hand imagery to make a thematic statement, the narrative contrasts Jake's invasive visual and sexual possession of Rennie with Daniel's healing touch. Believing in "the touch of the hand that could transform you, change everything, magic" (195), Rennie comes to crave Daniel's touch. But although she imagines that Daniel can somehow rescue her, she discovers, when she finally entices him to have sex with her, that she has rescued him. "She felt like a straw that had been clutched, she felt he'd been drowning. She felt raped" (238). In their sexual encounter, Rennie feels she has been used, violated, victimized. If Daniel is "a fantasy about the lack of fantasy, a fantasy of the normal" (237), he is also a potentially frightening figure. It is suggestive that Rennie comes to equate Daniel with his surgeon's knife to the man with the rope (287). Although Rennie craves human contact and an empathic, healing touch, she also unconsciously connects the male hand that heals with the hand wielding the phallic knife that wounds and mutilates the female body.

Capitulating yet again to the erotic plot, Rennie enacts a further variation on the romance pattern in her affair with Paul. When she shows Paul her disfigured breast, he does not look away from "the missing piece, the place where death kissed her lightly" (204). Suggestively called the "connection" (182) because of his involvement in illegal activities like drug- and gun-running, Paul, like Daniel, gives Rennie a momentary feeling of vital connection when he first touches her. "[S]he's being drawn back down, she enters her body again and there's a moment of pain, incarnation. . . ." Rennie is "grateful, he's touching her, she can still be touched" (204). And yet, despite the positive rhetoric used to describe the beginning of their affair, Rennie subsequently questions her experience. "She owes him something: he was the one who gave her back her body; wasn't he?" (248). Undercutting and dialogizing its own romantic discourse, the narrative describes Rennie's resistance to the romantic relationship. "Love or sex? Jocasta would ask, and this time

Rennie knows. Love is tangled, sex is straight. High-quality though, she'd say. Don't knock it" (223). If the masterplot of *Bodily Harm* follows the spy thriller/romance formula, the narrative also pronounces this plot banal. After making love to Paul, Rennie feels that she has "fallen into the biggest cliché in the book, a no-hooks, no-strings vacation romance with a mysterious stranger. She's behaving like a secretary . . ." (222). "A kiss is just a kiss, Jocasta would say, and you're lucky if you don't get trenchmouth" (258).

Questioning the traditional representation of the strong hero as the protector of women, *Bodily Harm* characterizes Paul as a "danger freak" (239) who rescues women because he enjoys taking risks. When, for example, Marsdon physically tortures the woman he is living with, Paul rescues the screaming woman. But "he wasn't being noble. . . . He did it because it was dangerous; he did it because it was fun" (215). Later, after the uprising on Ste. Agathe, when Paul negotiates Rennie's safe exit from the island, she realizes the "truth about knights": "the maidens were only an excuse. The dragon was the real business" (258). In accordance with the standardized spy thriller format, Paul does help Rennie escape from the dangers of Ste. Agathe, but that rescue is ultimately thwarted and Rennie ends up in prison on St. Antoine under suspicion of being a spy. Moreover, while Paul is typecast as a hero-rescuer, he is also associated with the menacing "faceless stranger" (99, 233), the sadistic male who terrorizes women.

If Rennie's story, with its Gothic fears about male persecution, expresses female anxieties about male brutality and female vulnerability, with Lora's entrance into the narrative as a speaking voice near the beginning of Part III, the text becomes increasingly marked by violence. Although Lora has an innocent, childlike appearance—she has a "doll-face" and has "round blue-china eyes" (95, 90)—she is a woman Griswold would designate as "flashy or cheap." For in the coded description used by the island men, Lora is a "nice lady" (122), that is, sexually promiscuous. That Rennie unconsciously perceives Lora as sexually contaminated and contaminating is revealed in her disgust at the sight of Lora's hands. Repelled by Lora's "stub-tipped, slightly grubby" fingers, the raw skin surrounding the nails "nibbled as if mice have been at them," Rennie "wouldn't want to touch this gnawed hand, or have it touch her" (86). In displacing onto Lora her anxiety about the "nibbled flesh" of her bad—contaminated, diseased—breast, Rennie expresses her unacknowledged fears about her own sexuality. If Lora is bodily punished in the novel's final scenes for her uncontrolled sexuality, Rennie is also bodily punished for her sexuality through the uncontrollable disease of cancer.

"Sometimes they give you a choice, fork out or put out," Lora tells Rennie, describing the sexual harassment of women by the police. "The worst times in my life I had choices all right. Shit or shit." "You wouldn't put out to save your granny, would you?" (93, 94, 285). The representative marginal woman and sexual victim, Lora is also the primary carrier of the text's anger. "Why are you being so aggressive?" Rennie wants to ask Lora during one of their initial encounters (90). "The Women's Movement would have loved Lora, back in the old days, back in the early seventies. . . . They'd have given her ten out of ten for openness, a word that always made Rennie think of a can of worms with the top off" (93). When Lora, who is aware that Rennie is a writer, comments that the "story" of her life could be "put . . . in a book," Rennie, "instantly bored," thinks of how Lora's appearance could be improved. "Rennie arranges her into a Makeover piece, before and after, with a series of shots in between showing the process, Lora being tweezed and creamed and coloured in and fitted with a Norma Klein sweater" (89). Later, in prison, Rennie tells Lora about the man with the rope and Lora responds that she would "rather be plain old raped." Realizing that Lora is describing something that has actually happened to her, Rennie decides that Lora has "better"—that is, more violent—stories. But although Rennie knows how she is supposed to respond—first with "horror" and then "sympathy"—she "can't manage it" (270, 271). Trying not to listen, Rennie watches Lora's mouth "open and close . . . it's a movie with the sound gone" (271). In describing Rennie's desire not to hear Lora's stories, the narrative anticipates the wish of many a reader not to listen to such stories. For in its depiction of the socialization of lower-class women like Lora, *Bodily Harm* directly challenges affluent thinking and forces readers to confront the potentially crippling effects of women's marginalization and powerlessness in a male-ordered system. If the dominant culture denies women like Lora a speaking voice, one of the narrative's goals is to invert common social and literary practices by telling Lora's story side by side with Rennie's. And by bringing Lora's speech into dialogue with Rennie's, Atwood also focuses attention on the importance of social class in women's experiences of social and sexual oppression.

Breaking the code of silence, Lora relates the horror of a childhood spent in fear of an angry, brutal stepfather. Recalling a newspaper story about a woman who, after marrying a man, conspired with him to kill her son, presumably because the man "didn't want him around," Lora comments: "It was like something that almost happened to me and I didn't even know it at the time, like you're sleepwalking and you wake up and you're standing on the edge of this cliff." Subject to frequent beatings from her stepfather, Lora learns to think of him as an "accident" that had happened to her, "like getting run over by a truck, I was just in the way" (113). When he hit her, "it was like the weather, sometimes it rains, sometimes it doesn't. He didn't hit me because I was bad, like I used to think. He hit me because he could get away with it and nobody could stop him. That's mostly why people do stuff like that, because they can get away with it" (113–14). Only when, some years later, her stepfather attempts to sexually assault her, does she attack him and subsequently leave home. Taking the stepfather's side and thus acting as an accomplice in the victimization of her own daughter, Lora's mother accuses Lora of "asking for it" by flaunting her sexuality. "[I]t's a wonder every man in the city didn't do the same thing a long time ago," her mother tells her (172).

A narrative full of pain, violence, and anger, Lora's story is clearly meant to discomfort readers. But Atwood also partially deflects reader attention away from the horror of what is being described and onto the novel's intricate structure in which the stories of Rennie and Lora coexist, provide commentary on, and thematically and imagistically in-teranimate each other. Although there is a quality of fragmentation and interruption in the brief narrative segments that make up the novel—this technique apparently meant to reflect the fact that these stories are told by Rennie and Lora as they share a prison cell—there is also an emerging sense of authorial design as the narrative unfolds. But if *Bodily Harm* attempts to aestheticize violence, it also becomes increasingly fixated on and ruptured by the horrors it is assigned to uncover.

"[A]ll that flesh, totally helpless because totally dead," Rennie thinks when she skims the 1940s Dell mystery novels which Paul procures for her. Suggestive evidence that Lora is, in essence, predetermined by the text to die a violent death is found in the narrative's discussion of the detective mystery formula. As Rennie examines the cast of characters recorded at the beginning of each novel, she tries to guess who the murder victim will be. Having little patience with "the intricacies of clues and deductions," she reads up to the crime and tries to guess who did it and then skips to the closure to see if she has guessed correctly. While Rennie has trouble identifying the murderers, she is eighty per-cent accurate in predicting who the victims will be, for in the coded world of detective fiction, the female victims are a predictable type. In such novels, sexually provocative women—blonds with "mouths like red gashes and swelling breasts" and "tempestuous redheads with eyes of green smouldering fire"—are punished for their sexuality (246). If *Bodily Harm* is partly modeled after the game of Clue, as the narrative suggests in the opening chapter, then the sexually promiscuous Lora is preassigned the cultural and literary role of murder victim.

"What art does is, it takes what society deals out and makes it visible, right? So you can *see* it," comments a male pornographic artist who stands in the text as the author's unacknowledged spokesperson (208). In the novel's final section, which describes the imprisonment of Rennie and Lora, the anger, fear, and violence that have punctuated the narrative erupt in two brutal and brutalizing beating scenes. Despite Rennie's characteristic desire to evade the reality of her situation in prison— "[s]he longs for late-night television, she's had enough reality for the time being. Popcorn is what she needs" (269)—the narrative relentlessly strips away her defenses and compels her to confront what she has long avoided.

When Rennie, gripped with a fear that "goes on and on, no end to it," tries to comfort herself with memories of the men she has loved, the romance plot fails her. "Acts of the body, of love, what's left? A change, a result, a trace, hand through the sea at night, phosphorescence" (283). In prison, she dreams of the man with the rope. "He is the only man who is with her now, he's followed her, he was here all along, he was waiting for her." While she "sometimes" thinks that the faceless man is Jake, who once climbed in the window with a stocking on his face, or Daniel with his knife, or Paul, the identity of the man remains elusive. "The face keeps changing, eluding her, he might as well be invisible, she can't see him, this is what is so terrifying, he isn't really there, he's only a shadow, anonymous, familiar, with silver eyes that twin and reflect her own" (287).

As self and other meld, Rennie discovers that there is no escape from the faceless man. An agent of male oppression, he is also an internalized aspect of self. For like the faceless man, Rennie is a "spectator, a voyeur" (125). With her tourist vision, Rennie looks but feels no connection to what she sees: to the women beggars in Mexico, for example, "with the fallen-in cheeks of those who have lost teeth, suckling inert babies, not even brushing the flies away from their heads, their hands held out, for hours on end it seemed, in one position as if carved"; or to the St. Antoine girl nursing a "pleated, shrivelled" baby (72, 125). "As soon as you take a picture of something it's a picture. Picturesque. This isn't," Rennie thinks to herself the first time she sees the deaf and dumb man undergoing a beating at the hands of the police. And yet, as the injured man struggles to his knees and the two policemen watch him "with what seems like mild curiosity," Rennie is appalled by her "own fascination" (146). Rennie's desire to see things from the surface and as picturesque reveals her own implication in the voyeuristic male gaze that looks at but feels disconnected from the suffering of others.

But the faceless man, as the text insists, is more than a mirror image, a projection of self. "There's only people with power and people without power," Paul tells Rennie (240). In prison, when Rennie again becomes an eyewitness to police brutality, she discovers the horrible truth of this political dictum. As Rennie watches a policeman implement a policy by cutting the long hair of the male prisoners—who suggestively resemble women—she realizes that he enjoys the "ceremony, precise as an operation." Bayonet in hand, the policeman brutalizes the deaf and dumb man: "he pulls the head back like a chicken's, the hair is grey, he slices again with the bayonet but he's not careful enough, the man howls, a voice that is not a voice, there are no teeth in his opened mouth, blood is pouring down his face." For the man with the bayonet, who is "an addict, this is a hard drug. Soon he will need more." As the deaf and dumb man, "who has a voice but no words," cries out in pain when he is subsequently beaten, Rennie feels "he can see her, she's been exposed, it's panic, he wants her to do something, pleading, *Oh please*." Validating Rennie's persecutory fears, the text insists that Rennie's Gothic imaginings reflect a horrifying reality. "She's afraid of men and it's simple, it's rational, she's afraid of men because men are frightening. She's seen the man with the rope, now she knows what he looks like. She has been turned inside out, there's no longer a *here* and a *there*. Rennie understands for the first time that this is not necessarily a place she will get out of, ever. She is not exempt. Nobody is exempt from anything" (289–90).

And yet the text does exempt Rennie from the ghastly fate that awaits Lora. Trying to gain both favors and access to her lover—who is supposedly being kept in the same prison—Lora has sex with the prison guards. When Lora learns that the guards have deceived her and that her lover was shot during the uprising, she angrily threatens to retaliate. Rennie looks on in horror as Lora is savagely beaten. "They go for the breasts and the buttocks, the stomach, the crotch, the head, jumping, *My God*, Morton's got the gun out and he's hitting her with it, he'll break her so that she'll never make another sound. Lora twists on the floor . . . surely she can't feel it any more but she's still twisting, like a worm that's been cut in half. . . ." Although Rennie "wants to tell them to stop," she cannot utter a sound for they will see her. Rennie "doesn't want to see, she has to see, why isn't someone covering her eyes?" (293). Beaten until she lies motionless, her pulped face no longer a face but a bruise, reduced to a featureless cipher, Lora is the very emblem of the silenced, victimized woman and the fragmented body/self.

If this moment of male violence and persecution threatens to rupture the patterned fabric of the text, there is also a countermovement in the narrative toward survival and a healing sense of connection. Asserting hermeneutic control at the point of incipient textual disruption and breakdown, the narrative insistently orders and connects, forcing the recovery of novelistic pattern, meaning, and structure. For at this point the novel defensively interrupts the description of Lora's bruised, beaten body to complete the recurring story of Rennie's grandmother's loss of her hands. "I can't find my hands," the grandmother says. "Here they are. Right where you put them," Rennie's mother responds as she "takes hold of the grandmother's dangling hands, clasping them in her own" (297, 298). Aestheticizing the violence that has so radically disrupted the text through this focus on the healing handclasp, which reverberates against all the other images of the healing hand used in the novel—the lucky handshake of the deaf-mute, Elva's magic hands, Daniel's and Paul's rescuing touch—the narrative acts out a reparative urge as it transforms Lora's violent beating into Rennie's moment of epiphany.

Offering two competing versions of reality, the narrative replaces the image of the dehumanizing hand that beats and mutilates with that of the healing hand that rescues. In a repetition of her mother's gesture, Rennie takes hold of Lora's left hand and pulls on it: "there's an invisible hole in the air, Lora is on the other side of it and she has to pull her through, she's gritting her teeth with the effort, she can hear herself, a moaning, it must be her own voice, this is a gift, this is the hardest thing she's ever done. . . . Surely, if she can only try hard enough, something will move and live again, something will get born." Acting out the reader's wish to see Lora rescued, the narrative also undercuts that rescue. "'Lora,' she says. The name descends and enters the body, there's something, a movement; isn't there? 'Oh God,' says Lora. Or was that real? She's afraid to put her head down, to the heart, she's afraid she will not be able to hear" (299). That the death of Lora occurs in the lacunae in the text is suggested in Rennie's subsequent fantasy about her return to Canada. "She can feel the shape of a hand in hers, both of hers, there but not there, like the afterglow of a match that's gone out" (300).

When Rennie takes Lora by the hand, hoping that "something will get born," the text suggests that she herself undergoes a rebirth experience. Indeed, the fact that 'Renata' means "reborn"—a detail critics repeatedly comment on—seems meant as an interpretive clue to an analysis of the novel's closure. And yet, despite the claim that the scene depicting Lora's beating "is not merely gratuitous horror, pleasure in brutality for its own sake" but instead "is essential to turn Rennie from an observer into an actor, a contributor" (McLay, "Real Story" 137), there is something disturbing about the text's brutal silencing of Lora and its displacement of the threatened male persecution of Rennie onto Lora. Even though the "importance of Lora's stories . . . is acknowledged by the narrative strategy of the novel as a whole," as Elaine Hansen has observed, Lora is nevertheless "silenced at the end" of the novel; she is "lost" to the reader, her voice absent (6, 20). Her troubling presence banished from the text, Lora is sacrificed so that Rennie's character may be redeemed.

Whether Rennie is or is not released from prison, as Atwood comments, "is open to question, because as soon as you start using the future tense at the end of a book then of course it's open as to whether this actually happened or whether this is just what she's postulated is happening" (Castro 221). Through such a closural strategy, *Bodily Harm* insists that the reader "uncover and examine the contradictions, the disequilibrium and insufficiency masked by the sense of an ending" (Hansen 19). In announcing Rennie's rescue in the future tense, the narrative also cross-questions the outworn but expected plot resolution that dictates the rescue of the heroine in distress.

And yet the narrative acts out a form of rescue by repairing Rennie's character. No longer a lifestyles writer but now a reporter, a subversive, Rennie "will pick her time; then she will report." What Rennie sees "has not altered; only the way she sees it" (301, 300). Even though her scar "prods at her, a reminder, a silent voice counting, a countdown" and she is aware that "[z]ero is waiting somewhere," she still feels a sense of gratitude. "She doesn't have much time left, for anything. But neither does anyone else. She's paying attention, that's all." Rennie "will never be rescued" and yet "has already been rescued"; although she "is not exempt," she is "lucky, suddenly, finally, she's overflowing with luck" (301). Although some readers find Rennie's rehabilitation suspect—she has been described as "an unlikely healer" and her fantasy of escape as "yet another hackneyed plot, in which jaded journalist becomes romantic reporter" (Kareda 72, Brydon 183)—most readers follow the text's directives and accept the positive change in Rennie's character depicted in the novel's closure.

Commenting that she likes the reader "to participate in writing the book," Atwood says that it is the "reader's choice" as to whether Rennie will get out of prison or not (Lyons 80). But although readers of *Bodily Harm* may be "trapped" with Rennie "into wishing for a conventionally happy ending" (Smith 260), critics like Jerome Rosenberg still find the "poignant hope" of the novel's ending unconvincing. As Rennie sits confined in her dark cell, "rotting away to the bitter end," her "final affirmation" that she is "'lucky'" is "difficult to credit." In Rosenberg's view, this is a "pretty assertion, certainly, contending heroically against reality: but this time the words fail" (133). And yet if critic/readers like Rosenberg distrust the positive rhetoric of the closure, others use it as a basis for surmising a positive outcome to Rennie's story. Roberta Rubenstein, for example, argues that the novel's final sections, narrated in the future tense, describe "what 'will happen' to assure Rennie's release from prison and from the country." In Rubenstein's view, not only does the reader have "knowledge that Rennie will escape," but Rennie pulls Lora "back to consciousness"; and as Rennie returns to Canada, now a subversive, the "future is literally in her hands" ("Pandora's Box" 272, 273, 274). Similarly, Nora Stovel, who feels that *Bodily Harm* "concludes on a new note of optimism," argues that the novel's "opening emblem of death is countered by a concluding confirmation of life. This heroine goes further than any of her predecessors, for not only does she save her own life, but she also resurrects another" (65). If Rennie, "the sold-out lifestyle writer," is freed from prison, according to Judith McCombs, "what she should do . . . is tell the truth and be the voice of those whose voices are still imprisoned and denied. And perhaps . . . she has: the end could mean that Rennie returns to Toronto and writes this novel, *Bodily Harm*" ("Atwood's Fictive Portraits" 85).

Because the ending is unresolved, some readers, as we have observed, feel the need to do what the text refuses to do: they, in effect, insert themselves into the narrative and act out the rescue of Rennie in their critical reconstructions of the novel. But for others, the rescue wish engendered by the text takes a different form. In the view of Ildikó de Papp Carrington, reader uncertainty about Rennie's fate serves an important function. "In making Rennie cling to her hope of rescue, in letting her imagine her wish-fulfillment, Atwood's purpose is to satirize spy thrillers and their readers, as well as Rennie, and to insist on the readers' duty of massive involvement" ("Margaret Atwood" 90). If Rennie is not rescued, as Carrington's comment seems to suggest, Atwood's readers are. Similarly, Coral Ann Howells—who argues that Rennie's "new optimism . . . dictates the ending" but that Rennie may "never have the chance to enact her new story about not being a victim"—sees Rennie's story as "a warning against disabling female fantasies of innocence and victimization which displace women's recognition of the dangers of real life" (61, 62). For Dorothy Jones, who reads the ending as "tentative and uncertain," *Bodily Harm* asks its readers "to contemplate both the fact of individual mortality and the conditions under which the great mass of the world's population have to live, so that through the exercise of imagination they may be led to a more aware, more compassionate, politically committed view of life" (98, 99). Arguing that "Atwood's plot challenges the reader to imagine unity of being in a world of oppression and death," Denise Lynch comments that the novel "speaks to its readers not as victims but as survivors" (56).

While *Bodily Harm* does speak to its readers as survivors, it also risks victimizing readers by making them witness a brutal murder. But although fiction like *Bodily Harm* isn't "pretty," it acts out an important political agenda in its insistent focus on the potential horrors of power and gender politics. An author who is concerned with the uses and abuses of power, Atwood describes herself as a political writer. "By 'political,'" she explains, "I mean having to do with power: who's got it, who wants it, how it operates; in a word, who's allowed to do what to whom, who gets what from whom, who gets away with it and how" ("An End to Audience?" 353). Such political material "enters a writer's work not because the writer is or is not consciously political but because a writer is an observer, a witness, and such observations are the air he breathes" ("Amnesty" 394). Although audiences, according to Atwood, may prefer art to be "a Disneyland of the soul, containing Romanceland, Spyland, Pornoland and all the other Escapelands which are so much more agreeable than the complex truth" ("Amnesty" 393), art is, in a profound way, political and the artist is a subversive who bears witness. "People will say, 'I don't want to hear about it' or 'I don't want to read about it,'" Atwood once commented, describing her view of the novel as a reflector of society. "You can destroy your Amnesty International newsletter without reading it. But that doesn't make it go away. The less you pay attention to it, the more it's going to be there for somebody else" (Twigg 126).

Recognizing the extent to which story demands sadism, refusing to cater to those readers who might prefer the solace of comforting bourgeois fictional illusions, Atwood warns in *Bodily Harm* and also in her next novel, *The Handmaid's Tale,* that late twentieth-century "postfeminist" women are not exempt from the power and sexual politics that structure and drive masculinist culture.

7

The Misogyny of Patriarchal Culture in *The Handmaid's Tale*

———————————————————————— ■ ————————————————————————

L ike *Bodily Harm*, *The Handmaid's Tale* reflects on the antifeminist backlash of the 1980s. Observing that every "backlash movement has had its preferred scapegoat," Susan Faludi remarks that feminist women became "a prime enemy" for the New Right in the 1980s (231, 232). Claiming that feminists were against the family, New Right spokesman Jerry Falwell, for example, warned that feminists had begun a "satanic attack on the home," and Howard Phillips charged that feminists were behind "the conscious policy of government to liberate the wife from the leadership of the husband" (232, 234). "Under the banner of 'family rights,'" observes Faludi, the leaders of the New Right lobbied for "every man's right to rule supreme at home—to exercise what Falwell called the husband's 'God-given responsibility to lead his family'" (239). Countering women's independence and autonomy, these so-called "pro-family" activists called for the restoration of women's traditional roles and for the return of women to the home.

"A lot of what writers do is they play with hypotheses . . . ," comments Atwood in a discussion of *The Handmaid's Tale*. "It's a kind of 'if this, then that' type of thing. The original hypothesis would be some of the statements that are being made by the 'Evangelical fundamentalist right.' If a woman's place is in the home, then what? If you actually decide to enforce that, what follows?" (Rothstein). In *The Handmaid's Tale*, which reflects on the antifeminist messages given to women by the fundamentalist New Right in the 1980s, Atwood delineates in chilling detail just what might follow: the virtual enslavement of women, their reduction to mere functions, to mute, replaceable objects. Described as "bleak, unnerving" and as "disturbingly believable" (Kendall 1; Glendinning, "Lady Oracle" 40), *The Handmaid's Tale*, like *Bodily Harm*, exposes female anxieties about male domination and sexual exploitation that have always plagued women. "I didn't invent a lot" in *The Handmaid's Tale,* Atwood remarks. "I transposed to a different time and place, but the motifs are all historical motifs" (Cathy Davidson, "Feminist 1984" 24). Atwood describes her novel as "a study of power" and as "[s]peculative fiction," a "logical extension of where we are now" (Rothstein; Cathy Davidson, "Feminist 1984" 26). Although Atwood "avoided writing" *The Handmaid's Tale* for some four years because she thought it was "zany," when she did begin working on it she discovered it to be "a *compelling* story," one she "had to write" (Cathy Davidson, "Feminist 1984" 24).

A novel that many readers also have found strangely compelling, *The Handmaid's Tale,* as the critical conversation surrounding the text indicates, provokes both affective and cognitive responses from readers. *The Handmaid's Tale* is "disquieting and not nearly as futuristic nor fantasmatic as we might wish," writes one critic (Bartkowski 151). "In a very real sense, the future presaged by 'The Handmaid's Tale' is already *our* history . . . ," comments another (Arnold Davidson, "Future Tense" 116). "History repeats itself with minimal variations and the major source of fear for the reader is that nothing in this futurist society is new," observes yet another (Howells 63). And yet, if Atwood's talent is ignited by "fear," there is also a "hyperliterary quality" to her work (Glendinning, "Lady Oracle" 40). *The Handmaid's Tale* has been described as "intricately written" and as "an intense good read, almost a game or a puzzle" (Snitow 59). Atwood makes her readers "into detectives, trying to reconstruct the political history from which Offred's daily chronicle emerges" (Kauffman 241). If Atwood draws readers into the persecutory world of her novel, she also prompts them to recognize and appreciate the literary puzzles and artistic complexities of her narrative.

Confining readers to Offred's subjectivity and then abruptly shifting to an objective academic discussion of Offred's tale in the "Historical Notes" which conclude the novel, *The Handmaid's Tale* uses a narrative strategy designed to call attention to the acts of reading and interpretation. In Offred's narrative, memories of her pre-Gilead and her Gilead past in the Red Center where she was indoctrinated are layered with descriptions of her present 'reality' as a Handmaid. Because Offred's memories are narrated in interrupted fragments, the reader is forced to assemble and construct her story. Moreover, the fact that Offred's narrative never reaches a definitive conclusion compels reader speculation about and participation in her story. Reader collaboration in the process of assembling the text is reinforced by the novel's inclusion, in direct addresses to an implied reader, of self-reflexive discussions about the difficulties inherent in the narrative reconstruction of events. Just as these devices serve to partially deflect attention away from the horrors being described, the "Historical Notes"—which are appended to Offred's narrative and which describe the Gileadean world from the perspective of twenty-second century historians—also diffuse or defuse some of the affective intensities of Offred's account. The epigraph taken from Swift's *A Modest Proposal* found at the beginning of the novel serves a similar purpose, and it also, as several critics have observed, points to the novel's use of satire (see, for example, Keith; Carrington, "A Swiftian Sermon"; Freibert, "Control and Creativity"). Like the historians who play the game of historical detective as they reconstruct Offred's story from some thirty tape recordings, critic/readers of Offred's narrative become involved in the process of reading clues and unraveling puzzles. Even though the "Historical Notes" section of the novel implicitly denounces what it dramatizes—the critical objectification of texts—*The Handmaid's Tale* nonetheless invites just such an interpretive process. But Atwood's novel is also designed to discomfort readers as it immerses them in a regressive—and voyeuristic—sadomasochistic fantasy. Indeed, while some readers find themselves "consumed" by the novel, others find themselves sinking, "not without intermittent spasms of resistance," into "the deepening masochism" of Offred's tale (Maynard 114; Ehrenreich 34). If sadism demands a story, the story of *The Handmaid's Tale* demands sadism as it dramatizes the sexual oppression of women who, bound in a master-slave relationship, are forced to consent to femininity.

A feminist dystopia, but also part lurid Gothic fantasy and domestic romance plot, *The Handmaid's Tale* lays bare the inherent misogyny of patriarchal culture. In the Republic of Gilead, a theocracy established in the United States by New Right fundamentalists, the masculine code is carried to its absolute extreme in the regime's consignment of women to various classes—the Wives, the Handmaids, the Marthas, the Econowives, the Aunts—according to their functions. Through its imposition of a rigid system of hierarchical classification, the Gilead regime effectively robs women of their individual identities and transforms them into replaceable objects in the phallocentric economy. The thirty-three-year-old narrator of the tale is named Offred, her name identifying the Commander to whom she temporarily belongs. She is "Of Fred." Her name, as numerous commentators have pointed out, also suggests the words "afraid," "offered," and "off-read" (misread). In prompting the decoding of Offred's name for hidden meanings, the text encourages readers not only to repeat Offred's act of reading and interpretation as she attempts to unravel the mystery of the hidden message left by the previous Handmaid, but also to participate in the same word-association game Offred plays as she rehearses litanies of words to assuage her anxiety. If Offred is "misread" by her culture and also by the misogynist historians who later reconstruct and comment on her narrative, she is also "afraid" as she is forced to "offer" her sexual services to the state. Echoing the novel's wordplay and pointing to its political aim, one critic describes *The Handmaid's Tale* as "an impassioned sermon" that is "offered" by Atwood "as a warning to make her readers afraid" (Carrington, "Swiftian Sermon" 127, 128). Moreover, the fact that Offred's real name is hidden in the narrative seems intended as a kind of "password into the text," observes another critic. Since careful readers of the novel can deduce Offred's name from the list of names provided at the outset—for all of the names, with the exception of "June," are assigned to other characters as the narrative unfolds—the fact that the historian who reconstructs and comments on Offred's tale does not know her real name is a "sign" of his "inability" to read Offred's story (Bergmann 853).

"Ordinary," the Handmaids are told, "is what you are used to. This may not seem ordinary to you now, but after a time it will" (45). Repeatedly and with didactic intention, the narrative contrasts Offred's pre-Gilead past—her life in the United States in the 1970s and 1980s—with her Gilead present. A "refugee from the past," Offred recalls how women once felt as if they "were free to shape and reshape forever the ever-expanding perimeters" of their lives and how they were once depicted in the glossy women's magazines as "bold, striding, confident, their arms flung out as if to claim space, their legs apart, feet planted squarely on the earth" (294, 201). In Gilead, in contrast, the Handmaids are infantilized. Like the Surfacer who feels that words come out of her "like the mechanical words from a talking doll" (105) when she speaks in an inauthentic, feminine voice, Offred responds mechanically when Serena Joy lays out the ground rules for their relationship. "They used to have dolls, for little girls, that would talk if you pulled a string at the back; I thought I was sounding like that, voice of a monotone, voice of a doll" (21). Treated "like a child" in the Commander's household, she "must not be told" certain things; allowed to watch television news on the evening of the ceremony, she is like "a child being allowed up late with the grown-ups"; when she asks one of the Marthas for a match, she feels "like a small, begging child" (70, 105, 268).

The Handmaids are forced to a life of utter passivity and submissiveness. They are "ladies in reduced circumstances. . . . The circumstances have been reduced; for those of us who still have circumstances" (10). Because they are women with "viable ovaries" (186) in a world of mass sterility, they are forcibly enlisted in the regime's project of reversing the precipitous decline in the Caucasian birthrate. Objectified by the culture and used solely for breeding purposes, the Handmaids, in Offred's description, are "containers," "two-legged wombs . . . sacred vessels, ambulatory chalices" (124, 176). Those Handmaids who do not capitulate to the new regime are severely punished or executed. Making a conscious allusion to and an intertextual comment on the paradigmatically female story of *The Red Shoes* which, as we have observed, occurs in other Atwood novels, *The Handmaid's Tale* describes the brutal foot punishment suffered by disobedient Handmaids. "It was the feet they'd do, for a first offense. They used steel cables, frayed at the ends." When Moira undergoes this punishment, her feet resemble "drowned feet, swollen and boneless, except for the color. They looked like lungs" (118). Although Offred's shoes are red, they are "not for dancing" (11). Observing the dangling feet of women who have been "salvaged"—that is, executed by hanging—Offred remarks that "[i]f it weren't for the ropes and the sacks it could be a kind of dance, a ballet, caught by flash-camera: midair" (356). Offred does not want to be such "a dancer, my feet in the air, my head a faceless oblong of white cloth" (368). "Women's Salvagings," as she observes, "are not frequent. There is less need for them. These days we are so well behaved" (351). Offred is part of the "transitional" generation. "For the ones who come after you," she is told, "it will be easier. They will accept their duties with willing hearts"; they will freely submit, she recognizes, because "they will have no memories, of any other way" (151).

Although Offred remembers the pre-Gilead era as a time of relative freedom and choice for women, she also describes another, partially censored, version of the past. Relentlessly exposing the misogyny underlying present-day culture, *The Handmaid's Tale* constructs a feminist reading position as it continues *Bodily Harm*'s critique of the sexual degradation and violence to which women are subjected. "Nothing changes instantaneously: in a gradually heating bathtub you'd be boiled to death before you knew it," Offred comments as she recalls the pre-Gilead world, the America of the 1970s and 1980s. "There were stories in the newspapers, of course, corpses in ditches or the woods, bludgeoned to death or mutilated, interfered with, as they used to say, but they were about other women, and the men who did such things were other men" (74). Similarly, the pornographic films from the same historical period which Offred sees in the Red Center make manifest the hidden cultural script of male violence against women. The films show "[w]omen kneeling, sucking penises or guns, women tied up or chained or with dog collars around their necks, women hanging from trees, or upside-down, naked, with their legs held apart, women being raped, beaten up, killed. Once we had to watch a woman being slowly cut into pieces, her fingers and breasts snipped off with garden shears, her stomach slit open and her intestines pulled out" (152). Providing a graphic depiction of the sexual victimization of women, these images disclose the diseased underside of patriarchal culture. Subject to the killing male rage which mutilates, dismembers, and destroys, woman is a sexualized and dehumanized object in a sadomasochistic master-slave relationship.

"In the days of anarchy, it was freedom to. Now you are being given freedom from. Don't underrate it," the Handmaids are told (33). In Gilead the Handmaids have been promised "freedom from" the sexual degradation and violence—the pornography and rape—which existed in the pre-Gilead period. But the clichéd messages Offred gets from her culture repeat the masculine discourse from the past: "Men are sex machines"; it is up to the woman to "set the boundaries"; men do not want sex to be "too easy"; and "[n]ature demands variety, for men" (186, 60, 273, 308). "Think of yourselves as pearls," the Handmaids are told (145), while other women perceive them as sexually debased and contaminated. "She thinks I may be catching, like a disease or any form of bad luck," Offred thinks to herself when one of the Marthas shuns her. After the ritual insemination ceremony, Offred hears "loathing" in the voice of the Commander's wife, "as if the touch of my flesh sickens and contaminates her." And at the Prayvaganza, the Handmaids are segregated, presumably to protect the other women from "contamination" (13, 123, 277).

The sexual object for male consumption and the marginalized woman who is shunned and despised by other women, the Handmaid is the good/bad woman, the saintly prostitute. Her red, nunlike uniform symbolizes her imprisonment in the Handmaid's role. "Everything except the wings around my face is red: the color of blood, which defines us." A domestic and sexual captive—a "Sister, dipped in blood" (11)—she is cast in the public gaze and yet remains invisible. The hostile male gaze that objectifies and obliterates what it sees becomes figured in the omnipresent Eyes—the Eyes of God—who are agents of surveillance and oppression. If to be seen, as Rennie recognizes in *Bodily Harm,* is to be violated, the enforced invisibility of the Handmaid serves as an even more insidious threat to the self. "Modesty is invisibility. . . . To be seen—to be *seen*—is to be . . . penetrated. What you must be, girls, is impenetrable," the Handmaids are taught (38). As the Handmaids walk in pairs, twinlike, they are iterable objects in the eyes of the body politic. Indeed, Offred imagines that she and Ofglen look "picturesque" from a distance, "like Dutch milkmaids on a wallpaper frieze . . . or anything that repeats itself with at least minimum grace and without variation" (275). Returning to a concern voiced in other Atwood novels we have investigated, *The Handmaid's Tale* depicts women participating in men's desires and renouncing their own as they perform the feminine masquerade. When Offred catches sight of herself in a mirror, she appears "like a distorted shadow, a parody of something, some fairy-tale figure in a red cloak" (11). Similarly, in the purple-sequined costume the Commander gives her to wear to Jezebel's, she is "a travesty, in bad make-up and someone else's clothes, used glitz" (330).

"I'm doing my best. . . . I'm trying to give you the best chance you can have," Aunt Lydia tells the Handmaids (73). The Aunts, who ironically place a high value on "camaraderie among women" (287), uphold the male supremist power structure of Gilead with its hierarchical arrangement of the sexes, and they play an active role in the state's sexual enslavement of the Handmaids. Anticipating *Cat's Eye*'s dramatization of the female-directed oppression of women which begins during the girlhood socialization process, *The Handmaid's Tale* describes the brutal reeducation of the Handmaids, who are coerced by the Aunts to forego the ideology of women's liberation and to revert to the "traditional" values of a male-dominant system. The "Historical Notes" describe the regime's use of women to control other women, explaining that in Gilead "there were many women willing to serve as Aunts, either because of a genuine belief in what they called 'traditional values,' or for the benefits they might thereby acquire. When power is scarce, a little of it is tempting" (390).

Repeating a pattern we have observed in other Atwood novels, *The Handmaid's Tale* is preoccupied with the bad mother, while the good mother is essentially absent from the text. Subject to the brutality of the Aunts—who are embodiments of the overcontrolling, fault-finding bad mother—Offred wants Serena Joy to be "a motherly figure, someone who would understand and protect" her (21). But she recognizes from the outset the Wife's hostility toward her. While the Wife is a menacing presence in Offred's life, her mother is both physically and emotionally absent. A "wiry, spunky" feminist (155), Offred's mother disappears soon after the Gileadean coup; branded an Unwoman, she is shipped to the Colonies where she is forced to sweep up toxic wastes—a certain death sentence. "I thought she was dead," Offred tells Moira. "She might as well be. . . . You should wish it for her" (327).

"Mother," Offred thinks to herself, "You wanted a women's culture. Well, now there is one. It isn't what you meant, but it exists" (164). While "patriarchal in form," Gilead is also "occasionally matriarchal in content" (390). Existing in an all-women's enclave, Offred is doomed to a "minimalist life" (141) which consists of shopping, eating, taking a bath, listening to the gossip of the Marthas, whispering to other Hand-maids, participating in the monthly insemination ceremony and the rare birthing rituals. Totally passive, Offred must endure long stretches of "blank time" (91) with nothing to do but wait. "I wait, washed, brushed, fed, like a prize pig" (90). Recalling nineteenth-century erotic art and its obsession with depictions of harems, she recognizes the true subject matter of these "[s]tudies of sedentary flesh." "They were paintings about suspended animation; about waiting, about objects not in use. They were paintings about boredom" (89). For Offred, the "amount of unfilled time, the long parentheses of nothing" (89), be-comes oppressive. "Now there's a space to be filled, in the too-warm air of my room, and a time also; a space-time, between here and now and there and then, punctuated by dinner. The arrival of the tray, carried up the stairs as if for an invalid. An invalid, one who has been invalidated. No valid passport. No exit" (290).

Treated as subordinate other—as body without mind—Offred is defined and confined by her reproductive role. "I used to think of my body as an instrument, of pleasure, or a means of transportation, or an implement for the accomplishment of my will. . . . There were limits, but my body was nevertheless lithe, single, solid, one with me. Now the flesh arranges itself differently. I'm a cloud, congealed around a central object, the shape of a pear, which is hard and more real than I am and glows red within its translucent wrapping." Submissively, Offred undergoes the monthly ceremony and attunes herself to her body's monthly cycle. "I become the earth I set my ear against, for rumors of the future. Each twinge, each murmur of slight pain, ripples of sloughed-off matter, swellings and diminishings of tissue, the droolings of the flesh, these are signs, these are the things I need to know about. Each month I watch for blood, fearfully, for when it comes it means failure. I have failed once again to fulfill the expectations of others, which have become my own" (95).

But encoded in Offred's fervent—and orthodox—desire for pregnancy is the hidden fantasy that enforced pregnancy not only entails a loss of control but also poses a threat to the self. While the Handmaids are taught to intone "Blessed be the fruit," Offred sardonically likens herself, at one point, to "a queen ant with eggs" (25, 175). More significantly, Janine, the Handmaid who is depicted as utterly compliant and broken, is the only character in the novel who becomes pregnant and gives birth. At one point during the birthing process, Janine crouches "like a doll, an old one that's been pillaged and discarded, in some corner, akimbo" (160). In a related description of childbearing, Offred recalls a film depicting childbirth in a pre-Gilead hospital: it shows a woman "wired up to a machine, electrodes coming out of her every which way" so that she resembles "a broken robot" (146). Convinced that it is her fault that she has given birth to an Unbaby—a "shredder"—Janine subsequently appears depleted, "as if the juice is being sucked out of her" (278). And in the monstrous image of the Unbaby—"with a pinhead or a snout like a dog's, or two bodies, or a hole in its heart or no arms, or webbed hands and feet" (143)—*The Handmaid's Tale,* like other Atwood novels we have examined, acknowledges female anxieties about pregnancy and motherhood.

"Maybe the life I think I'm living is a paranoid delusion," Offred says at one point (139), as she struggles to retain a sense of sanity in an insane world of sexual slavery. Examining the psychological origins of the sexual oppression of women, *The Handmaid's Tale* makes visible the pattern of desire laid down during female oedipal development by staging the female oedipal fantasy, in which the girl wishes to marry the father and take the place of the mother, who is viewed as a rival for the father's affection. "If female readers of a particular culture share certain fantasies, it is because particular child-raising patterns, shared across a culture, embed common fantasy structures in their daughters," remarks Jean Wyatt (20). Not only are family relations "the principal conduits between cultural ideology and the individual unconscious," but cultural ideology "is most subtle and insidious when it comes in the form of interpersonal relations in the family" (104). In female oedipal development, the daughter's relationship to her father "trains her to idealize a distant and mysterious figure whose absences she can fill with glamorous projections." Some of the "behaviors that speak directly to the quirks of a female unconscious patterned by life in a patriarchal family are waiting, flirting, and the oedipal triangle," writes Wyatt (27). Because the "father's homecoming" is the "exciting event of a child's day," the waiting daughter comes to associate novelty and stimulation with the arrival of the father—a behavior that is repeated later in the romance scenario where "lover and waiting woman assume the active and passive roles first played out by father and daughter" (27, 28). The father enacts an important developmental role by "diverting his daughter's erotic impulses, first oriented toward her mother, into heterosexual channels"; he also engages in "sexual flirtation" with the daughter but does not follow through because of the incest taboo (29).

Providing a thinly disguised dramatization of the female oedipal situation in which the daughter views the mother as a rival and is drawn to the father, *The Handmaid's Tale* presents Serena Joy as a "malicious and vengeful woman" and the Commander as "not an unkind man" (208, 330). And the narrative also enacts the "waiting" and "flirting" behavior typical of the father-daughter relationship. When asked to meet secretly with the Commander in his study, Offred finds that these visits give her "something to do" and "to think about" (210) and thus relieve the tedium of her life of passive waiting. But she also realizes that she is "only a whim" for the Commander (205), who likes it when she distinguishes herself, showing "precocity, like an attentive pet, prick-eared and eager to perform. . . . [H]e is positively daddyish. He likes to think I am being entertained; and I am, I am" (238). But what is culturally repressed in this developmental scenario—because of the taboo against incest—is acted out in the novel's staging of the monthly insemination ceremony. If the narrative risks victimizing readers by positioning them as voyeurs and subjecting them to the obscene spectacle of the Ceremony, it also partially conceals what it reveals as it minimizes the horror of what is being depicted. For Offred protectively distances herself from what she is experiencing: she "detaches" herself, she "describes," she finds "something hilarious" about the impregnation ritual (123). Similarly, at least one critic claims to find a "humorous correspondence" between Atwood's description of the Ceremony and its biblical source in the Rachel and Bilhah story, which is quoted in one of the epigraphs to the novel. For the barren Rachel's desire that Jacob impregnate her handmaid, Bilhah—"go in unto her; and she shall bear upon my knees, that I may also have children by her"—is dramatized in the novel not only in the birthing ritual but also in the impregnation ritual since in "both crucial moments, the Handmaid is between the Wife's knees" (Freibert, "Control and Creativity" 283). And another critic remarks that *The Handmaid's Tale* deliberately and with parodic intent deflates the Gothic suspense it has invoked in the description leading up to the Ceremony by depicting the impregnation ritual as "not so much dreadful as boring" (Banerjee, "Alice in Disneyland" 84).

Although readers are encouraged to participate in the narrative's defenses by recognizing Atwood's parody of Gothic form in this scene or by locating the connections between the Gileadean Ceremony and its biblical counterpart, this pornographic and voyeuristic scene is, nevertheless, profoundly disturbing. As Offred lies between the legs of the Commander's wife, "my head on her stomach, her pubic bone under the base of my skull, her thighs on either side of me," the Commander services her. "What he is fucking is the lower part of my body. I do not say making love, because this is not what he's doing. Copulating too would be inaccurate, because it would imply two people and only one is involved. Nor does rape cover it . . ." (121). Despite the text's denial, this passage does dramatize a terrible kind of rape. Because the Handmaid takes on the role of the dutiful child-daughter in the father-commander's household, the Ceremony is presented as a thinly disguised incest drama. The actors in this degrading oedipal flesh triangle are the complicitous mother, the sexually violating father, and the sexually abused—and mute, silenced—daughter. In the displaced drama of Janine, the narrative explicitly refers to the forbidden theme of incest. "[S]o well behaved. . . . More like a daughter to you. . . . One of the family," Offred imagines the Wives saying when the pregnant Janine is "paraded" before them. "Little whores, all of them," is the remark made when Janine has left the room (147). And yet although the novel deliberately stages an incest drama, it also defends against it by focusing attention on Offred's involvement in an all "too banal" plot. In her relationship with the Commander, she has become the mistress of a man whose wife doesn't understand him (203).

"Is there no end to his disguises, of benevolence?" Offred asks at one point (113) as she compares the Commander to a series of innocuous male figures: to a museum guard, a midwestern bank president, a man in a vodka ad, and the shoemaker character in a fairy tale (111–13). Yet another Atwoodian split male, the Commander is both the father-protector and the father-persecutor. For although he wants to make Offred's life more bearable and although he can be "positively daddyish" in his behavior, he also affirms the male supremist ideology which subordinates and sexually enslaves women. In Gilead, he claims, women are "protected" so that they "can fulfill their biological destinies in peace." The pre-Gilead years, in the Commander's view, "were just an anomaly, historically speaking. . . . All we've done is return things to Nature's norm" (284, 285). What lies behind the benevolent paternalism of the Commander and the culturally conservative ideal of protected womanhood, as *The Handmaid's Tale* makes apparent, is a rigid belief in the male use and control of female sexuality.

"Sexual objectification," remarks Catharine MacKinnon, "is the primary process of the subjection of women. . . . Man fucks woman; subject verb object" (541). The fact that "consent rather than nonmutuality is the line between rape and intercourse . . . exposes the inequality in normal social expectations." Asking whether "consent is a meaningful concept" when sex is "ordinarily accepted as something men do *to* women," MacKinnon observes how "[r]ape in marriage expresses the male sense of entitlement to access to women they annex" and "incest extends it." As the experience of women "blurs the lines between deviance and normalcy, it obliterates the distinction between abuses *of* women and the social definition of what a woman *is*" (532).

Depicting the male objectification and sexual control of women, *The Handmaid's Tale* exposes the horror of women's consent to femininity. But if the novel concerns itself with the troubling issues of incest and forced sex, it also incorporates an antagonistic, feminist-dialogic speech which serves to partially contain and master the female fears it dramatizes. Describing how this tactic works, Offred muses that "[t]here is something powerful in the whispering of obscenities, about those in power. . . . It's like a spell, of sorts. It deflates them, reduces them to the common denominator where they can be dealt with" (287–88). "What'd you do wrong? Laugh at his dick?" Moira asks when Offred suddenly appears at Jezebel's with the Commander. When Offred explains that her Commander smuggled her in, Moira responds, "Who? . . . That shit you're with? I've had him, he's the pits" (315, 316). Indulging in a form of penis ridicule, Offred likens the Commander's penis to a stub, an extra thumb, a tentacle, a stalked slug's eye (113). When she attends a Gileadean group wedding, she imagines the impressive-looking Commander, who is officiating, in bed with his Wife and Handmaid. "[F]ertilizing away like mad" and "pretending to take no pleasure in it," he is "like a rutting salmon," in her view. "When the Lord said be fruitful and multiply, did he mean this man?" (282). And she imagines sex among the Angels and their new brides as "momentous grunts and sweating, damp furry encounters; or, better, ignominious failures, cocks like three-week-old carrots, anguished fumblings upon flesh cold and unresponsive as uncooked fish" (288).

Externally compliant, Offred expresses her defiance through her "inner jeering" at the Commander and her "mean-minded bitter jokes" about Serena Joy (177, 195–96). To Offred, the Wife's name is stupid-sounding, recalling the brand name of "something you'd put on your hair, in the other time, the time before, to straighten it." Serena Joy, who once made speeches about "the sanctity of the home, about how women should stay home," now stays in her home, but "it doesn't seem to agree with her. How furious she must be, now that she's been taken at her word" (60, 61). When Serena Joy wears one of her best dresses with flowers on it on the night of the Ceremony, Offred is scornful. "No use for you, I think at her, my face unmoving, you can't use them anymore, you're withered. They're the genital organs of plants. I read that somewhere, once" (104–05).

Despite Offred's cynical inner voice, her anger remains largely censored. Although at one point in her narrative reconstruction of events she claims that she fantasizes stabbing the Commander when he first asks her to kiss him—"I think about the blood coming out of him, hot as soup, sexual, over my hands"—she subsequently denies this impulse. "In fact I don't think about anything of the kind. I put it in only afterwards. . . . As I said, this is a reconstruction" (181). Whereas the film version of *The Handmaid's Tale* not only privileges this angry fantasy, it also enacts it, in the novel, Offred acts out her killing rage against her male oppressors only in the displaced drama of the state-sanctioned Particicution ceremony. When a man accused of rape is thrown at the mercy of a group of Handmaids, he is mobbed and brutally killed. "[T]here is a bloodlust; I want to tear, gouge, rend," as Offred describes it (358). On the fringes of her tale we find the partially expressed drama of female rage.

"Like physical abuse," writes Christine Froula, "literary violence against women works to privilege the cultural father's voice and story over those of women, the cultural daughters, and indeed to silence women's voices" (121). Treating the Handmaid as an abused cultural daughter, the Gilead regime also attempts to silence her. *"Blessed are the silent,"* according to the revised Gileadean Bible (115). In Gilead, men have "the word" (114) and women are rendered speechless. When

Offred first meets her double Ofglen—the Handmaid she is assigned to go shopping with and to spy on—they exchange the "orthodox" platitudes sanctioned by the regime:

> "The war is going well, I hear," she says.
> "Praise be," I reply.
> "We've been sent good weather."
> "Which I receive with joy." (26)

Later, after Ofglen informs Offred that she is a member of the anti-regime Mayday organization, their whispered conversations change but still their speech is, of necessity, "more like a telegram, a verbal sema-phore. Amputated speech" (260). Offred comes to feel that speech is "backing up inside" her (239). "Our big mistake," says one of the officials of the regime's original think tank, "was teaching them [women] to read. We won't do that again" (389). In Gilead, women are forbidden by law to read books; after the third conviction, the offender's hand is cut off.

Ordered to make secret visits to the Commander's private, book-filled study, Offred does there what has become a perversity and crime in the new culture: she reads while he watches. His "watching is a curiously sexual act" and her "illicit reading . . . seems a kind of performance" (239). And she and the Commander play Scrabble, a language game that is now banned and thus dangerous. As she uses "all the old tricks with consonants" she can recall, her tongue feels "thick with the effort of spelling," and her mind lurches and stumbles "among the sharp R's and T's, sliding over the ovoid vowels as if on pebbles" (199). When the Commander, on one occasion, allows her to write with a pen, the pen seems "sensuous, alive almost" and she can "feel its power, the power of the words it contains." As Offred holds the pen, she remembers a Red Center saying—"Pen Is Envy"—which is meant to warn the Handmaids to avoid such forbidden objects (241). Since this Gileadean motto en-codes yet another motto—"Penis envy"—it also may be a self-conscious allusion on Atwood's part to Sandra Gilbert and Susan Gubar's analysis of the "metaphor of literary paternity," the notion that the pen is a "metaphorical penis." In our phallocentric culture, as Gilbert and Gubar observe, "the text's author is a father, a progenitor, a procreator, an aesthetic patriarch whose pen is an instrument of generative power like his penis" (3, 6).

Because Offred recognizes the connection between the male control of language and male power, her dialogic resistance to the official, monologic discourse of Gilead is a conscious form of political disobedience. When, for example, Aunt Lydia tells the Handmaids to think of themselves as pearls, Offred resists this reeducation effort. "We, sitting in our rows, eyes down, we make her salivate morally. We are hers to define, we must suffer her adjectives. I think about pearls. Pearls are congealed oyster spit" (145). Responding to another one of Aunt Lydia's sayings, "All flesh is weak," Offred mentally replies, "All flesh is grass . . ." (60). When greeting another Handmaid, Offred is compelled to use the orthodox speech of Gilead: " 'Blessed be the fruit,' she says to me, the accepted greeting among us. 'May the Lord open,' I answer, the accepted response" (25). But she also listens avidly to the "unofficial news"—the subversive discourse—exchanged among the Marthas. "*Stillborn, it was.* Or, *Stabbed her with a knitting needle, right in the belly. Jealousy, it must have been, eating her up.* Or, tantalizingly, *It was toilet cleaner she used. Worked like a charm, though you'd think he'd of tasted it*" (14). Trapped in the male supremist world of Gilead, Offred recalls her mother's oppositional discourse. What "use" are men, Offred's mother once commented, "except for ten seconds' worth of half babies. A man is just a woman's strategy for making other women" (155). Gratified when she finds the "taboo message" left by the former Handmaid—"*Nolite te bastardes carborundorum*"—Offred feels that the written message is meant for her and is pleased that it has "made it through" (69). If the mock-Latin phrase— "Don't let the bastards grind you down"—is alternately a prayer, a command, and a joke to Offred, it is also a whispered obscenity about those in power which is secretly passed from one Handmaid to another.

Through her dialogic wordplay and focus on words, Offred not only registers her resistance to the official speech and totalizing discourse of the state, she also signals her desperate desire to retain some sense of control. "I sit in the chair and think about the word *chair*. It can also mean the leader of a meeting. It can also mean a mode of execution. It is the first syllable in *charity*. It is the French word for flesh. None of these facts has any connection with the others. These are the kinds of litanies I use, to compose myself" (140). Words, to Offred, are more than precious commodities. They are also signposts to the reality she is determined to hold on to. While the world can be read as if it were a text, it is not equivalent to a text. At one point Offred notices, on the white cloth bag covering the head of a hanged man, that blood has seeped through the bag, making a "smile of blood" on the white cloth (43). Associating the blood red smile of the executed man with red tulips, she thinks: "The red is the same but there is no connection. The tulips are not tulips of blood, the red smiles are not flowers, neither thing makes a comment on the other. The tulip is not a reason for disbelief in the hanged man, or vice versa. Each thing is valid and really there. It is through a field of such valid objects that I must pick my way, every day and in every way. I put a lot of effort into making such distinctions. I need to make them. I need to be very clear, in my own mind" (44–45).

Realizing that a "danger" of her existence is "grayout" (258), Offred also needs to make distinctions and be "very clear" in her "own mind" as she reconstructs her past and describes her present; for what she retains of her identity is bound up in her memories of what she was and is. "I wait. I compose myself," she says. "My self is a thing I must now compose, as one composes a speech" (86). In the "Historical Notes" appended to Offred's tale, we learn that her narrative is really an oral diary, a transcription of some thirty cassette tapes. For Offred—who is "a blank . . . between parentheses. Between other people" (295)—to compose her story, to speak herself into agency, is to attempt to recuperate herself.

To her imaginary audience, Offred admits that she wishes her story were "different" and "more civilized," that it had "more shape" and showed her "more active, less hesitant, less distracted by trivia" (343). She would like to believe that the story she is telling is *only* a story because then she would have "control" over its ending (52). "I'm sorry there is so much pain in this story. I'm sorry it's in fragments, like a body caught in crossfire or pulled apart by force," she says. "But I keep on going with this sad and hungry and sordid, this limping and mutilated story, because after all I want you to hear it. . . . By telling you anything at all I'm at least believing in you, I believe you're there, I believe you into being. Because I'm telling you this story I will your existence. I tell, therefore you are" (343–44). Although there are postmodernist appeals in the novel's repeated and self-conscious meditations on the act of narration, *The Handmaid's Tale,* as W. F. Garrett-Petts remarks, "invokes the conventions and themes of postmodernism . . . in order to reinsert them back into the narrative of daily experience" (75). Despite its muted "postmodernist echoes," *The Handmaid's Tale* conforms to the purpose informing all of Atwood's novels: "her desire to teach her audience how to read the world" (74). While Atwood's narrative thematizes the collaboration between writer and readers, it uses direct address to draw in readers, who assume the role of confidant and who "listen, sympathize, and learn from Offred's testimony" (80). Moreover, Offred's open appeal to her imaginary audience—in particular to a female audience—is also designed to strengthen the reader's desires to make sense out of her fragmentary text and to see her rescued.

"I'm too tired to go on with this story. I'm too tired to think about where I am. Here is a different story, a better one. This is the story of what happened to Moira," Offred says at one point (166), interrupting her description of her life in Gilead to describe her "irreverent, resourceful" (69) feminist friend from earlier times, who actively rebels against the Gilead system. Despite the horrible foot punishment Moira suffers after her first attempted escape from the Red Center, she remains undaunted. "I left that old hag Aunt Elizabeth tied up like a Christmas turkey behind the furnace. I wanted to kill her, I really felt like it . . . ," Moira later tells Offred, as she describes, in her characteristic feminist-dialogic speech, her second escape attempt (317). After her disappearance from the Red Center, Moira becomes a "fantasy" for the other Handmaids. Because of her rebellion, the Aunts are "less fearsome and more absurd," for their power is somehow flawed. And yet, the Handmaids also find something frightening in Moira's freedom. "Already we were losing the taste for freedom, already we were finding these walls secure. In the upper reaches of the atmosphere you'd come apart, you'd vaporize, there would be no pressure holding you together" (172).

Ultimately cross-questioning the possibility of female heroism in such a regime, the narrative, while typecasting Moira as a feminist rebel, also dramatizes her defeat. Caught, tortured, and then forced into prostitution, Moira ultimately loses her volition and becomes indifferent. "I don't want her [Moira] to be like me. Give in, go along, save her skin," says Offred. "I want gallantry from her, swashbuckling, heroism, single-handed combat. Something I lack." Although Moira's story does not "end with something daring and spectacular" (324, 325) as Offred and many readers wish it would, Offred's story does in the film version's rewriting of the novel: for in the film, which enacts a female revenge fantasy, Offred kills the Commander at the end and then is helped to escape Gilead by a Mayday rescue team.

If the text's rage is acted out in the film version of *The Handmaid's Tale,* the narrative, in contrast, intertwines its increasing anger about male oppression—which culminates in the displaced drama of the Particicution ceremony—with Offred's love affair with Nick and her at times lyrical, sensuous celebrations of the "minimalist life." Offred takes deep pleasure, for example, in observing the egg she is about to eat for breakfast. "The shell of the egg is smooth but also grained; small pebbles of calcium are defined by the sunlight, like craters on the moon. It's a barren landscape, yet perfect; it's the sort of desert the saints went into, so their minds would not be distracted by profusion. . . . The egg is glowing now, as if it had an energy of its own" (141). She also takes delight in Serena Joy's garden: "A Tennyson garden, heavy with scent, languid; the return of the word *swoon*. . . . To walk through it in these days, of peonies, of pinks and carnations, makes my head swim" (196). Having, from the beginning, hungered to "commit the act of touch," Offred finds it "good" to be touched by Nick, "to be felt so greedily, to feel so greedy" (14, 127–28). "Can I be blamed for wanting a real body, to put my arms around? Without it I too am disembodied" (132).

"*Falling in love,* we said; *I fell for him.* We were falling women. We believed in it, this downward motion: so lovely, like flying, and yet at the same time so dire, so extreme, so unlikely," Offred thinks as she recalls the pre-Gilead ideology of romantic love. In the past, falling in love "was the central thing; it was the way you understood yourself" (292). But in Gilead, this culture-specific notion of romantic fulfillment has been replaced with the arranged marriages that existed before the rise of romantic marriage in Western society. "Don't let me catch you at it," Aunt Lydia warns Offred (June) and the other Handmaids. "No moon-ing and June-ing around here, girls. . . . *Love* is not the point" (285).

If Offred's situation "recalls that of a romantic heroine" who must choose between two men—the older, paternal Commander and the younger, dangerous and thus more sexually desirous, Nick—the "grim realities of Offred's actual existence resemble those of a concentration camp inmate, far more than those of a gothic heroine" (Hammer 41). That some readers may take comfort in the novel's love plot—which provides Offred temporary escape from the sexually repressive world of Gilead—is suggested in Lucy Freibert's remark that "Offred's real break-through to her courageous sexual self" occurs in her relationship with Nick, and that Offred's "joyous reaction to her desire embodies precisely the French *jouissance*" ("Control and Creativity" 288). But despite the common claim that love is presented as a "subversive force" in *The Handmaid's Tale,* the narrative's representation of romantic love is, in fact, "highly qualified, highly ambivalent" (Ehrenreich 34; Madonne Miner 164).

Although Offred's affair with Nick is presented as a form of female opposition to the State, the novel's invocation of the conventional romance plot may also appear to present a culturally conservative mes-sage: namely, that falling in love is the "central" thing, that a woman reaches self-fulfillment only in the love relationship. And yet if *The*

Handmaid's Tale seems to recuperate the romance plot, it also interrupts it by having Offred tell two radically different versions of her initial sexual encounter with Nick. The first version is erotic. "His mouth is on me, his hands, I can't wait and he's moving, already, love, it's been so long, I'm alive in my skin, again, arms around him, falling and water softly everywhere, never-ending." Claiming that she invented this version of events, Offred then tells another story which actively undercuts and dialogizes the erotic discourse of the first description. In a telling role reversal, Nick becomes the sexual object and commodity. When he tells her that he could "just squirt it into a bottle" and she could "pour it in," she thinks that perhaps he wants something from her, "some emotion, some acknowledgment that he too is human, is more than just a seedpod." When they subsequently engage in "corny and falsely gay sexual banter" adopted from the late movies—"And what's a nice girl like me doing in a spot like this"; "Abstinence makes the heart grow fonder"—Offred realizes the purpose of such borrowed, stylized speech. "I can see now what it's for, what it was always for: to keep the core of yourself out of reach, enclosed, protected" (338–39). That Offred subsequently admits that it "didn't happen that way either" (340) points to the narrative's reluctance to commit itself to the romance plot. And if Offred's sexual relationship with Nick is presented as an important act of defiance against the Gilead regime, it is also entrapping; for when Nick becomes Offred's lover, she loses her desire to escape Gilead. Above all else, she wants to be near Nick; with him she feels she can make some kind of life for herself. "Humanity is so adaptable, my mother would say. Truly amazing, what people can get used to, as long as there are a few compensations" (349).

"Thinking can hurt your chances, and I intend to last," Offred says at the outset of the novel, even as she contemplates the potential escape of suicide. "I know why there is no glass, in front of the watercolor picture of blue irises, and why the window opens only partly and why the glass in it is shatterproof. It isn't running away they're afraid of. We wouldn't get far. It's those other escapes, the ones you can open in yourself, given a cutting edge" (10). "Oh God oh God. How can I keep on living?" Offred says on another occasion (253). "I could burn the house down. Such a fine thought, it makes me shiver. An escape, quick and narrow" (271). Although the narrative repeatedly warns that Offred's story will end in the prescribed closure of suicide, it, instead, acts out the threatened ending of suicide in the displaced drama of Offred's predecessor, the Handmaid who defiantly leaves behind a written message. "I look up at the ceiling, the round circle of plaster flowers. . . . From the center was the chandelier, and from the chandelier a twisted strip of sheet was hanging down. That's where she was swinging, just lightly, like a pendulum; the way you could swing as a child, hanging by your hands from a tree branch. She was safe then . . ." (274). When Serena Joy discovers that Offred has been secretly seeing the Commander, she condemns Offred to the same fate. "Just like the other one. A slut. You'll end up the same" (369). Although Offred thinks about setting fire to the house or killing the Wife, she finds herself unable to act. She is the victim of circumstances, not an active agent capable of directing the plot of her own life. In scenes that anticipate Atwood's next novel, *Cat's Eye*, Offred imagines herself freezing to death in the snow and she hears the former Handmaid—whose voice she has internalized just as Elaine internalizes the voice of Cordelia—telling her to kill herself. "Get it over, she says. I'm tired of this melodrama, I'm tired of keeping silent. There's no one you can protect, your life has value to no one. I want it finished" (375).

Refusing the preestablished closure of suicide, *The Handmaid's Tale*, like *Bodily Harm*, intentionally leaves the reader in a state of suspense even as it invokes and promotes a rescue fantasy. As the Eyes help Offred into the black van, she is uncertain whether she is going to her "end or a new beginning," whether she is stepping up "into the darkness within; or else the light" (378). Because Nick may be an Eye or a member of the Mayday organization—that is, a persecutor or a rescuer—readers do not know for certain whether Offred has been betrayed by Nick and ultimately sent to her death or rescued by the secret Mayday organization and the Underground Femaleroad. Although Offred's fate is left hanging in the balance at the end of her narrative, the "Historical Notes" section appended to her tale partially acts out the rescue fantasy generated by the narrative. Speculating on what probably happened to her, Professor Pieixoto, the twenty-second century historian who transcribes Offred's tapes, comments that while her "ultimate fate" (393) is unknown, the weight of evidence suggests that Nick engineered her escape. And her narrative, he claims, has "a certain reflective quality. . . . It has a whiff of emotion recollected, if not in tranquillity, at least *post facto*" (384).

Some critic/readers have similarly speculated about Offred's fate. In the view of Arnold Davidson, although "Offred's end is uncertain" in the main narrative, "the very existence of the tapes suggests that, aided by Nick, she did elude the rule of Gilead" ("Future Tense" 116). In contrast, Leslie-Ann Hales argues that not only does Offred's narrative "not reach the security of conclusion," but readers never learn whether Offred "safely escapes Gilead, dies in the attempt, or is recaptured only to be hanged from a meathook on the Wall in Gilead. It is possible that only the tapes, not the maker of the tapes, survives Gilead" (260). But for Coral Ann Howells, even though Offred's ultimate fate does remain uncertain, the fact that history proves that Gilead is "not invulnerable" builds "a shadowed optimism" into the novel (69). And Barbara Rigney feels that *The Handmaid's Tale* is "a novel about survival" (119). Describing her intention in the closure, Atwood comments that *The Handmaid's Tale* "isn't totally bleak and pessimistic," for not only does Offred get out but also a future society exists which "is not the society of Gilead and is capable of reflecting about the society of Gilead in the same way that we reflect about the 17th century. Her little message in a bottle has gotten through to someone—which is about all we can hope, isn't it?" (Rothstein). And yet despite the epilogue's reassurance that "there are nightmares from which one does eventually wake up" (Gardam 30), some critic/readers, like Arnold Davidson, find the professor's comments "in crucial ways . . . the most pessimistic part of the book" ("Future Tense" 120).

Presented as a partial transcription of a scholarly meeting held in the far north of Canada in a nation ruled by native North Americans, the epilogue is set in 2195 at the Twelfth Symposium on Gileadean Studies at the University of Denay, Nunavit, a name that carries a hidden message to readers—namely, to "deny none of it" (see Norris 361; Murphy 34). The setting, the names of the participants—Professor Maryann Crescent Moon who chairs the session and Professor Pieixoto—and the fact that Caucasian Anthropology is now a subject of academic study all serve to suggest a multicultural future in which the power of white patriarchy has been successfully challenged. But disturbing signs of the staying power of sexism soon emerge. Describing the joke behind the naming of Offred's story by a male colleague, Professor Pieixoto comments that "all puns were intentional, particularly that having to do with the archaic vulgar signification of the word *tail;* that being, to some extent, the bone, as it were, of contention, in that phase of Gileadean society of which our saga treats" (381). This comment provokes laughter from the academicians, as does the professor's remark that "The Underground Femaleroad" has been "dubbed by some of our historical wags 'The Underground Frailroad'" (381). It is also telling that the professor seems to admire the "ingenuity" of the original members of the Sons of Jacob Think Tank while he belittles the intelligence of Offred who, in his words, "appears to have been an educated woman, insofar as a graduate of any North American college of the time may be said to have been educated" (391, 387). As he assumes an air of scholarly objectivity, Professor Pieixoto reveals his moral obtuseness. "[A]llow me to say that in my opinion we must be cautious about passing moral judgment upon the Gileadeans," he tells his academic audience. "Surely we have learned by now that such judgments are of necessity culture-specific" (383). Because history's voices are "imbued with the obscurity of the matrix out of which they come," we "cannot always decipher them precisely in the clearer light of our own day," remarks Professor Pieixoto, who is blind to his own interpretive biases as he reconstructs the history of Offred's society (394–95).

Atwood comments that one of her purposes in the "Historical Notes" is to provide the reader with information about Offred's society which Offred, given her limited circumstances, could not have known (Hancock 284). But her pedantic, misogynistic history professor, who is obsessed with facts but ignores (or denies) the feelings generated by Offred's narrative, is also clearly designed to provoke reader outrage. Again and again, critic/readers have dialogically contested the authoritative speech of Atwood's fictional professor. Leslie-Ann Hales finds the professor's "pompous attitude of moral objectivity . . . appalling in the wake of the handmaid's own story" (262). For Linda Kauffman, the archivist not only "has little sensitivity to Offred's predicament or her pain" but he and his cohorts "appropriate the female voice for their own purposes—fame, fortune, power, self-aggrandizement, and self-congratulation" (224, 225). According to Amin Malak, the epilogue reveals not only the "absurdity and futility of certain academic writings that engage in dull, clinically sceptic analysis of irrelevancies and inanities," it also shows that the scholar who avoids taking a moral or political stand about issues such as totalitarianism "will necessarily become an apologist for evil" (14, 15).

In providing a potent critique of the male appropriation and objectification of the female voice, the "Historical Notes" expose the ideological biases of literary interpretation. But if the epilogue "calls forth strange emotions" and if the professor's witticisms "set the teeth on edge" (Cowart 108), the "Historical Notes" also function to disrupt and defuse the powerful emotions generated by the novel and to focus attention, instead, on the act of interpretation. Designed to make critic/readers aware of the author's presence behind the text—indeed, Roberta Rubenstein imagines Atwood "wryly anticipating her commentators at the annual rites of MLA" ("Nature and Nurture" 111)—the epilogue also forces academic commentators to cross-question their own critical activity. "Do we, as scholars, contribute to the dehumanizations of society by our own critical work . . . ?" asks Arnold Davidson, who observes how Professor Pieixoto objectifies just as the state objectified Offred. "Is this what history is for? To round out the vitae of historians?" ("Future Tense" 115, 119). Lucy Freibert thinks that "'serious' academics will turn bloody as they hear themselves echoed" in the professor's "pedantic analysis." In the epilogue, "the small-mindedness of academe in dealing with reality cannot be missed" ("Control and Creativity" 289). And for Michael Foley, the epilogue shows how "even in one of the temples of liberal democracy, namely the Western university, the deeply rooted sexual, racial or other biases of academics can anesthetize their critical faculties." Although "ostensibly a scene from the distant future," this is "actually the book's clearest depiction of a worrisome present" (44, 45).

Decrying the power politics of literary interpretation in the "Historical Notes," Atwood also asserts authorial power by urging commentators to reflect on their own critical practices and by suggesting that there are appropriate and inappropriate ways of responding to literary texts. In calling for a reading that, in the words of Harriet Bergmann, "combines emotional and intellectual perception" (847), Atwood dramatizes her desire to save her novel from those readers who, like her fictional professor, treat the text as a verbal artifact to be coldly dissected and ultimately dismissed. And judging from the critical commentary *The Handmaid's Tale* has provoked, many readers find it difficult to dismiss Atwood's novel and its warning against the fundamentalist backlash against feminism. For David Cowart, readers who refuse "to concede any real prophetic plausibility" to *The Handmaid's Tale* miss "the contemporary actuality that fuels Atwood's speculation" (109). Finding something "sickeningly familiar" in the novel's description of the pre-Gilead society, W. J. Keith feels that the "very suggestion" that Gilead represents a possible future for America is "a crushing indictment of our own times" (125). "However we choose to look at it," writes Michele Lacombe, "Offred's world is not far removed from our own" (5). While Atwood's fictional professor refuses to pass judgment, many readers do, as they are meant to. If Atwood wants to chill her readers, she is also determined to force them to pay attention. Indeed, as W. F. Garrett-Petts remarks, for Atwood the role of the reader "is one of considerable responsibility" and "reading is a matter of fierce interpretation" (88).

"I would like to believe this is a story I'm telling. I need to believe it. I must believe it. Those who can believe that such stories are only stories have a better chance," Offred comments at one point (52). Although *The Handmaid's Tale* contains postmodernist echoes in passages that self-consciously reflect on the narrative process, it also insists on the existence of an historical reality that exists beyond the words of the text. Encouraging readers to speculate on the semifictive process of history-making and the ideological biases involved in any historical interpretation of the past, Atwood also enjoins her audience to recognize the terrifying reality—the material presence—of history. While history is an account we must attempt to decipher, it is also a lived experience. To reduce history to a mere story, as Offred recognizes, is to attempt to make it "less frightening" (187). But history is more than a story we tell ourselves, Atwood reminds her "postfeminist" women readers, and it is a mistake to think that we can easily explain away its blood-stained smiles or use fiction to shield ourselves from the oppressive practices perpetuated by patriarchal ideology, with its hierarchical arrangement of the sexes—practices exemplified in the New Right's deliberate scapegoating of independent, autonomous women and its insistence on the restoration of women's traditional roles.

8

The
Power Politics
of Women's
Relationships
in
Cat's Eye

━━━━━━━━━━━━━━━━━━━━━━━━━ ■ ━━━━━━━━━

I t takes something of a heroine—and Margaret Atwood is definitely a
heroine to both readers and writers of women's fiction—to turn the
tables on her own kind," writes Anita Brookner in an early review of
Cat's Eye (32). Atwood describes *Cat's Eye* as "a more personal,
unpretentious book" and a novel it was "important" for her to write
(Timson 57). In it, she deals with the "Best Girlfriend" theme. Remarking that "women's friendships are now firmly on the literary map as valid
and multidimensional novelistic material," Atwood observes that the
treatment of this theme in fiction by women writers "runs the gamut,
from selfless idealism to pointy-toothed ego-devouring" ("That Certain
Thing" 39). A novel that questions what Atwood describes as the
nineteenth-century notion that "women somehow are more morally
wonderful than men" (Timson 58), *Cat's Eye* explores the potential
power politics of female relationships and contradicts the feminist ideology that idealizes female relationships, viewing them as inherently egalitarian and cooperative. In *Cat's Eye*, Atwood retrieves an oft-forgotten
stage of female development: the "in-between time" of girlhood friendship. "We got a real dish of Freud," Atwood comments, "so we were told
that the early years were very, very important. And then we have a whole
cult of romance and sex . . . so the later period becomes important. The
in-between time I think we've forgotten because it's been indicated to us
that it's not important . . ." (Peri 30). Deliberately evoking the popular
myth of the vampire in its exploration of the "pointy-toothed ego-
devouring" brand of friendship, *Cat's Eye* reveals just how important—
and emotionally crippling—these forgotten years of girlhood friendship
can be.

Likening time to "a series of liquid transparencies, one laid on top of another" (3), *Cat's Eye* searches out the girlhood origins of the artist's memory-haunted and tormented life. "The past isn't quaint while you're in it. Only at a safe distance, later, when you can see it as decor, not as the shape your life's been squeezed into" (384). So comments the narrator of *Cat's Eye,* Elaine Risley, a middle-aged painter who undertakes a mental review of the five decades of her life when she returns to Toronto for a retrospective exhibition of her art. Narrated in the first-person present tense and deftly structured by interweaving chronological installments of present and past time, *Cat's Eye* is a lyrical novel of memory but also an anxiety-ridden narrative preoccupied with the notion of psychic vampirism: the invasion by and loss of the self to a malignant other. Although *Cat's Eye* deliberately locates the point of origin of Elaine's damaged self in girlhood, the narrative's idealistic but emotionless description of early family life and its narrative silence over the absent mother are, as we shall see, psychologically suggestive. Also significant is the narrative's obsessive return to the verbally assaultive Mrs. Smeath and its verbal—indeed, painterly—assault on her.

As *Cat's Eye* excavates the buried secrets and childhood traumas that have permanently marked Elaine's adult personality, it also erects defenses against the painful memories that threaten to rupture and overwhelm the narrative by embedding these memories in a formidable mass of accumulated detail. Calling attention to the narrative's remarkable specificity, one commentator says that Atwood chooses "to unload onto the page an atticful of memorabilia," and thus the novel reads, in part, like "an anthropological catalogue of the evolution of Toronto's tribal customs from the forties to the eighties" (Manguel 67). According to another commentator, the reader of *Cat's Eye* "is nearly overwhelmed by the mass of documentation. A social historian of the next century could find no better source for what middle-class children in Toronto . . . wore, ate, sang, or played with during the 1940s and 1950s" (Towers 50). Indeed, for some readers, although Atwood writes "convincingly, sometimes wincingly well" about the vicissitudes of girlhood friendships, the "narrative sags somewhat" after Elaine reaches puberty (Mackay 113). "Inevitably, the emotional intensity of these early scenes makes the more familiar material of Elaine's later life seem somewhat anticlimactic" (McDermott 35). A novel about memory and forgetting, *Cat's Eye* is also a narrative that both inscribes and defends against the childhood terrors at its core. It is an "elegiac" work, a novel "about mourning" (Brookner 32), but it is also a novel about female rage and resentment. By focusing attention on the link between Elaine's paintings and her life,

Cat's Eye reveals that Elaine's art finds its source not only in loss and yearning but also in fear and anger. At once an intensely painful and yet a carefully constructed narrative, Atwood's novel enacts what it depicts: the transformation of deep emotional trauma into a complex and coded work of art.

"As a novelist, Margaret Atwood never seems out of control. Whatever rage or disappointment may smolder underneath, the surfaces of her fiction are unusually cool and dry," observes Robert Towers, who feels that *Cat's Eye* is "an intensely personal novel, much of which reads like barely mediated autobiography" (50). Despite Atwood's frequent complaints throughout her writing career about readers who naively assume that her fiction is autobiographical, and despite her warning that readers of *Cat's Eye* should avoid the "autobiographical fallacy" when interpreting the novel (Hubbard 206), *Cat's Eye* invites critic/readers to ferret out the similarities between Elaine's life and Atwood's. Indeed, "serious readers" of Atwood, who are familiar with her many interviews and thus with the general outlines of her early life, are "enticed" to see Atwood's character "as at least partly" the author's "own reflection" (Ingersoll, "Margaret Atwood's 'Cat's Eye'" 18). For like Elaine Risley, Atwood spent the early years of her life with her family in the northern Canadian bush; Atwood's father, like her character's, was an entomologist; and Atwood also found the customs of girls odd when the family moved to Toronto. Moreover, one of the impulses behind *Cat's Eye,* as Atwood comments, was to celebrate "a physical world that's vanished." "I wanted a literary home for all those vanished *things* from my own childhood—the marbles, the Eaton's catalogues, the Watchbird Watching You, the smells, sounds, colors" (Ingersoll, "Waltzing Again" 10, 9–10). "Certainly, this novel feels more 'personal' than any other in the Atwood *oeuvre;* it may also be more metafictional," writes Constance Rooke, who describes how she had the "eerie sense" that all of Atwood's other novels "were present" in *Cat's Eye.* And yet if reading *Cat's Eye* feels "illicit, and heady," the "voyeuristic glimpses" of Atwood's life that the narrative seems to provide are "made of paint or printer's ink, and not of flesh—of art, not autobiography," as Rooke comments (131).

Atwood's Elaine Risley is a familiar character. A middle-aged version of characters we have encountered in other Atwood novels, Elaine feels deeply inadequate. "I should get bifocals. But then I'd look like an old biddy"; "aging begins at the elbows and metastasizes," she thinks as she reflects on her aging body (19, 119). And she imagines that younger women view her as a "middle-aged frump" or as "teetering on the brink of matronhood" (92, 119). Although Elaine has a "real life," she some-times has "trouble believing in it," for it does not seem like the sort of life she "could ever get away with, or deserve" (15). "I'm supposed to have accumulated things by now: possessions, responsibilities, achievements, experience and wisdom. I'm supposed to be a person of substance." But when she returns to Toronto, a city associated with the traumas of her past, she feels not "weightier" but "lighter," as if she is "shrinking," "filling with cold air, or gently falling snow" (13). Prone to feelings of depression and nothingness, she feels she is "without worth," that noth-ing she does "is of any value." "Last night I felt the approach of noth-ing," she comments (43).

Because Elaine associates these feelings with her girlhood friend, Cordelia, it becomes the task of the narrative to decipher the buried puzzle of this formative relationship and to locate the lost connections between Elaine's past experiences and her present self-state. And yet, as if to provide a buffer against the virulent feelings that threaten to erupt in the text, the narrative first provides positive memories of Elaine's rela-tionship with Cordelia as a teenager and then, abruptly and unaccount-ably, undercuts these memories by staging a series of revenge fantasies. Elaine takes "some satisfaction" in the image of Cordelia as a broken-down, aging bag lady and "more in worse things": Cordelia being chased and physically attacked by a man; or Cordelia, unconscious, in an oxygen tent; or Cordelia, conscious but immobilized, in an iron lung (7–8). The fact that there is a prolonged delay before Cordelia makes her real entry into the novel is also significant. It is as if the narrative wants to accumulate and store up a hoard of positive childhood memories to shield against the psychic horrors it is assigned to uncover. Also acting as a protective device are the theoretical discourses on time and space which interlace the text and serve to partially deflect reader attention away from the novel's painful content and onto its intellectual and speculative framework. Moreover, Atwood's use of voice in *Cat's Eye* serves a defensive function: whereas the voice of the middle-aged Elaine, which narrates the present, is "social, engaged in a telling," the "voice of remembrance," which narrates the past, is "almost toneless" (Banerjee, "Atwood's Time" 514, 515).

"Until we moved to Toronto I was happy," Elaine announces early in the narrative (22) as she chronicles her family's nomadic life in northern Canada where her father worked as a forest-insect field researcher. Pre-senting two radically different versions of the past, *Cat's Eye* contrasts Elaine's "happy" childhood with her devastatingly unhappy girlhood.

And yet, although the narrator's memorialization of her early life is overly rich in descriptive details and imagery, she also largely avoids describing her relationship with her family. Instead, she recalls a proliferating array of objects: a black, oblong Brownie box camera; the silver paper from cigarette packages; a blue balloon; a red plastic purse; the black cats of Halloween and the red paper hearts of Valentine's day; childhood drawings, comic books, coloring books and scrapbooks. And she describes places associated with childhood: the caterpillar-infested woods; the shabby housekeeping cottage; the unfinished yellow-brick house in Toronto; the zoology building at the university. If, through the sheer weight of the specific details it records, the novel highlights the objects and places of this remembered world, it also suggestively pushes family members—and the narrator's feelings about them—to the periphery.

"Such are my pictures of the dead," Elaine says of her family members in a flat, unemotional voice early in the narrative (27). Suggesting a pattern of narrative avoidance and omission, members of Elaine's family have only a muted, shadowy existence in the narrative and eventually simply vanish from the text. Indeed, Elaine seems to observe and record details of family life, rather than emotionally experience it. Her sense of yearning and loss—but also of emotional absence and detachment—is conveyed in a scene in which she, alone and outside in the dark, looks in at her parents through a lighted window and sees them as "a far-away picture with a frame of blackness." Finding it "disquieting" to observe her parents without their awareness, she feels that "[i]t's as if I don't exist; or as if they don't" (72–73). Similarly, she dreams that her parents "are dead but also alive" as they, lying beside each other, sink into the hard but transparent earth, looking up "sorrowfully" at her "as they recede" (178). Also revealing is Elaine's artwork, *Pressure Cooker*, a six-panel series of images of her mother. In the top three panels, which show her mother cooking in the kitchen of her Toronto house, the same figure appears first in colored pencil, then in collage formed from pictures cut out of women's magazines, and finally in white on white in which pipe cleaners are used for the raised parts. When the top panels are read from left to right, it appears as if her mother is "slowly dissolving, from real life into a Babylonian bas-relief shadow." The bottom three panels, which show her mother making jam over an outdoor fire, reverse the order and thus can be "read" as a "materialization, out of the white pipe cleaner mist into the solid light of day." Commenting on these images, completed soon after the death of her mother, Elaine says, "I suppose I wanted to bring her back to life. I suppose I wanted her timeless, though there is no such thing on earth" (160–61). But this serial artwork may also reflect Elaine's adult desire to assume omnipotent control in her relationships with others, to make people "appear and vanish, at will" (339), as she later puts it.

While the narrative strategically splits off and preserves family life, depicting it as a safe but lonely world, the social sphere of girlhood friendships is cast as a dangerous, threatening world where the female self is shaped and irrevocably damaged in the process. Significantly, while Elaine's mother is idealized as the good but emotionally remote mother—indeed, she is characterized as "airy and hard to pin down" (166)—Mrs. Smeath takes on the role of the bad, destructive mother and thus becomes the focal point not only for much of Elaine's surrealistic and angry art but also for the text's rage and retaliatory rhetoric. Although it can be argued that *Cat's Eye,* in its thematization of the in-between time of girlhood friendships, deliberately deemphasizes the family relationship, the narrative also leaves unanswered an important question. For in asserting that Elaine was "happy" until her family moved to Toronto, *Cat's Eye,* as Judith Thurman has observed, begs the question which is "central" to the text: "What happens to a child that disposes her to self-punishment?" And "[w]hy does the sturdy, observant, tomboyish Elaine become the victim?" (109).

The novel remains largely silent about what, in Elaine's early childhood, predisposes her to assume the victim's role. Instead, *Cat's Eye* suggests that when Elaine becomes the victim of her girlhood friends, she also becomes subject to the repressive cultural code that her friends enforce, in a childish but effective imitation of their parents. In the novel's analysis of the origins of gender-identity, the social construction of feminine identity is viewed as a formative trauma. "How is going in through a door different if you're a boy? What's in there that merits the strap, just for seeing it?" Elaine pointedly asks when she and her brother begin to attend public school in Toronto (49). Because Elaine's earliest life is spent in the northern Canadian bush where her brother is her chief playmate, and because she continues to identify, in part, with the rough-and-tumble world of boys when she moves to Toronto, she becomes an astute observer of the culturally constructed differences between boys and girls. Elaine knows the "unspoken rules of boys," but because she is unfamiliar with the "customs" of girls when she is introduced to their world at the age of eight, she feels "awkward" in their presence. Sensing that she is "always on the verge of some unforeseen, calamitous blunder," she finds playing with girls "different," and she feels "strange" and "self-conscious," as if she is "doing an imitation of a girl" (50, 55). "You didn't know what a *cold wave* is?" (55), asks an incredulous Carol as she guides Elaine through the unfamiliar terrain of pageboys and hairdressers, twin beds and coat trees, twin sets and rubber gloves, rooms that one can look at but not enter, and cupboards full of clothes.

Insistently, the narrative contrasts the unruly world of boys, which Elaine partially inhabits with her brother, and the orderly world of girls. Elaine and her brother practice burping at will, they fill their mouths with water to see how far they can spit, they send coded messages to each other, and they kick and nudge each other under the table. In contrast, Elaine and her first two girlfriends, Carol Campbell and Grace Smeath, play school, a game in which Elaine is taught the feminine virtues of obedience and decorum. "Grace is always the teacher, Carol and I the students. . . . We can't pretend to be bad, because Grace doesn't like disorder" (56). Similarly, when Elaine and Carol color in Grace's Veronica Lake and Esther Williams coloring books, they must "stay inside the lines. She likes to get these books all colored in. She tells us what colors to use, on which parts. I know what my brother would do—green skin for Esther, with beetle antennae, and hairy legs for Veronica, eight of them—but I refrain from doing it" (56). Under the tutelage of Grace and Carol, Elaine cuts figures and household objects out of the *Eaton's Catalogue* and pastes them into a scrapbook. Although this activity seems "implausible" to Elaine when she and her family return to the Canadian bush the following summer (71), the effortless world of girlhood play does have an odd appeal. For with girls, unlike with boys, Elaine does not have to "keep up with anyone, run as fast, aim as well. . . . All I have to do is sit on the floor and cut frying pans out of the *Eaton's Catalogue* with embroidery scissors, and say I've done it badly. Partly this is a relief" (57). And yet Elaine retains her loyalty to the world of her brother who is "on the side of ox eyeballs, toe jam under the microscope, the outrageous, the subversive. Outrageous to whom, subversive of what? Of Grace and Mrs. Smeath, of tidy paper ladies pasted into scrapbooks" (132–33).

Predisposed by the narrative to give priority to Elaine's relationship with Cordelia, the reader is also provided an unmistakable narrative signal in Elaine's description of her first encounter with Cordelia. "I look at her, empty of premonition," Elaine comments (73). Initially Elaine feels a bond with Cordelia because of her apparent breach of female decorum. When Cordelia tells Elaine that she has "dog poop" on her shoe and Elaine replies, "It's only a rotten apple," Cordelia's response is telling. "'It's the same color though, isn't it? . . . Not the hard kind, the soft squooshy kind, like peanut butter.' This time her voice is confiding, as if she's talking about something intimate that only she and I know about and agree on. She creates a circle of two, takes me in" (75). But although Cordelia initially "creates a circle of two," she soon becomes the key player in a very cruel game of social intimidation in which Elaine is repeatedly forced to assume the role of the beleaguered outsider who is terrorized by the group. *Cat's Eye,* in its focus on Elaine's torments at the hands of her "friends," elaborates on descriptions of girlhood found in Atwood's earlier novels, recalling how other Atwood characters—the Surfacer, Joan Foster, and Lesje—are taunted and bullied by their girl-hood companions (see *Surfacing* 82–83, *Lady Oracle* 58–67, *Life Before Man* 244).

With ideological intent, *Cat's Eye* describes the methods by which femininity is constructed in our culture. Repeating what has been done to them, Elaine's friends determine to "improve" Elaine; that is, they attempt to coerce her to be a proper little girl and to mimic culturally prescribed feminine behavior. In an unconscious imitation of their parents' disciplinary behavior and speech, they tell her she is "not measuring up" and "will have to do better"; they torment her for her "own good" because they are her "best friends"; and they insist that they want to help her "improve" (123, 122). Under the surveillance of her friends, Elaine becomes plagued by self-doubt. And as she internalizes the monitoring voices of her friends, she begins the process of self-monitoring. "I worry about what I've said today, the expression on my face, how I walk, what I wear, because all of these things need improvement. I am not normal, I am not like other girls. Cordelia tells me so, but she will help me. Grace and Carol will help me too. It will take hard work and a long time" (124–25). In girlhood, as *Cat's Eye* reveals, we find early evidence of the inflexible social control of the female body.

Like an overcontrolling, fault-finding bad mother, Cordelia badgers Elaine. "'Stand up straight! People are looking! . . . Don't hunch over. . . . Don't move your arms like that'" (126). "'Look at yourself! Just look!'" Cordelia says, holding a mirror up to Elaine's face. "Her voice is disgusted, fed up, as if my face, all by itself, has been up to something, has gone too far" (168). "'Wipe that smirk off your face,'" Cordelia commands Elaine (183). Striving to be perfect in her pathetic desire to win the approval of others, Elaine feels that she is "always being watched" and that she may "step over some line" she doesn't know exists

(127). And yet, despite her growing paranoia and sense of victimization, she continues to believe that Cordelia wants to "help" her, that "they all do. They are my friends, my girl friends, my best friends. I have never had any before and I'm terrified of losing them. I want to please" (126).

"When I was put into the hole I knew it was a game; now I know it is not one," Elaine says, recalling how her friends buried her in a hole in Cordelia's backyard. This incident is presented as deeply traumatic—as Elaine's first entry into the abyss of girlhood anxiety and despair. But the narrative also aestheticizes the pain of what is being described by strategically focusing attention both on the difficulty of the narrative reconstruction of the past and on the text's thematic preoccupation with the experience of self-in-time.

Claiming that she felt "sadness, a sense of betrayal" and then "terror" as the darkness pressed down on her, Elaine also asserts that she cannot "really remember" what happened to her or what she "really felt" while she was buried in the hole. "Maybe nothing happened, maybe these emotions I remember are not the right emotions," she remarks. "I have no image of myself in the hole; only a black square filled with nothing, a square like a door. Perhaps the square is empty; perhaps it's only a marker, a time marker that separates the time before it from the time after. The point at which I lost power" (112–13). Although this incident is carefully marked in the text as deeply meaningful—as a key metaphor for unraveling the mystery of Elaine's narcissistically damaged self—it is also presented as a narrative gap, an omission. "I close my eyes, wait for pictures. I need to fill in the black square of time, go back to see what's in it. It's as if I vanish at that moment and reappear later, but different, not knowing why I have been changed." In an attempt to fill in time's black square, Elaine conjures up a picture of deadly nightshade, envisioning "a thicket of dark-green leaves with purple blossoms, dark purple, a sad rich color, and clusters of red berries, translucent as water." She presents this as an authentic memory only to insist, once again, that "it's the wrong memory" (113–14). Despite the fact that Elaine subsequently describes the "grief" attached to this text-identified screen memory (114), there remains in the narrative a continuing suggestion not only of buried or omitted information but also of buried emotion.

Because the reader of *Cat's Eye* is positioned as an empathic insider—both as Elaine's confidant and as a privileged observer of what is largely hidden from others—proximity to Atwood's character can be unsettling, if not anxiety-provoking, most particularly in those scenes that describe her intensifying victimization at the hands of her girlfriends and her resultant dissociation from reality and acts of self-mutilation. But, as is characteristic of Atwood's fiction, even as the narrative focuses on Elaine's experiences of self-dissolution, it also involves the reader in the process of pattern-hunting and consistency-building as images and fantasies associated with the narrator's buried past—such as the cat's eye marble and the fantasy of falling from a great height—repeat and circulate in the text and ultimately find their way into the novel's descriptions of Elaine's surrealistic art.

Learning to defend her fragile self by distancing herself from reality, Elaine fantasizes that her favorite marble—the blue cat's eye—has "power" and can protect her from her friends. Fascinated with the blue "eye part of it," which is like "something frozen in the ice," she imagines that she can "see" in the same way that the marble sees. "I can see people moving like bright animated dolls, their mouths opening and closing but no real words coming out. I can look at their shapes and sizes, their colors, without feeling anything else about them. I am alive in my eyes only" (150–51). As the novel reveals in such passages, Elaine's girlhood torments are what "decisively form and catalyze the creating self," for it is in moments of "fear, hatred, and shame" that the powerless girl "begins to see, eidetically and iconically" (McCombs, "Contrary Rememberings" 10). From the detached cat's eye perspective, Elaine's friends look "like puppets" and Elaine can "see them or not, at will" (165). Similarly, when Elaine faints, she discovers that there is "a way out of places you want to leave, but can't. Fainting is like stepping sideways, out of your own body, out of time or into another time. When you wake up it's later. Time has gone on without you" (182). Subsequently accused by Cordelia of fainting on purpose, Elaine begins to spend time "outside" her body without fainting. "At these times I feel blurred, as if there are two of me, one superimposed on the other, but imperfectly. There's an edge of transparency, and beside it a rim of solid flesh that's without feeling, like a scar. I can see what's happening, I can hear what's being said to me, but I don't have to pay any attention. My eyes are open but I'm not there. I'm off to the side" (184).

In a desperate attempt to retain a sense of self-reality, Elaine peels the skin off her feet in "narrow strips" going "down as far as the blood." Although her peeled feet make it "painful to walk, but not impossible," the pain also gives her "something definite to think about, something immediate," and thus "something to hold on to" (120). Despite the narrator's factual, dispassionate voice, this description of Elaine's self-mutilation is a deliberately disturbing one. Clearly meant to provoke a visceral response from readers, this passage may also promote the act of literary detection, calling to mind not only Atwood's frequent use of the red shoes motif in her novels but, more particularly, her earlier descriptions in *Lady Oracle* and *The Handmaid's Tale* of Joan Foster's and Moira's bloodied, injured feet.

Elaine feels more and more threatened as Cordelia, seemingly driven by the "urge to see how far she can go," becomes "harsher, more relentless" in her bullying (164). Elaine's heightening disintegration anxiety is reflected in her fantasies. She imagines she will "burst inward . . . implode"; she thinks that if she seeks comfort from her mother, who tells her to "have more backbone," the "little backbone" she has left "will crumble away to nothing"; she feels that Cordelia is backing her "toward an edge, like the edge of a cliff: one step back, another step, and I'll be over and falling" (151, 167, 164). As her situation becomes unendurable, she thinks about eating the deadly nightshade berries or drinking poison, and she imagines jumping off the ravine bridge, "smashing down there like a pumpkin, half of an eye, half of a grin." Although she does not want to do such things, for indeed she is "afraid of them," she nevertheless imagines Cordelia telling her to do them, "not in her scornful voice, [but] in her kind one. I hear her kind voice inside my head. *Do it. Come on.* I would be doing these things to please her" (165–66). While the text insists that Elaine's self-fragility stems solely from her relationship with her girlhood friends, it also tells us that her friends are impersonating "someone much older" (205): that Cordelia is imitating her father and Grace her mother. This suggests not only a much earlier point of origin for the psychic wounds inflicted on Elaine and thus for her consequent narcissistic vulnerability, but also that the girlhood drama in *Cat's Eye* stages scenes which are denied in, and thus omitted from, the family drama.

A scene charged with emotion, the ravine incident is meant both to provoke an angry response from readers and to generate a powerful wish to see Elaine rescued. That this incident happens on one of Cordelia's "friendly days," when Elaine allows herself to laugh in her "grab at the ordinary" (196), makes it all the more poignant. When, predictably, the mood turns ugly and Cordelia punishes the narrator by throwing her hat into the ravine and then commanding her to retrieve it, Elaine feels that her laughter "was unreal after all, merely a gasp for air" (198). Subsequently abandoned by her friends, Elaine falls through the ice and almost freezes to death. Suffering not only physical but also psychic endangerment, she imagines that she will become like the dead people who are dissolved in the cold water of the creek. "If I don't move soon I will be frozen in the creek. I will be a dead person, peaceful and clear, like them" (199).

But then, as Elaine succumbs to the cold, her head filling with "black sawdust" and her body feeling "weightless" (200), she sees the Virgin Mary walking on the air toward her. Disrupting the realistic surface of the text with this sudden intrusion of the fantastic, the narrative acts out a reparative urge through its dramatization of a healing union with the idealized mother. "I can see the white glimmer of her face. . . . She holds out her arms to me and I feel a surge of happiness. Inside her half-open cloak there's a glimpse of red. . . . It must be her heart, on the outside of her body, glowing like neon, like a coal. Then I can't see her any more. But I feel her around me, not like arms but like a small wind of warmer air" (201). Suggestively, when Elaine's mother, who has been searching for her, embraces her, the Virgin Mary "is suddenly gone" and "[p]ain and cold shoot back" into her (203). As the delusion is dispelled, Elaine abruptly returns to the real world of childhood bereavement and numbing despair. Despite the narrative's depiction of the ravine incident as a near fatal accident, it also is a thinly veiled enactment both of the suicidal fantasies that long have plagued Elaine and of a fantasy of restitution, an attempt by the narrative to convert trauma into a magical—and purely fictional—rescue.

And yet, if *Cat's Eye* acts out the dramatic rescue of Elaine, it is also, to quote Hermione Lee, "horrifyingly brilliant" in its depiction of Elaine's torture and thus is able to "strike home to anyone who was ever involved in childhood gang warfare, whether as bullier or bullied" (39). A narrative that both communicates and generates intense feelings, *Cat's Eye* prompts readers not only to come to Elaine's defense, but also to accuse her accusers. The "point" of the ravine incident, writes Anita Brookner, "is that had the girls been older this would have been a clear case of attempted murder" (32). Directed by the text, commentators have harshly judged Cordelia, who has been variously described as Elaine's "torturer" and "guide through the hell of childhood"; as a "mean-spirited brat"; and as "an incarnation of evil" (Manguel 67; Kanfer; Brookner 32).

Just as commentators participate in the text's condemnation of Cordelia, so they praise its "gruesome description" of the "puritanical and censorious Mrs. Smeath" (Lee 39) and its retaliatory plot against her. "This woman inspired a virulent and justified hatred in the child Elaine, and the adult took an artist's time-honoured revenge: Mrs. Smeath . . . hangs in slug-like nakedness for all to see," writes one commentator

(Mackay). Elaine, writes another, "has a delicious, nasty way of using details from childhood in her paintings," many of which "involve unclothed versions of Grace's lumpish, self-righteous mother" (Caryn James). A character readers love to hate and a target of much of the text's rage, Mrs. Smeath is described in minute, malicious detail and her physically grotesque body is deliberately put on display. A big-boned woman, she has large, red, knuckly hands; she wears metal-rimmed glasses on her bland, rounded potato face; she has a slight mustache and large teeth; she has sagging breasts that seem, under her bibbed apron, to be a single breast that reaches to her thick waist. Rendered immobile in the afternoons because of her bad heart, she lies "unmoving, like something in a museum, with her head on the antimacassar pinned to the arm of the chesterfield, a bed pillow under her neck, the rubber plant on the landing visible behind her" (62). Fascinated with Mrs. Smeath's "bad heart," Elaine pictures it "hidden, underneath her woolen afghan and the billow of her apron bib, pumping in the thick fleshy darkness of the inside of her body: something taboo, intimate." To Elaine, Mrs. Smeath's bad heart is "compelling," a "curiosity, a deformity. A horrible treasure" (61, 62).

One of the reasons that the prepubescent Elaine finds this fetishized body part so compelling is that she unconsciously equates it with the sexually mature female body, which seems "alien and bizarre, hairy, squashy, monstrous" (97). Although Elaine finds it difficult to think of her mother as having a body—and indeed, her mother's physical being is all but erased from the text—she studies and comments on Mrs. Smeath's fleshy body. Similarly, Elaine imagines not her parents, but instead the Smeaths, having sexual intercourse, envisioning them in a repulsive, insectlike embrace, the two of them naked, with Mr. Smeath "stuck to the back of Mrs. Smeath" (99). When years later Elaine tries to draw a naked woman who is posing for her Life Drawing art class, her disgust at the monstrousness of the uncontained, uncontrollable female body all but overwhelms her. "There is a lot of flesh to her, especially below the waist; there are folds across her stomach, her breasts are saggy and have enormous dark nipples." Repeating an image that recurs in Atwood's fiction, Elaine comments that the "massiveness" of the woman's body "makes her head look like an afterthought" and admits that she is "afraid of turning into that" (284).

"Why do I hate her so much?" Elaine asks of Mrs. Smeath (62, also 369). If Mrs. Smeath stands in the text as an image of the female as alien other—as grotesque woman/body—she also belongs to the long line of Atwoodian bad mothers. Indeed, her cardiac condition is an apt symbol of her maternal malevolence. Asserting the right to interpret and judge Elaine—to assume a kind of hermeneutic control over her—Mrs. Smeath speaks in the disciplinary, punishing voice of religious conservatism. And she is also, in effect, an accessory to the crime of Elaine's victimization as Elaine learns when she overhears a conversation between Mrs. Smeath and her sister. Motivated by a desire "to be good, to follow instructions" (131), Elaine accompanies the Smeath family to church only to be described as "exactly like a heathen" by Mrs. Smeath's sister. When the sister asks whether the other girls are being "too hard" on Elaine, Mrs. Smeath responds, "It's God's punishment. . . . It serves her right" (190–91).

Recognizing that the righteous, puritanical Mrs. Smeath knows and approves of how the other girls are treating her and that she has done nothing to stop it, Elaine becomes enraged. Her hatred is palpable: it is a "heavy, thick hatred" associated, interestingly enough, with the primal fantasy of the bad breast—"with a particular shape, the shape of Mrs. Smeath's one breast and no waist." In a vivid fantasy of revenge, Elaine imagines Mrs. Smeath going, legs first, through the wringer of a washing machine, her "bones cracking and flattening, skin and flesh squeezing up toward her head, which will pop in a minute like a huge balloon of blood" (191). When Mrs. Smeath, suddenly aware that Elaine has been eavesdropping, gives her "smug" smile, Elaine imagines that Mrs. Smeath's "bad heart floats in her body like an eye, an evil eye, it sees me" (192). Now imagining that God is on Mrs. Smeath's side—"Mrs. Smeath has God all sewed up, she knows what things are his punishments. He's on her side, and it's a side from which I'm excluded"— Elaine begins to pray to the Virgin Mary, which is "something dangerous, rebellious, perhaps even blasphemous" (192, 194). In the coded world of the text, Mrs. Smeath, with her bad heart and her damaging words, represents the bad mother, and the Virgin Mary, with her glowing red heart and warm nurturing touch, the good mother. It is revealing, then, that the idealized mother is all but absent from the text while the monstrous Mrs. Smeath recurs again and again, her image doubling and redoubling and ultimately undergoing multiple transformations in Elaine's art.

If Elaine's artistic renderings of Mrs. Smeath grow out of a desire for retaliation, they also are driven by the need to master this persecutory figure from the past. Taking artistic revenge on the woman who injured her, Elaine depicts a naked Mrs. Smeath flying heavily through the air with Mr. Smeath stuck to her back; Mrs. Smeath reclining on her velvet sofa and ascending to a heaven filled with rubber plants; Mrs. Smeath peeling potatoes with her sickle-moon paring knife; Mrs. Smeath clad only in indigo blue bloomers or wrapped in white tissue paper; Mrs. Smeath with half of her face peeling off; Mrs. Smeath with her one large breast sectioned to show her dark-red, diseased heart. "One picture of Mrs. Smeath leads to another. She multiplies on the walls like bacteria, standing, sitting, flying, with clothes, without clothes, following me around with her many eyes . . . ," as Elaine comments (354). By subjecting the condemning Mrs. Smeath to the artist's condemnation and by regarding Mrs. Smeath voyeuristically as the framed object of the artist's disciplinary gaze, Elaine attempts to subdue and contain the monstrous mother/female.

The tenuousness of this artistic containment is suggested in a scene in which Elaine, attending the opening of an all-women group show which includes her varied renderings of Mrs. Smeath, mistakenly identifies a woman who comes to protest the exhibit first as Mrs. Smeath and then as her daughter, Grace. "It's as if she's stepped down off the wall, the walls: the same round raw potato face, the hulky big-boned frame, the glittering spectacles and hairpin crown. My gut clenches in fear; then there's that rancid hate, flashing up in an instant." Although Elaine feels that she is "in control" when the woman makes a "spectacle" of herself, the woman's condemnation of Elaine—"You are disgusting. . . . You are taking the Lord's name in vain. Why do you want to hurt people?" (370)—is also a repetition of girlhood traumas. But in this adult duplication of the past, which seems deliberately staged by the narrative, the powerful and overcontrolling Mrs. Smeath is rendered impotent and her injurious, judgmental speech is dialogically contested and turned against her. Not only is the Mrs. Smeath stand-in judged by the onlookers to be a "religious nut case" and a "reactionary," but her symbolic attack on one of Elaine's paintings of Mrs. Smeath, ironically enough, instantly transforms Elaine into an artist who commands the respect and confirming attention of others. As Elaine comments, "[P]aintings that can get bottles of ink thrown at them, that can inspire such outraged violence, such uproar and display, must have an odd revolutionary power. I will seem audacious, and brave. Some dimension of heroism has been added to me" (371).

Yet, despite Elaine's heroic public image and her artistic success, she retains an inner sense of depletion and despair. "Cordelia. . . . You made me believe I was nothing," she thinks as she recalls the traumas of her girlhood (211). Whereas Elaine paints multiple versions of Mrs. Smeath in an attempt to master the past, she does only one painting of Cordelia. Entitled *Half a Face,* it reflects the psychic horror of Elaine's adolescent relationship with Cordelia. Although, after the ravine incident, Elaine attempts to free herself from the lethal influence of her girlhood friend by simply walking away—a defensive behavior she will repeat again and again in her adult relationships—she does not escape. Instead, she internalizes Cordelia as an aspect of her own personality. Thus, when Elaine becomes an adolescent, her lurking fears are provoked by a horror comic book story in which a pretty sister looks into a mirror and sees her disfigured sister, who has a burn covering half of her face, gazing back at her. Reacting to the story, Elaine fantasizes that she will discover that there is somebody else "trapped" in her body: "I'll look into the bathroom mirror and see the face of another girl, someone who looks like me but has half of her face darkened, the skin burned away" (224). In *Half a Face,* Elaine reflects her psychic twinship with Cordelia. It depicts Cordelia's face in the foreground, and hanging on the wall behind her is another face, which is covered with a white cloth. Although she attempted to paint Cordelia as belligerent, Cordelia's eyes, which give the face a hesitant, fearful look, "sabotaged" her. "Cordelia is afraid of me, in this picture. I am afraid of Cordelia. I'm not afraid of seeing Cordelia. I'm afraid of being Cordelia. Because in some way we changed places, and I've forgotten when" (239). Similarly, at one point, Cordelia puts on a pair of sunglasses and Elaine suggestively sees herself, "in duplicate and monochrome, and a great deal smaller than life-size," in Cordelia's "mirror eyes" (317).

When Elaine, who is missing time from her past and thus has "forgotten" (213) how Cordelia once tormented her, becomes friends once again with Cordelia in high school, they exchange roles. Now Elaine learns about Cordelia's traumatic childhood and how she was subjected to her father's verbal assaults. "'Wipe that smirk off your face,'" Cordelia's father would tell her—this being one of the commands Cordelia used when she bullied Elaine (268, 183). Repeating what was done to her by Cordelia, Elaine, by the eleventh grade, becomes known for her "mean mouth." "I don't use it unless provoked, but then I open my mean mouth and short, devastating comments come out of it" (247). When she hurts other people, she wants her hurts to "be intentional," and the person she uses her mean mouth on the most is Cordelia: "She doesn't even have to provoke me, I use her as target practice." Although Elaine's father warns her that her "sharp tongue" will one day get her "in trouble," she realizes that she has come to "enjoy the risk, the sensation of vertigo" when she recognizes that she has "shot right over the border of the socially acceptable," that she is "walking on thin ice, on empty air" (248). As this allusion to the pivotal ravine incident suggests, Elaine attempts to achieve active mastery over passive suffering by verbally terrorizing others. And through her aggressive and transgressive dialogic speech, she also openly challenges the "socially acceptable" voices of bourgeois culture.

In the kind of energic exchange we have observed in other dramatizations of the dyadic relationship in Atwood's art, Elaine seems to grow stronger at Cordelia's expense. Having incorporated the poisonous aspects of Cordelia's personality, Elaine becomes a sadistic persecutor who feeds off Cordelia's energy. Indeed, she tells Cordelia that she is a "vampire," one of a pair of identical twins. "'I have a coffin full of earth where I sleep; it's down in, down in'—I search for a likely place—'the cellar.' . . . 'You're my friend, I thought it was time you knew. I'm really dead. I've been dead for years.'" Taking pleasure in Cordelia's uneasiness, Elaine also has "a denser, more malevolent little triumph to finger: energy has passed between us, and I am stronger" (245, 246).

Unlike Elaine, who is successful in her high school studies, Cordelia fails more and more exams as she finds it increasingly difficult to concentrate. Both Cordelia's mental distraction and her physical decline—she becomes a physical "wreck" (271)—are signs of her growing psychic disintegration. Visiting Cordelia some years later in the "rest home"—a "discreet private loony bin" (373)—Elaine sees in Cordelia's fleshy body an image of the monstrous, uncontained femininity which has long disturbed her. "[S]he has put on weight. Or has she? Flesh has been added, but it has slid down, toward the middle of her body, like mud sliding down a hill. The long bones have risen to the surface of her face, the skin tugged downward on them as if by irresistible gravitational pull. I can see how she'll be when she's old" (374–75). When Cordelia explains why she tried to commit suicide—"It just came over me. I was tired"—Elaine feels that Cordelia "has placed herself beyond me, out of my reach, where I can't get at her. She has let go of her idea of herself. She is lost" (376). Despite Cordelia's affected bravado, Elaine recognizes her friend's narcissistic vulnerability. "There's a frantic child in there, behind that locked, sagging face" (377).

Although Elaine "gently" refuses Cordelia's request for help in escaping from the rest home, she does not feel gentle toward her friend. "I am seething, with a fury I can neither explain nor express. *How dare you ask me*? I want to twist her arm, rub her face in the snow." After depositing

Cordelia at the rest home, Elaine feels "free, and weightless." But, of course, she is "not free," as her dreams indicate. In a potent dream image of self-dissolution resuscitated from her own childhood, Elaine envisions, not herself, but Cordelia falling from a cliff or bridge, her arms spread out and her skirt opened like a bell. "She never hits or lands; she falls and falls, and I wake with my heart pounding and gravity cut from under me, as in an elevator plummeting out of control." And in another dream of body-self fragmentation, Elaine envisions a mannequin. "[H]acked apart and glued back together," the statue "ends at the neck. Underneath its arm, wrapped in a white cloth, is Cordelia's head" (378, 379). Although Elaine physically escapes Cordelia, she is unable to expel the Cordelia within. "The last time I saw Cordelia, she was going through the door of the rest home. That was the last time I talked to her. Although it wasn't the last time she talked to me" (384).

That Elaine's forgetting is also a form of remembering becomes evident in her adult relationships with men. The painting *Falling Women,* for example, in which Elaine expresses her anxiety about men, also contains the residue of much earlier fears. *Falling Women* shows three women falling off a bridge, their wind-blown skirts opened into bells as they approach the unseen men who, "jagged and dark," lie far below. In Elaine's analysis, this painting depicts women who have hurt themselves by falling onto men. But *Falling Women* also conflates imagery associated with Elaine's girlhood anxieties about self-disintegration, as well as her dream image of Cordelia falling from a height, her skirt blown open like a bell. To fall in love, as this painting suggests, is not only to suffer a loss of self-control but also to put the self at serious risk. If the painting of *Falling Women* begins in Elaine's "confusion about words" (282), the words behind this painterly conception can be found in *The Handmaid's Tale: "Falling in love,"* Offred thinks at one point as she recalls the romantic ideology of the pre-Gilead world. "We were falling women. We believed in it, this downward motion: so lovely, like flying, and yet at the same time so dire, so extreme, so unlikely" (292). Similarly, Elaine remarks of "fallen women": "There was some suggestion of downward motion, against one's will. . . . Fallen women were not pulled-down women or pushed women, merely fallen" (282).

Like other Atwood novels, *Cat's Eye* contrives to undermine the romance plot and to dialogize romantic discourse. Although Elaine, as an art student, feels that she is "beyond marriage," and indeed views love as "obsession, with undertones of nausea" (311, 307), she nevertheless falls in love with her art teacher, Josef. But even before her affair begins, the novel purposefully describes a conversation between two women about an exhibitionist. "So I looked him in the eye—the *eye*—and I said, 'Can't you do any better than that?' I mean, talk about weenies. No wonder the poor boob runs around in train stations trying to get somebody to look at it!" Similarly, female sexuality is denigrated by men in their discussions of women: "'Cunt like an elephant's arse,' 'How would you know, eh, screw elephants much?'" (307, 294). And yet, despite its resistance to romantic discourse, *Cat's Eye* also reveals how easily women can become ensnared in the romance plot. As in other novels by Atwood we have examined in the course of this study, *Cat's Eye* views the love relationship as a potential form of bondage and persecution which endangers, rather than enhances, female selfhood.

In her affair with Josef, Elaine initially falls in love with "his need" which seems, at times, "helpless and beyond his control" (310). Yet, she also becomes helpless as he, in a reenactment of Elaine's girlhood friends' attempts to "improve" her, begins to assume control over her: "Josef is rearranging me. 'You should wear your hair loose,' he says, unpinning it. . . . I stand still and let him do this. I let him do what he likes. It's August and too hot to move. . . . I move through the days like a zombie. . . . 'You should wear purple dresses,' says Josef. 'It would be an improvement'" (319). Relentlessly, Josef rearranges her to fulfill his ideal of feminine beauty. Catching a glimpse of herself in the mirror on one occasion, Elaine is aware of what he sees in her: "a slim woman with cloudy hair, pensive eyes in a thin white face. I recognize the style: late nineteenth century. Pre-Raphaelite. I should be holding a poppy." When Josef tells her she is "mysterious," she realizes that she does not feel mysterious but instead "vacant" (320, 321). For Elaine, as for other Atwoodian characters we have encountered, the enactment of the feminine masquerade—in which the woman participates in the man's desire but at the cost of renouncing her own—leads to a sense of self-alienation and inauthenticity.

Elaine recognizes that she might find Josef "silly" if she could only see him "objectively"; instead she finds him "a source of power, nebulous and shifting." He also is an object of fear. "He tells me, casually, in the same way he told me about shooting a man in the head, that in most countries except this one a woman belongs to a man: if a man finds his woman with another man, he kills both of them and everyone excuses him" (333, 332). Although Josef poses a potential threat to Elaine, that threat is acted out, interestingly enough, in the peripheral, displaced drama of the Susie-Josef love affair.

While Elaine feels zombielike and vacant, as if Josef is vampiristically feeding off her energy, Susie is rendered "drained and boneless" as a result of her affair with Josef and consequent abortion (339). "Everything that's happened to her could well have happened to me," Elaine thinks while another "small, mean voice, ancient and smug" that comes from "deep inside" her says, "*It serves her right*" (337). Elaine both empathizes with Susie's plight and, repeating Mrs. Smeath's words, is harshly judgmental. Now perceiving a guilt-stricken Josef as "weak . . . clinging, gutted like a fish," Elaine finds herself unable to respect a man "who can allow himself to be reduced to such rubble by women" and so she walks away from the relationship. "It's enormously pleasing to me, this act of walking away. It's like being able to make people appear and vanish, at will" (338, 339).

Although Elaine assumes control in her affair with Josef, she experiences a frightening loss of control when she discovers that her relationship with Jon has resulted in pregnancy. "I feel as if I'm at the center of nothingness, of a black square that is totally empty; that I'm exploding slowly outward, into the cold burning void of space," she says (353). While *Cat's Eye* suggests that Elaine's anxieties about pregnancy originate in her fear that Jon will insist she have an abortion, the narrative, nevertheless, contains traces of the pregnancy fears that surface in other novels by Atwood. "[C]ocooned" in her body, which swells "like a slow flesh balloon," she lapses "into a voluptuous sloth." In a revival of the vampiristic fantasy of energic exchange, she thinks that perhaps the foetus is "sponging up" her adrenaline. After giving birth to a daughter, Sarah, Elaine not only imagines that she is "bulbous by comparison" with the young women she sees on the street, she also finds it difficult to paint, for she feels "clogged," as if she is swimming with her clothes on. "[P]erhaps all I will ever be is what I am now," she fears (357, 356, 359). But although Elaine temporarily succumbs to the gender code and its received categories that identify women not with the mind and culture but instead with the body and nature, she also openly contests male assumptions. When she overhears Jon telling another painter that "[s]he's mad because she's a woman," Elaine recalls how this was once "a shaming thing to say, and crushing to have it said about you, by a man. It implied oddness, deformity, sexual malfunction." Using a feminist-dialogic tactic, she turns his hostile words against him. "I'm not mad because I'm a woman. . . . I'm mad because you're an asshole" (362–63).

"I begin to see how the line is crossed, between histrionics and murder," Elaine says, describing her stormy marriage to Jon (362).

Inverting the myth of romantic fulfillment, *Cat's Eye* describes, instead, the "explosions" and "Technicolor wreckage" and days of "evasion, suppressed anger, [and] false calm" in Elaine's troubled marriage (280, 390). Insistently, the narrative describes the force of Elaine's retaliatory anger against Jon, her power to victimize him: "We have been shark to one another . . ."; "I think, I once threw things at this man. . . . I once thought I was capable of murdering him"; "I don't feel overmatched by him. Whatever he did to me, I did back, and maybe worse" (17, 279–80, 398). But it also reveals her feelings of vulnerability. In an oblique reference to the fear of male persecution dealt with more directly in earlier Atwood novels, *Cat's Eye* describes Jon's "shatter patterns"—art constructions made by smashing things and then gluing the pieces into the position of the breakage (18, 362). And in Jon's Toronto studio, Elaine finds "hacked-up" body parts, an image that calls to mind earlier Atwoodian depictions of female victimization, most particularly in *Bodily Harm* and *The Handmaid's Tale*. Also suggestive is the fact that Jon's current special effects film project is a chain-saw murder (18, 17).

Despite Elaine's insistence that she is not "overmatched" by Jon, her self-cohesion becomes more and more threatened as the failure of her marriage revives girlhood feelings of rejection and worthlessness. "I lie in the bedroom with the curtains drawn and nothingness washing over me like a sluggish wave. Whatever is happening to me is my own fault. I have done something wrong, something so huge I can't even see it, something that's drowning me. I am inadequate and stupid, without worth. I might as well be dead" (392–93). When, one night, Jon does not come back, Elaine's primitive anxieties about separation and abandonment resurface. In a recapitulation of girlhood terrors, she feels she has been left behind, "in the cold." As her disintegration anxiety heightens, she imagines the "pull of the earth" on her and "the spaces between the atoms" which she could "fall so easily through." Responding to the voice of Cordelia which urges her to "*Do it. Come on. Do it,*" she slashes her left wrist. As if Cordelia is now vampiristically feeding off her, Elaine feels "white, drained of blood" but also "purified" and "[p]eaceful" (393, 394). After the suicide attempt, Elaine finds the pressure of her relationship with Jon too much to bear and repeats what she has done time and again in the past: she leaves. "The trick is to close yourself off. Don't hear, don't see. Don't look back" (396). In a textual enactment of the desire to gain active mastery over passive suffering, Jon, who has injured and abandoned Elaine, is depicted as being injured and abandoned in return. "He's twisting now, because he misses Sarah. He calls long distance, his voice on the phone fading in and out like a wartime broadcast, plaintive with defeat, with an archaic sadness that seems, more and more, to be that of men in general" (398–99).

In her refusal to overvalue love, the middle-aged Elaine asserts her own dialogic authority as she contests the notion that romantic affiliation is at the center of a woman's life. "Old lovers go the way of old photographs, bleaching out gradually as in a slow bath of acid . . . until nothing remains but the general outlines," Elaine says of the men in her life (280). Describing her middle-aged response to having a sexual encounter with a stranger, she comments, "I'm losing the appetite for strangers. Once I would have focused on the excitement, the hazard; now it's the mess, the bother" (18). Elaine also undermines the ideology of romantic fulfillment in her description of her marriage to Ben, a man she once would have considered "too obvious, too dull, practically simple-minded." That she does not "require him," that he is "no transfusion," becomes evident in the novel's immediate dismissal of him (401). Moreover, in her painting *Life Drawing,* which depicts both Josef and Jon at their easels painting their own distinct versions of the female model (Elaine) who sits between them, her head a sphere of bluish glass, Elaine acts out a kind of painterly defeat of the men who once had power over her. In a feminist inversion of the female nude tradition in Western art, she shows both men "stark-naked but turned with a twist half away from the viewer, so what you get is the ass end" (386). Not only does *Cat's Eye* demystify the ideology of romantic love, it also openly enacts a fantasy of female revenge.

With its provocative punitive plotting and feminist-dialogic speech, *Cat's Eye* gives voice to a powerful female anger. But it also acts out a reparative urge in its closing scenes. Looking at her many paintings of Mrs. Smeath, Elaine sees that she put "a lot of work into that imagined body," that she "labored on it, with . . . considerable malice." And yet the paintings are "not only mockery, not only desecration," for she "put light into them too. Each pallid leg, each steel-rimmed eye, is there as it was, as plain as bread. I have said, *Look*. I have said, *I see*." Now in Mrs. Smeath's painted eyes, Elaine discerns not only self-righteousness and smugness but also defeat and uncertainty. Recognizing that she "went for vengeance," Elaine realizes that "[a]n eye for an eye leads only to more blindness" (427).

In a similar desire for restitution, the narrative returns, in the closing scenes, to the formative trauma of Elaine's relationship with Cordelia. Although the text encourages readers to share Elaine's irrational belief that her mental obsession with Cordelia will magically summon up her lost friend, Cordelia remains conspicuously absent from the Toronto exhibition of Elaine's art. "I've been prepared for almost anything; except absence, except silence" (435). Only when Elaine returns to the ravine—the scene of her greatest childhood terror—does she confront her lost friend, not as an adult but rather as a child. "I know she's looking at me . . . the face closed and defiant. There is the same shame, the sick feeling in my body, the same knowledge of my own wrongness, awkwardness, weakness; the same wish to be loved; the same loneliness; the same fear. But these are not my own emotions any more. They are Cordelia's; as they always were." Now the "older" and "stronger" one, Elaine, in a gesture of healing and reconciliation, reaches out her arms to the child-Cordelia. "*It's all right,* I say to her. *You can go home now*" (443).

Yet if revenge turns to reparation in this fantasy, *Cat's Eye,* while remaining silent about the actual fate of the adult Cordelia, presents and re-presents her defeat. When, for example, Elaine helps a drunken woman who has fallen on the street, she has an imaginary encounter with Cordelia. "In the clutch of the helpless I am helpless," Elaine thinks. In this reenactment of the ravine incident, Cordelia's stand-in—the drunken woman—is the frantic, abandoned child-victim and Elaine is the helping "Lady." " 'You're Our Lady and you don't love me,' " the woman says. " 'No,' I say. She's right, I don't love her. Her eyes are not brown but green. Cordelia's" (162, 163). Similarly, Elaine fantasizes Cordelia as a bag lady, dressed "in a worn coat and a knitted hat like a tea cosy, sitting on a curb, with two plastic bags filled with her only possessions, muttering to herself" (7). Counterpoised with the narrator's final gesture of reconciliation with the child-Cordelia and her yearning for the female camaraderie she and Cordelia will never experience as they get older are these potent fantasies of Cordelia's defeated adult self, which reverberate against all the other depictions of the damaged female self in the text. That the outcast Cordelia is also Elaine's cast-off mirror image is revealed in Elaine's fear that with "a slight push, a slip over some ill-defined edge," she herself "could turn into a bag lady" (406). "We are like the twins in old fables, each of whom has been given half a key" to the personality of the other, Elaine realizes (434). Thus, although it has been claimed that *Cat's Eye,* in its treatment of the friendship theme, "continues" the movement toward "a healing of the rift" between women begun in Atwood's previous novels (Rooke 132), the healing gestures in the closing scene are, at best, ambiguous.

Remarking in an interview that she finds it "curious that women should love all other women," Atwood comments that women "are not angels, nor should they be considered angels. That's a hangover from the 19th Century" (Anderson 6). According to Atwood, one of her purposes in *Cat's Eye* is "to deal with the idea that women somehow are more morally wonderful than men" (Timson 58). The essentialist notion of women's moral superiority, which Atwood attacks in *Cat's Eye*, is an outgrowth of feminist critiques of the hierarchical relations between the sexes. In this view, as Joan Cocks explains, the power of men is connected to "vice" and the powerlessness of women to "virtue or innocence" (174). According to this ideology, "when women are what they truly are, they are nurturant, caring, co-operative, and egalitarian" and they are "innocent of the will to power." Moreover, the "subterranean" life of women within the masculine order is one "in which women act in instinctual sympathy with all victims of domination, provide asylum and solace for those who have borne the brunt of male abuse, and enjoy mutually respectful and loving relations among themselves that stand in stark contrast to all they suffer through men" (178).

In dialogic opposition to the feminist ideology that views women as innocent of the will to power and that celebrates female relationships as egalitarian and nonexploitative, *Cat's Eye* describes the female community as a site of possible oppression. Elaine avoids "gatherings" of feminists. "I think they are talking about me, behind my back. They make me more nervous than ever, because they have a certain way they want me to be, and I am not that way. They want to improve me." With feminists, in other words, Elaine experiences a repetition of girlhood patterns of subordination and domination. "At times I feel defiant: what right have they to tell me what to think? I am not Woman, and I'm damned if I'll be shoved into it. *Bitch,* I think silently. *Don't boss me around*" (399). With the women at the Toronto gallery where the retrospective of her art is being planned, Elaine feels "outnumbered, as if they are a species" of which she is "not a member" (92). Thus, while Elaine envies feminists "their conviction, their optimism, their carelessness, their fearlessness about men, their camaraderie," she nevertheless defensively watches "from the sidelines," retaining the position of the detached outsider (399).

Elaine resents the attempts of feminists to appropriate and commodify her art, and she resists the label often attached to her—that of "feminist painter"—insisting that she hates "party lines" and "ghettos" (94). When Elaine first begins to paint objects—such as a silver toaster, a coffee percolator, a wringer washing machine—the images "arrive detached from any context"; similarly, images of Mrs. Smeath float up "without warning" (353, 354). Although Elaine's art finds its source in her girlhood world of objects and people, it is interpreted for its use-value to the feminist movement. Thus Elaine's early depictions of domestic objects are described as "forays . . . into the realm of female symbolism," and her painting of some people who were kind to her as a child is interpreted as a "disconcerting deconstruction of perceived gender and its relationship to perceived power" (426, 428). Similarly, the labels *"post-feminist"* and "post-modern" are attached to her work (238, 427). While others, through their critical pronouncements, attempt to assume hermeneutic control over Elaine's art, she "can no longer control these paintings, or tell them what to mean. Whatever energy they have came out of me. I'm what's left over," she insists (431). Elaine does not "like it that this is where paintings end up, on these neutral-toned walls with the track lighting, sterilized, rendered safe and acceptable. It's as if somebody's been around spraying the paintings with air freshener, to kill the smell. The smell of blood on the wall" (90). It is ironic that the gallery where Elaine's paintings are being exhibited is called Sub-Versions, for the social institutionalization of art, as this passage suggests, can affect the way others perceive it by legitimizing it and thus neutralizing its emotional appeal, its power to shock and transgress.

Directing asides to her critic/readers in these passages, as is her wont, Atwood warns against the misreading or misappropriation of her art. But even though Atwood may distrust the label "feminist," her work is decidedly feminist not only in its woman-centered approach and oppositional appeal but also in its continuing critique of patriarchy and its politics of domination and subordination. That Atwood has the courage "to turn the tables on her own kind" in *Cat's Eye* does not make her antifeminist. For as we have seen in the course of this study, Atwood despairs of the power politics inherent in all human relationships: in women's friendships, in parent-child relationships, and, most particularly, in heterosexual romance.

In *Cat's Eye,* as in her other works of fiction, Margaret Atwood deliberately sets out to transgress, to shock her readers into seeing and feeling. Because she does not shy away from the brutal, she also risks brutalizing her readers. Dealing relentlessly and repeatedly with outlawed emotions and urged by the need to shape complex narrative patterns, Atwood designs her brutal yet carefully choreographed fictions to elicit both an intellectual and emotional response from readers. If, fulfilling the critic/reader's need for omnipotent control, the patterns and themes of Atwood's fiction can be traced and schematized, there remains something impervious to analysis in Atwood's art. For her fiction puts blood on the wall as it brings into public view the dark female anxieties and passions that art can never truly frame or control.

Works
Cited

For a detailed publishing history of Atwood's writings and for an annotated bibliography of writings about Atwood (published through 1987 but with some 1988 publications included) see Judith McCombs and Carole Palmer's *Margaret Atwood: A Reference Guide* (Boston: G. K. Hall, 1991). For current information on Atwood's writings and lists of secondary sources, see "Current Atwood Checklist," which is published in the *Newsletter of the Margaret Atwood Society* at Miami University, Oxford, Ohio.

Primary Sources—Fiction

Bodily Harm. Toronto: McClelland and Stewart, 1981. New York: Bantam, 1983.

Cat's Eye. Toronto: McClelland and Stewart, 1988. New York: Doubleday, 1989.

The Edible Woman. Toronto: McClelland and Stewart, 1969. New York: Warner, 1983, 1989.

The Handmaid's Tale. Toronto: McClelland and Stewart, 1985. New York: Ballantine/ Fawcett Crest, 1987.

Lady Oracle. Toronto: McClelland and Stewart, 1976. New York: Avon/Bard, 1982. New York: Ballantine/Fawcett Crest, 1987.

Life Before Man. Toronto: McClelland and Stewart, 1979. New York: Ballantine/Fawcett Crest, 1987.

Murder in the Dark: Short Fictions and Prose Poems. Toronto: Coach House, 1983.

Surfacing. Toronto: McClelland and Stewart, 1972. New York: Warner, 1983.

Primary Sources—Nonfiction

"Amnesty International: An Address." *Second Words* 393–97.

"The Curse of Eve—Or, What I Learned in School." *Second Words* 215–28.

"An End to Audience?" *Second Words* 334–57.

"Great Unexpectations: An Autobiographical Forward." VanSpanckeren and Castro xiii– xvi.

"An Introduction to *The Edible Woman*." *Second Words* 369–70.

"On Being a 'Woman Writer': Paradoxes and Dilemmas." *Second Words* 190–204.

Second Words: Selected Critical Prose. Toronto: Anansi, 1982. Boston: Beacon, 1984.

Survival: A Thematic Guide to Canadian Literature. Toronto: Anansi, 1972.

"That Certain Thing Called the Girlfriend." *New York Times Book Review* 11 May 1986: 1, 38–39.

"Where Is How." *Publishers Weekly* 8 August 1991: 8–11.

"Writing the Male Character." *Second Words* 412–30.

Secondary Sources

Anderson, Jon. "Margaret Atwood Reigns." *Chicago Tribune* 19 March 1989, sec. 6: 1, 6.

Assiter, Alison. "Romance Fiction: Porn for Women?" *Perspectives on Pornography: Sexuality in Film and Literature.* Ed. Gary Day and Clive Bloom. New York: St. Martin's Press, 1988. 101–09.

"An *Atlantis* Interview with Margaret Atwood." *Atlantis: A Women's Studies Journal* 5.2 (Spring 1980): 202–11.

Bakhtin, Mikhail. *The Dialogic Imagination: Four Essays.* Ed. Michael Holquist. Trans. Caryl Emerson and Michael Holquist. Austin: University of Texas Press, 1981.

———. *Problems of Dostoevsky's Poetics.* Trans. R. W. Rotsel. Ann Arbor: Ardis, 1973.

Banerjee, Chinmoy. "Alice in Disneyland: Criticism as Commodity in *The Handmaid's Tale.*" *Essays on Canadian Writing* 41 (Summer 1990): 74–92.

———. "Atwood's Time: Hiding Art in *Cat's Eye.*" *Modern Fiction Studies* 36.4 (Winter 1990): 513–22.

Barry, Kathleen. *Female Sexual Slavery.* New York: New York University Press, 1979.

Bartkowski, Frances. *Feminist Utopias.* Lincoln: University of Nebraska Press, 1989.

Bartlett, Donald. "'Fact' and Form in *Surfacing.*" *University of Windsor Review* 17.1 (Fall–Winter 1982): 21–28.

Bauer, Dale M. *Feminist Dialogics: A Theory of Failed Community.* Albany: State University of New York Press, 1988.

Benjamin, Jessica. *The Bonds of Love: Psychoanalysis, Feminism, and the Problem of Domination.* New York: Pantheon, 1988.

Beran, Carol. "The Canadian Mosaic: Functional Ethnicity in Margaret Atwood's *Life Before Man.*" *Essays on Canadian Writing* 41 (Summer 1990): 59–73.

Berger, John. *Ways of Seeing.* London: Penguin, 1972.

Bergmann, Harriet. "'Teaching Them to Read': A Fishing Expedition in *The Handmaid's Tale.*" *College English* 51.8 (December 1989): 847–54.

Berman, Jaye. "A Quote of Many Colors: Women and Masquerade in Donald Barthelme's Postmodern Parody Novels." *Feminism, Bakhtin, and the Dialogic.* Ed. Dale M. Bauer and Susan Jaret McKinstry. Albany: State University of New York Press, 1991. 123–33.

Bettelheim, Bruno. *The Uses of Enchantment: The Meaning and Importance of Fairy Tales.* 1975. New York: Vintage, 1977.

Boone, Joseph Allen. *Tradition Counter Tradition: Love and the Form of Fiction.* Chicago: University of Chicago Press, 1987.

Bordo, Susan. "The Body and the Reproduction of Femininity: A Feminist Appropriation of Foucault." *Gender/Body/Knowledge: Feminist Reconstructions of Being and Knowing.* Ed. Alison M. Jaggar and Susan R. Bordo. New Brunswick: Rutgers University Press, 1989. 13–33.

Bouson, J. Brooks. *The Empathic Reader: A Study of the Narcissistic Character and the Drama of the Self.* Amherst: University of Massachusetts Press, 1989.

Brans, Jo. "Using What You're Given: An Interview with Margaret Atwood." *Southwest Review* 68.4 (Autumn 1983): 301–15. (Rpt. in *Listen to the Voices: Conversations with Contemporary Writers.* Dallas: Southern Methodist University Press, 1988. 125–47. Also in Ingersoll, *Margaret Atwood: Conversations* 140–51.)

Bromberg, Pamela. "The Two Faces of the Mirror in *The Edible Woman* and *Lady Oracle.*" VanSpanckeren and Castro 12–23.

Brookner, Anita. "Unable to Climb Out of the Abyss." *Spectator* 28 Jan. 1989: 32–33.

Brown, Rosellen. "Anatomy of Melancholia." *Saturday Review* 2 Feb. 1980: 33–35. (Excerpted in Gunton 39.)

Brydon, Diana. "Caribbean Revolution and Literary Convention." *Canadian Literature* 95 (Winter 1982): 181–85.

Campbell, Josie P. "The Woman as Hero in Margaret Atwood's *Surfacing.*" *Mosaic* 11.3 (Spring 1978): 17–28.

Caper, Robert. *Immaterial Facts: Freud's Discovery of Psychic Reality and Klein's Development of His Work.* Northvale: Aronson, 1988.

Carrington, Ildikó de Papp. "Another Symbolic Descent." *Essays on Canadian Writing* 26 (Summer 1983): 45–63.

———. "Demons, Doubles, and Dinosaurs: *Life Before Man, The Origin of Consciousness,* and 'The Icicle.'" *Essays on Canadian Writing* 33 (Fall 1986): 68–88. Rpt. in McCombs, *Critical Essays* 229–45.

———. "'I'm Stuck': The Secret Sharers in *The Edible Woman.*" *Essays on Canadian Writing* 23 (Spring 1982): 68–87.

———. "Margaret Atwood." *Canadian Writers and Their Works.* Ed. Robert Lecker, Jack David, and Ellen Quigley. Toronto: ECW Press, 1987. 9:25–116.

———. "A Swiftian Sermon." *Essays on Canadian Writing* 34 (Spring 1987): 127–32.

Castro, Jan Garden. "An Interview with Margaret Atwood, 20 April 1983." VanSpanckeren and Castro 215–32.

Chodorow, Nancy. *The Reproduction of Mothering: Psychoanalysis and the Sociology of Gender.* Berkeley and Los Angeles: University of California Press, 1978.

Christ, Carol. *Diving Deep and Surfacing: Women Writers on Spiritual Quest.* Boston: Beacon Press, 1980.

Cocks, Joan. *The Oppositional Imagination: Feminism, Critique, and Political Theory.* London: Routledge, 1989.

"A Conversation with Margaret Atwood." Mendez-Egle 172–80.

Cowart, David. *History and the Contemporary Novel.* Carbondale: Southern Illinois University Press, 1989.

Cranny-Francis, Anne. *Feminist Fiction: Feminist Uses of Generic Fiction.* New York: St. Martin's Press, 1990.

Davey, Frank. *Margaret Atwood: A Feminist Politics.* Vancouver: Talonbooks, 1984.

Davidson, Arnold E. "Future Tense: Making History in *The Handmaid's Tale.*" VanSpanckeren and Castro 113–21.

Davidson, Arnold E., and Cathy N. Davidson. "The Anatomy of Margaret Atwood's *Surfacing.*" *Ariel: A Review of International English Literature* 10.3 (July 1979): 38–54.

———, eds. *The Art of Margaret Atwood: Essays in Criticism.* Toronto: Anansi, 1981.

———. "Margaret Atwood's *Lady Oracle:* The Artist as Escapist and Seer." *Studies in Canadian Literature* 3 (1978): 166–77.

———. "Prospects and Retrospects in *Life Before Man.*" Arnold and Cathy Davidson, *The Art of Margaret Atwood* 205–21.

Davidson, Cathy. "A Feminist *1984:* Margaret Atwood Talks about Her Exciting New Novel." *Ms.* 14 (Feb. 1986): 24–26.

de Lauretis, Teresa. *Alice Doesn't: Feminism, Semiotics, Cinema.* Bloomington: Indiana University Press, 1984.

Doane, Mary Ann. "Film and the Masquerade: Theorising the Female Spectator." *Screen* 23.3–4 (Sept.–Oct. 1982): 74–87.

Donaldson, Mara. "Woman as Hero in Margaret Atwood's *Surfacing* and Maxine Hong Kingston's *The Woman Warrior.*" *Heroines of Popular Culture.* Ed. Pat Browne. Bowling Green: Bowling Green State University Popular Press, 1987. 101–13.

Draine, Betsy. "An Interview with Margaret Atwood." *Interviews with Contemporary Writers: Second Series, 1972–1982.* Ed. L. S. Dembo. Madison: University of Wisconsin Press, 1983. 366–81.

DuPlessis, Rachel Blau. *Writing Beyond the Ending: Narrative Strategies of Twentieth-Century Women Writers.* Bloomington: Indiana University Press, 1985.

Ehrenreich, Barbara. "Feminism's Phantoms." *New Republic* 17 March 1986: 33–35. (Rpt., slightly cut, in Hall 155–56.)

Ewell, Barbara. "The Language of Alienation in Margaret Atwood's *Surfacing.*" *Centennial Review* 25.2 (Spring 1981): 185–202.

Faludi, Susan. *Backlash: The Undeclared War Against American Women.* New York: Crown, 1991.

Felski, Rita. *Beyond Feminist Aesthetics: Feminist Literature and Social Change.* Cambridge: Harvard University Press, 1989.

Fitzgerald, Judith. "Fiction: 'Bodily Harm.'" *Quill and Quire* Oct. 1981: 34. Excerpted in Stine 66.

Flax, Jane. *Thinking Fragments: Psychoanalysis, Feminism, and Postmodernism in the Contemporary West.* Berkeley and Los Angeles: University of California Press, 1990.

Foley, Michael. "Satiric Intent in the 'Historical Notes' Epilogue of Margaret Atwood's *The Handmaid's Tale.*" *Commonwealth Essays and Studies* 11.2 (Spring 1989): 44–52.

Freibert, Lucy. "The Artist as Picaro: The Revelation of Margaret Atwood's *Lady Oracle.*" *Canadian Literature* 92 (Spring 1982): 23–33.

———. "Control and Creativity: The Politics of Risk in Margaret Atwood's *The Handmaid's Tale.*" McCombs, *Critical Essays* 280–91.

French, Marilyn. "Spouses and Lovers." *New York Times Book Review* 3 Feb. 1980: 1, 26. (Excerpted in Gunton and Harris 39–40.)

Froula, Christine. "The Daughter's Seduction: Sexual Violence and Literary History." *Daughters and Fathers.* Ed. Lynda Boose and Betty Flowers. Baltimore: Johns Hopkins University Press, 1989. 111–35.

Frye, Joanne S. *Living Stories, Telling Lives: Women and the Novel in Contemporary Experience.* Ann Arbor: University of Michigan Press, 1986.

Fulford, Robert. *Best Seat in the House: Memoirs of a Lucky Man.* Toronto: Collins, 1988.

———. "The Images of Atwood." *Malahat Review* 41 (Jan. 1977): 95–98.

Gardam, Jane. "Nuns and Soldiers." *Books and Bookmen* 365 (March 1986): 29–30. (Excerpted in Hall 152–53.)

Garebian, Keith. "*Surfacing:* Apocalyptic Ghost Story." *Mosaic* 9.3 (Spring 1976): 1–9.

Garrett-Petts, W. F. "Reading, Writing, and the Postmodern Condition: Interpreting Margaret Atwood's *The Handmaid's Tale*." *Open Letter* 7th ser., no. 1 (Spring 1988): 74–92.

Gibson, Graeme. "Margaret Atwood." *Eleven Canadian Novelists*. Toronto: Anansi, 1973. 5–31. (Rpt. in Ingersoll, *Margaret Atwood: Conversations* 3–19.)

Gilbert, Sandra, and Susan Gubar. *The Madwoman in the Attic: The Woman Writer and the Nineteenth-Century Literary Imagination*. New Haven: Yale University Press, 1979.

Givner, Jessie. "Mirror Images in Margaret Atwood's *Lady Oracle*." *Studies in Canadian Literature* 14.1 (1989): 139–46.

Glendinning, Victoria. "Lady Oracle." *Saturday Night* 101 (Jan. 1986): 39–41. (Rpt. in Hall 146–47.)

———. "Survival of the Fittest." *Washington Post Book World* 27 Jan. 1980: 4. (Excerpted in Gunton and Harris 38–39.)

Godard, Barbara. "My (m)Other, My Self: Strategies for Subversion in Atwood and Hébert." *Essays on Canadian Writing* 26 (Summer 1983): 13–44.

———. "Telling It Over Again: Atwood's Art of Parody." *Canadian Poetry* 21 (Fall–Winter 1987): 1–30.

Goetsch, Paul. "Margaret Atwood's *Life Before Man* as a Novel of Manners." *Gaining Ground: European Critics on Canadian Literature*. Ed. Robert Kroetsch and Reingard M. Nischik. Western Canadian Literary Documents Series. Vol. 6. Edmonton: NeWest Press, 1985. 137–49.

Grace, Sherrill. "In Search of Demeter: The Lost, Silent Mother in *Surfacing*." VanSpanckeren and Castro 35–47.

———. "'Time Present and Time Past': *Life Before Man*." *Essays on Canadian Writing* 20 (Winter 1980–81): 165–70.

———. *Violent Duality: A Study of Margaret Atwood*. Montréal: Véhicule, 1980.

Grace, Sherrill, and Lorraine Weir, eds. *Margaret Atwood: Language, Text, and System*. Vancouver: University of British Columbia Press, 1983.

Greene, Gayle. *Changing the Story: Feminist Fiction and the Tradition*. Bloomington: Indiana University Press, 1991.

———. "*Life Before Man:* 'Can Anything Be Saved?'" VanSpanckeren and Castro 65–84.

———. "Margaret Atwood's *The Edible Woman:* 'Rebelling Against the System.'" Mendez-Egle 95–115.

Griffin, Susan. *Pornography and Silence: Culture's Revenge Against Nature*. New York: Harper, 1981.

Guédon, Marie-Françoise. "*Surfacing:* Amerindian Themes and Shamanism." Grace and Weir 91–111.

Gunton, Sharon, and Laurie Harris, eds. *Contemporary Literary Criticism*. Vol. 15. Detroit: Gale, 1980.

Hales, Leslie-Ann. "Genesis Revisited: The Darkening Vision of Margaret Atwood." *The Month*, 2nd n.s. 20.7 (July 1987): 257–62.

Hall, Sharon K. ed. *Contemporary Literary Criticism Yearbook*. Vol. 44. Detroit: Gale, 1987.

Hammer, Stephanie Barbé. "The World as It Will Be? Female Satire and the Technology of Power in *The Handmaid's Tale*." *Modern Language Studies* 20.2 (Spring 1990): 39–49.

Hammond, Karla. "An Interview with Margaret Atwood." *American Poetry Review* 8 (Sept.–Oct. 1979): 27–29. (Rpt. in Ingersoll, *Margaret Atwood: Conversations* 109–120.)

———. "A Margaret Atwood Interview with Karla Hammond." *Concerning Poetry* 12.2 (Fall 1978): 73–81. (Rpt. in Ingersoll, *Margaret Atwood: Conversations* 99–108.)

Hancock, Geoff. "Margaret Atwood." *Canadian Writers at Work: Interviews with Geoff Hancock*. Toronto: Oxford University Press, 1987. 256–87. (Rpt. in Ingersoll, *Margaret Atwood: Conversations* 191–220.)

Hansen, Elaine. "Fiction and (Post)Feminism in Atwood's *Bodily Harm*." *Novel* 19.1 (Fall 1985): 5–21.

Harcourt, Joan. "Atwood Country." *Queen's Quarterly* 80.2 (Summer 1973): 278–81.

Harkness, David. "Alice in Toronto: The Carrollian Intertext in *The Edible Woman*." *Essays on Canadian Writing* 37 (Spring 1989): 103–11.

Harrison, James. "The 20,000,000 Solitudes of *Surfacing*." *Dalhousie Review* 59.1 (Spring 1979): 74–81.

Hirsch, Marianne. *The Mother/Daughter Plot: Narrative, Psychoanalysis, Feminism*. Bloomington: Indiana University Press, 1989.

Hite, Molly. *The Other Side of the Story: Structures and Strategies of Contemporary Feminist Narrative*. Ithaca: Cornell University Press, 1989.

Howells, Coral Ann. *Private and Fictional Words: Canadian Women Novelists of the 1970s and 1980s*. London: Methuen, 1987.

Hubbard, Kim. "Reflected in Margaret Atwood's *Cat's Eye*, Girlhood Looms as a Time of Cruelty and Terror." *People Weekly* 8 March 1989: 205–06.

Hutcheon, Linda. *The Canadian Postmodern: A Study of Contemporary English-Canadian Fiction*. Oxford and Toronto: Oxford University Press, 1988.

———. "From Poetic to Narrative Structures: The Novels of Margaret Atwood." Grace and Weir 17–31.

Ingersoll, Earl. "Evading the Pigeonholers: A Conversation with Margaret Atwood." *Midwest Quarterly* 28.4 (Summer 1987): 525–39. (Rpt. in Ingersoll, *Margaret Atwood: Conversations* 131–39.)

———, ed. *Margaret Atwood: Conversations*. Princeton: Ontario Review Press, 1990. [Contains shortened and edited versions of a number of Atwood interviews.]

———. "Margaret Atwood's 'Cat's Eye': Re-Viewing Women in a Postmodern World." *Ariel: A Review of International English Literature* 22.4 (October 1991): 17–27.

———. "Waltzing Again: A Conversation with Margaret Atwood." *Ontario Review* 32 (Spring-Summer 1990): 7–11. (Rpt. in Ingersoll, *Margaret Atwood: Conversations* 234–38.)

Irigaray, Luce. *This Sex Which Is Not One*. Trans. Catherine Porter and Carolyn Burke. Ithaca: Cornell University Press, 1985.

———. "When Our Lips Speak Together." Trans. Carolyn Burke. *Signs* 6.1 (Autumn 1980): 69–79. (Rpt. in *This Sex Which Is Not One* 205–218.)

Irvine, Lorna. "Atwood's Parable of Flesh." *Sub/version*. Toronto: ECW Press, 1986. 39–53. (Rpt., slightly rev., in VanSpanckeren and Castro 85–100.)

Jaggar, Alison M. "Love and Knowledge: Emotion in Feminist Epistemology." *Gender/Body/Knowledge: Feminist Reconstructions of Being and Knowing*. Ed. Alison M. Jaggar and Susan R. Bordo. New Brunswick: Rutgers University Press, 1989. 145–71.

James, Caryn. "Women's Friendships Thrive in Ambiguity." *New York Times* 28 Jan. 1989 (Arts/Entertainment): 15.

James, William. "Atwood's *Surfacing*." *Canadian Literature* 91 (Winter 1981): 174–81.

Jamkhandi, Sudhakar. "An Interview with Margaret Atwood." *Commonwealth Novel in English* 2.1 (Jan. 1983): 1–6.

Jardine, Alice A. *Gynesis: Configurations of Woman and Modernity*. Ithaca: Cornell University Press, 1985.

Jeannotte, M. Sharon. "Tension Between the Mundane and the Cosmic." *Sphinx* 3.4 (1981): 74–82.

Jones, Dorothy. "'Waiting for the Rescue': A Discussion of Margaret Atwood's *Bodily Harm*." *Kunapipi* 6.3 (1984): 86–100.

Kahane, Claire. "The Gothic Mirror." *The (M)other Tongue: Essays in Feminist Psychoanalytic Interpretation*. Ed. Shirley Nelson Garner, Claire Kahane, and Madelon Sprengnether. Ithaca: Cornell University Press, 1985. 334–51.

Kanfer, Stefan. "Time Arrested." *Time* 6 Feb. 1989: 70.

Kareda, Urjo. "Atwood on Automatic." *Saturday Night* 96 (Nov. 1981): 70, 72.

Kauffman, Linda. "Special Delivery: Twenty-first Century Epistolarity in *The Handmaid's Tale*." *Writing the Female Voice: Essays on Epistolary Literature*. Ed. Elizabeth Goldsmith. Boston: Northeastern University Press, 1989. 221–44.

Keitel, Evelyne. *Reading Psychosis: Readers, Texts and Psychoanalysis*. Trans. Anthea Bell. Oxford: Basil Blackwell, 1989.

Keith, W. J. "Apocalyptic Imaginations: Notes on Atwood's *The Handmaid's Tale* and Findley's *Not Wanted on the Voyage*." *Essays on Canadian Writing* 35 (Winter 1987): 123–34.

Kendall, Elaine. "*The Handmaid's Tale* by Margaret Atwood." *Los Angles Times Book Review* 9 Feb. 1986: 1, 12. (Rpt., slightly cut, in Hall 149–50.)

Kerr, Michael, and Murray Bowen. *Family Evaluation: An Approach Based on Bowen Theory*. New York: W. W. Norton, 1988.

King, Bruce. "Margaret Atwood's *Surfacing*." *Journal of Commonwealth Literature* 12.1 (August 1977): 23–32.

Kirtz, Mary K. "The Thematic Imperative: Didactic Characterization in *Bodily Harm*." Mendez-Egle 116–30.

Klein, Melanie. *Envy and Gratitude and Other Works, 1946–1963*. New York: Delacorte Press, 1975.

Kohut, Heinz. "Introspection, Empathy, and the Semicircle of Mental Health." *International Journal of Psycho-Analysis* 63 (1982): 395–408. Rpt. in *Empathy*. Ed. Joseph Lichtenberg, Melvin Bornstein, and Donald Silver. 2 vols. Hillsdale: Analytic Press, 1984. 1: 81–100.

———. *The Restoration of the Self*. New York: International Universities Press, 1977.

———, and Ernest S. Wolf. "The Disorders of the Self and Their Treatment: An Outline." *International Journal of Psycho-Analysis* 59 (1978): 413–25.

Kroetsch, Robert. "Unhiding the Hidden: Recent Canadian Fiction." *Journal of Canadian Fiction* 3.3 (1974): 43–45.

Lacombe, Michele. "The Writing on the Wall: Amputated Speech in Margaret Atwood's *The Handmaid's Tale*." *Wascana Review* 21.2 (Fall 1986): 3–20.

Larkin, Joan. "Soul Survivor." *Ms.* May 1973: 33–35. Rpt. in McCombs, *Critical Essays* 48–52.

Laurence, Margaret. "Review of *Surfacing*." *Quarry* 22.4 (Spring 1973): 62–64. Rpt. in McCombs, *Critical Essays* 45–47.

Lecker, Robert. "Janus Through the Looking Glass: Atwood's First Three Novels." Arnold Davidson and Cathy Davidson, *The Art of Margaret Atwood* 177–203.

Lee, Hermione. "Little Women." *New Republic,* 10 April 1989: 38–40.

Leonard, John. "The Heroine: A Contraption of Attitudes." *New York Times Book Review* 21 March 1982: 3, 20–21.

Lynch, Denise. "Personalist Plot in Atwood's *Bodily Harm*." *Studies in the Humanities* 15.1 (June 1988): 45–57.

Lyons, Bonnie. "An Interview with Margaret Atwood." *Shenandoah* 37.2 (1987): 69–89. (Rpt. in Ingersoll, *Margaret Atwood: Conversations* 221–33.)

McCombs, Judith. "Atwood's Fictive Portraits of the Artist: From Victim to Surfacer, from Oracle to Birth." *Women's Studies* 12.1 (1986): 69–88.

———. "Contrary Re-memberings: The Creating Self and Feminism in *Cat's Eye*." *Canadian Literature* 129 (Summer 1991): 9–23.

———, ed. *Critical Essays on Margaret Atwood*. Boston: G. K. Hall, 1988.

———. "Introduction." McCombs, *Critical Essays* 1–28.

———. "'Up in the Air So Blue': Vampires and Victims, Great Mother Myth and Gothic Allegory in Margaret Atwood's First, Unpublished Novel." *Centennial Review* 33.3 (Summer 1989): 251–57.

McDermott, Alice. "What Little Girls Are Really Made Of." *New York Times Book Review* 5 Feb. 1989: 1, 35.

Mackay, Shena. "The Painter's Revenges." TLS 3–9 Feb. 1989: 113.

MacKinnon, Catharine. "Feminism, Marxism, Method, and the State: An Agenda for Theory." *Signs* 7 (Spring 1982): 515–44.

McLay, Catherine. "The Dark Voyage: *The Edible Woman* as Romance." Arnold Davidson and Cathy Davidson, *The Art of Margaret Atwood* 123–38.

———. "The Divided Self: Theme and Pattern in Margaret Atwood's *Surfacing*." *Journal of Canadian Fiction* 4.1 (1975): 82–95.

———. "The Real Story." *Journal of Canadian Fiction* 35–36 (1986): 130–37.

———. "Triple Solitaire." *Journal of Canadian Fiction* 35–36 (1986): 122–29.

MacLean, Susan. "*Lady Oracle*: The Art of Reality and the Reality of Art." *Journal of Canadian Fiction* 28–29 (1980): 179–97.

MacLulich, T. D. "Atwood's Adult Fairy Tale: Levi-Strauss, Bettelheim, and *The Edible Woman*." *Essays on Canadian Writing* 11 (Summer 1978): 111–29.

McMillan, Ann. "The Transforming Eye: *Lady Oracle* and Gothic Tradition." VanSpanckeren and Castro 48–64.

Mahler, Margaret, Fred Pine, and Anni Bergman. *The Psychological Birth of the Human Infant: Symbiosis and Individuation*. New York: Basic Books, 1975.

Malak, Amin. "Margaret Atwood's *The Handmaid's Tale* and the Dystopian Tradition." *Canadian Literature* 112 (Spring 1987): 9–16.

Manguel, Alberto. "First Impressions." *Saturday Night* 103 (Nov. 1988): 66–67, 69.

Martens, Cathrine. "Mother-Figures in *Surfacing* and *Lady Oracle*: An Interview with Margaret Atwood." *American Studies in Scandinavia* 16 (1984): 45–54.

Massé, Michelle. *In the Name of Love: Women, Masochism, and the Gothic*. Ithaca: Cornell University Press, 1992.

Maynard, Joyce. "Briefing for a Descent into Hell." *Mademoiselle* March 1986: 114, 118, 120. (Excerpted in Hall 153–55.)

Meese, Elizabeth. "An Interview with Margaret Atwood." *Black Warrior Review* 12.1 (Fall 1985): 88–108. (Rpt. in Ingersoll, *Margaret Atwood: Conversations* 177–90.)

Mendez, Charlotte Walker. "Loon Voice: Lying Words and Speaking World in Atwood's *Surfacing*." Mendez-Egle 89–94.

Mendez-Egle, Beatrice, ed. *Margaret Atwood: Reflection and Reality.* Living Author Series No. 6. Edinburg: Pan American University, 1987.

Miller, Nancy K. "Emphasis Added: Plots and Plausibilities in Women's Fiction." *PMLA* 96.1 (January 1981): 36–48. (Rpt. in *Subject to Change: Reading Feminist Writing.* New York: Columbia University Press, 1988. 25–46.)

Miner, Madonne. "'Trust Me': Reading the Romance Plot in Margaret Atwood's *The Handmaid's Tale*." *Twentieth Century Literature* 37.2 (Summer 1991): 148–68.

Miner, Valerie. "Atwood in Metamorphosis: An Authentic Canadian Fairy Tale." *Her Own Woman: Profiles of Ten Canadian Women.* Ed. Myrna Kostash, et al. Toronto: Macmillan, 1975. 173–94.

Modleski, Tania. *Loving with a Vengeance: Mass-Produced Fantasies for Women.* 1982. London and New York: Routledge, 1984.

———. *The Women Who Knew Too Much: Hitchcock and Feminist Theory.* 1988. New York and London: Routledge, 1989.

Mulvey, Laura. "Visual Pleasure and Narrative Cinema." *Screen* 16.3 (Autumn 1975): 6–18. Rpt. in *Feminisms: An Anthology of Literary Theory and Criticism.* Ed. Robyn Warhol and Diane Price Herndl. New Brunswick: Rutgers University Press, 1991. 432–42.

Murphy, Patrick D. "Reducing the Dystopian Distance: Pseudo-Documentary Framing in Near-Future Fiction." *Science-Fiction Studies* 17.1 (March 1990): 25–40.

Nodelman, Perry. "Trusting the Untrustworthy." *Journal of Canadian Fiction* 21 (1977–78): 73–82.

Norris, Ken. "'The University of Denay, Nunavit': The 'Historical Notes' in Margaret Atwood's *The Handmaid's Tale*." *American Review of Canadian Studies* 20.3 (Autumn 1990): 357–64.

Oates, Joyce Carol. "A Conversation with Margaret Atwood." *Ontario Review* 9 (Fall–Winter 1978–79): 5–18. (Rpt. in Ingersoll, *Margaret Atwood: Conversations* 74–85.)

Onley, Gloria. "Power Politics in Bluebeard's Castle." *Canadian Literature* 60 (Spring 1974): 21–42. Rpt. in McCombs, *Critical Essays* 70–89.

Patterson, Jayne. "The Taming of Externals: A Linguistic Study of Character Transformation in Margaret Atwood's *The Edible Woman*." *Studies in Canadian Literature* 7.2 (1982): 151–67.

Patton, Marilyn. "*Lady Oracle*: The Politics of the Body." *Ariel: A Review of International English Literature* 22.4 (October 1991): 29–48.

Peri, Camille. "Witchcraft." *Mother Jones* 14.3 (April 1989): 28, 30–31, 44–45.

Piercy, Marge. "Margaret Atwood: Beyond Victimhood." *Parti-Colored Blocks for a Quilt.* Poets on Poetry. Ann Arbor: University of Michigan Press, 1982. 281–99. Rpt. in McCombs, *Critical Essays* 53–66.

Pratt, Annis. "*Surfacing* and the Rebirth Journey." Arnold Davidson and Cathy Davidson, *The Art of Margaret Atwood* 139–57.

194 ▪ Works Cited

Quigley, Theresia. "*Surfacing:* A Critical Study." *Antigonish Review* 34 (Summer 1978): 77–87.

Rainwater, [Mary] Catherine. "The Sense of the Flesh in Four Novels by Margaret Atwood." Mendez-Egle 14–28.

Rao, Eleonora. "Margaret Atwood's *Lady Oracle:* Writing Against Notions of Unity." *British Journal of Canadian Studies* 4.1 (1989): 136–56.

Rich, Adrienne. *Of Woman Born: Motherhood as Experience and Institution.* New York: Norton, 1976.

Rigney, Barbara. *Margaret Atwood.* Totowa: Barnes and Noble, 1987.

Rimmon-Kenan, Shlomith. "Narration as Repetition: The Case of Günter Grass's *Cat and Mouse.*" *Discourse in Psychoanalysis and Literature.* Ed. Shlomith Rimmon-Kenan. London: Methuen, 1987. 176–87.

Robinson, Sally. "The 'Anti-Logos Weapon': Multiplicity in Women's Texts." *Contemporary Literature* 29.1 (Spring 1988): 105–24.

Rooke, Constance. "Margaret Atwood, *Cat's Eye.*" *Malahat Review* 85 (December 1988): 131–32.

Rosenberg, Jerome H. *Margaret Atwood.* Boston: Twayne, 1984.

Rosowski, Susan. "Margaret Atwood's *Lady Oracle:* Social Mythology and the Gothic Novel." *Research Studies* 49.2 (June 1981): 87–98.

Ross, Catherine. "Nancy Drew as Shaman: Atwood's *Surfacing.*" *Canadian Literature* 84 (Spring 1980): 7–17.

Ross, Jean. "Contemporary Authors Interview." *Contemporary Authors.* Ed. Deborah Straub. Vol. 24. New rev. ser. Detroit: Gale, 1988. 22–25.

Rothstein, Mervyn. "No Balm in Gilead for Margaret Atwood." *New York Times* 17 Feb. 1986: C11.

Rubenstein, Roberta. *Boundaries of the Self: Gender, Culture, Fiction.* Urbana: University of Illinois Press, 1987.

———. "Nature and Nurture in Dystopia: *The Handmaid's Tale.*" VanSpanckeren and Castro 101–12.

———. "Pandora's Box and Female Survival: Margaret Atwood's *Bodily Harm.*" *Journal of Canadian Studies* 20.1 (Spring 1985): 120–35. Rpt. in McCombs, *Critical Essays* 259–75.

———. "*Surfacing:* Margaret Atwood's Journey to the Interior." *Modern Fiction Studies* 22.3 (Autumn 1976): 387–99.

Russ, Joanna. "Somebody's Trying to Kill Me and I Think It's My Husband: The Modern Gothic." *Journal of Popular Culture* 6.4 (Spring 1973): 666–91.

St. Andrews, Bonnie. *Forbidden Fruit: On the Relationship Between Women and Knowledge in Doris Lessing, Selma Lagerlöf, Kate Chopin, Margaret Atwood.* Troy: Whitston, 1986.

St. Clair, Michael. *Object Relations and Self Psychology: An Introduction.* Monterey: Brooks/Cole, 1986.

Sandler, Linda. "Interview with Margaret Atwood." *Malahat Review* 41 (January 1977): 7–27. (Rpt. in Ingersoll, *Margaret Atwood: Conversations* 40–57.)

Schaeffer, Susan. "'It Is Time That Separates Us': Margaret Atwood's *Surfacing.*" *Centennial Review* 18 (Fall 1974): 319–37.

Schreiber, Le Anne. "Female Trouble: Margaret Atwood and Her Haunting New Novel." *Vogue* Jan. 1986: 208–09.

Sciff-Zamaro, Roberta. "The Re/membering of the Female Power in *Lady Oracle.*" *Canadian Literature* 112 (Spring 1987): 32–38.

Smith, Rowland. "Margaret Atwood and the City: Style and Substance in *Bodily Harm* and *Bluebeard's Egg.*" *World Literature Written in English* 25.2 (Autumn 1985): 252–64.

Snitow, Ann. "Back to the Future." *Mother Jones* 11.3 (April-May 1986): 59–60. (Rpt., slightly cut, in Hall 156–58.)

Sontag, Susan. "The Third World of Women." *Partisan Review* 40. 2 (1973): 180–206.

Stine, Jean C., ed. *Contemporary Literary Criticism.* Vol. 25. Detroit: Gale, 1983.

Stone, Laurie. "Dinosaur Dance." *Village Voice* 7 Jan. 1980: 32. Excerpted in Gunton and Harris 38.

Stovel, Nora. "Reflections on Mirror Images: Doubles and Identity in the Novels of Margaret Atwood." *Essays on Canadian Writing* 33 (Fall 1986): 50–67.

Stow, Glenys. "Nonsense as Social Commentary in *The Edible Woman.*" *Journal of Canadian Studies* 23.3 (Fall 1988): 90–101.

Struthers, J. R. "An Interview with Margaret Atwood." *Essays on Canadian Writing* 6 (Spring 1977): 18–27. (Rpt. in Ingersoll, *Margaret Atwood: Conversations* 58–68.)

Sullivan, Rosemary. "Breaking the Circle." *Malahat Review* 41 (Jan. 1977): 30–41.

Tennant, Emma. "Margaret Atwood in Conversation with Emma Tennant." *Women's Review* (London) 21 (July 1987): 8–11.

Thurman, Judith. "When You Wish Upon a Star." *New Yorker* 29 May 1989: 108–10.

Timson, Judith. "Atwood's Triumph." *Maclean's* 3 Oct. 1988: 56–58, 60–61.

Towers, Robert. "Mystery Women." *New York Review of Books* 27 April 1989: 50–52.

Twigg, Alan. "Margaret Atwood." *Strong Voices: Conversations with Fifty Canadian Authors.* Madeira Park, B.C.: Harbour, 1988. 6–11. Rpt. in Ingersoll, *Margaret Atwood: Conversations* 121–30.

VanSpanckeren, Kathryn, and Jan Garden Castro, eds. *Margaret Atwood: Vision and Forms.* Carbondale: Southern Illinois University Press, 1988.

Vincent, Sybil. "The Mirror and the Cameo: Margaret Atwood's Comic/Gothic Novel, *Lady Oracle.*" *The Female Gothic.* Ed. Juliann Fleenor. Montréal: Eden, 1983. 153–63.

Waugh, Patricia. *Feminine Fictions: Revisiting the Postmodern.* New York: Routledge, 1989.

Wilson, Sharon. "Deconstructing Text and Self: Mirroring in Atwood's *Surfacing* and Beckett's *Molloy.*" *Journal of Popular Literature* 3.1 (Spring–Summer 1987): 53–69.

———. "Fairy-Tale Cannibalism in *The Edible Woman.*" *Cooking by the Book: Food in Literature and Culture.* Ed. Mary Anne Schofield. Bowling Green: Bowling Green State University Popular Press, 1989. 78–88.

Wolf, Naomi. *The Beauty Myth: How Images of Beauty Are Used Against Women.* New York: William Morrow, 1991.

Woodcock, George. "Surfacing to Survive: Notes of the Recent Atwood." *Ariel* 4.3 (July 1973): 16–28.

Wyatt, Jean. *Reconstructing Desire: The Role of the Unconscious in Women's Reading and Writing.* Chapel Hill: University of North Carolina Press, 1990.

Yaeger, Patricia. "Afterword." *Feminism, Bakhtin, and the Dialogic.* Ed. Dale M. Bauer and Susan Jaret McKinstry. Albany: State University of New York Press, 1991. 239–45.

———. *Honey-Mad Women: Emancipatory Strategies in Women's Writing.* New York: Columbia University Press, 1988.

Index